...with ears like radar tuned in for danger, and eyes darting in all directions, we forged ahead. Our eyes had to readjust to the dark as we entered; the sounds of our footfalls bounced off the blasted caverns, causing echoes that vibrated in our heads. All our sense were thrown off and we stayed closed together as instinct reminded us that there is safety in numbers.

The grinding noise, which had been a loud hum, began to grow in intensity. Although we couldn't see a train, we knew that something was just not right. "Hey, Reg, I'm not sure what that sound is or where it's coming from, but I have one suggestion...RUN!!" Somewhere on the track a speeding train was coming right for us. We couldn't tell if it was from behind or ahead, but it really didn't matter.

Running as quick as our feet could land on every second cross-tie, we ran towards the light at the end of the tunnel. Although Dixie led the way, closely followed by Reggie and myself, we ran as a unit; men and dog as one. Our hearts pounded, our lungs gasped for breath, and adrenalin rushed through our bodies. Knowing that two men, one dog and three backpacks were just about to be cross-stitched into the railroad track, we ran with hardly a stumble, relying on the muscles and talents we had developed over the roads of Washington. The faster we ran the greater the vibrations that encompassed us. We could just feel the hot breath of the steaming locomotive on our heels. "HURRY!" we cried as our legs pumped like pistons. "Faster, FASTER!"

"We laughed and cried and couldn't wait to find out if they would complete the walk."

Susan Roberts
President,
The Arc of Washington State

"Walkabout is really about exploration — of ourselves and of the differences and similarities of all those around us. There is a little bit of discovery for each of us here...a great story to share."

Nancy White
March of Dimes Foundation

"Reggie Feckley's determination and hard work are truly an inspiration. I know you will enjoy Steve Breakstone's entertaining description of their many adventures."

Ralph Munro
Secreatary of State, Washington

"...the journey of a lifetime for two men and their dog as they walked around the Evergreen State. Their accomplishments prove in dramatic fashion what can be done by any person regardless of their apparent disabilities."

Ronald L. Gibbs
Executive Director,
United Ways of Washington

Washington WALKABOUT

by Steve Breakstone
with Reggie Feckley and Janet Phipps

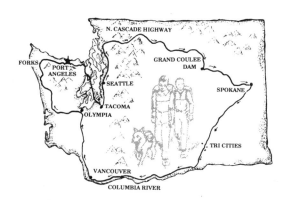

BALANCE PUBLICATIONS
Port Angeles, Washington

*In memory of my friend and housemate, Chuck Hanby.
Thank you for sharing yourself with Dixie, me and all of us
at the Lauridsen Group Home and Diversified Industries.*

Published by
Balance Publications, P.O. Box 447 Port Angeles, WA 98362-0069

First printing 1992
Typesetting by Words & Deeds
Printed by Griffin Printing
Cover design by Steve Breakstone and Words & Deeds
Photos reproduced by Gordon Coyier
Front cover photo by Steve Breakstone
Back cover photo by Janet Phipps

Long distance and/or walking along highways is dangerous! The
author and publisher do not recommend nor suggest that others
should attempt such walks and do not accept the responsibility of
others who attempt to do so.

Library of Congress Catalog Card Number: 92-81897
Steve Breakstone
A walk around the state of Washington by a man with a
developmental disability

ISBN 0-9632724-4-6

Printed in the United States of America
Printed with soybean ink on recycled paper

10 9 8 7 6 5 4 3 2 1

DEDICATIONS

This book is dedicated to all the people I promised I would dedicate this book:

...My mother, Pearl; my father, Arnold; my sister, Karen. And in memory of my forever friend, my brother, Benson. I always knew that no matter whatever I decided to do in my life, I could always count on all your love and support. Without you, I would not have become me.

...My friends Mike and Karen Drieblatt and Tyler and Drake. I knew that with every step I took, you were right there with me spiritually. Your love and friendship have kept me going at those times I began to question it all. And thanks for all your help.

...Dixie—you are my daughter, we are one. We will always be together, and perhaps we always have been.

...I also dedicate this book to my Grandma Minnie Yurik; Aunt Lily Levy; Howard, Sherrie, & Mitchell Katz; Gilda, Barry, Michael, Richard, and Todd Miller; Billy, Carol, Michelle, Susan Breakstone and Rob and Francine Nereroff. And of course all the wonderful people, friends and relatives in the Bronx, Sun Ranch, Spring Valley and all across America. You know who you are. Thank you, thank you, thank you for being a part of my wonderful life.

This book is also dedicated to:

...The folks at the Lauridsen Group Home, you are my friends and family. Dixie and I have loved being with you, sharing fun and destiny. You have been the adventure at the end of an adventure. Thank you all for enhancing our lives:

Anita Weems	Art Karjola
Ben Kinney	Cal Roedell
Carol Curren	Tracy Pittenger
Clover Brockman	Dan Briones Sr.
David Chastain	Dorothy Tomlinson
Eddie Newell	Erin Wallner
Fred Cnockaert	Greg Brack
Harry Thomas	Harvey Reise

Howie Gorton	Jim Melick
Jody Markham	Kellianne McNeil-O'Hagan
Lauralei Olson	Lee Martin
Leonard Cruz	Leslie Arrowsmith
Mark Goshorn	Mary Ann Peters
Mary Hofer	Melissa Lewis
Mike Soiseth	Niki Leilani
Rebecca Donelson	Ricky Ewing
Robert Campbell	Robert McComb
Shannon Slome	Sharon Meyers
Shirley Knight	Steven Schoos
John Rye	Sharon Jacobson

And, of course, Reggie Feckley and Janet Phipps.

...Reggie—What we shared will tie us together forever. I thank you for that. Not only did your perseverence and determination make one of your dreams come true, you helped me make one of my dreams come true. What more can a person ask of a friend?

...Janet—You became one of the best reasons for Dixie and me to stay in a great town in Washington State. It's been a lot of fun!

I hope I got everyone. I hope I fulfilled my promise. If I didn't get you on paper, you must know that it is in my heart. You must feel the love in the air, not only through these pages. It's there. Trust me.

CONTENTS

ACKNOWLEDGMENTS

Thanks to the caring, wonderful, supportive people within Diversified Industries of Port Angeles. Without your insight and open-mindedness, we never would have taken step one. Thank you Chris Brandt, Karen Higgens, Judy Ware, Rob Campbell, Mary Holden, Rosalie Rieck, Carol Liljedahl, Marion Hedin, Barbara L. Holman, Judy Hewitt. And thank you Danielle Cayner and Sue Romeo for lending your wonderful artistic talents.

Thank you, Pat Barnard, for your love and support. I'll never forget all the fun and love we shared. It will always be a wonderful part of who I am.

WALKABOUT, the walk as well as the book, succeeded only through the contributions of so many caring, knowledgeable people. All of us within the WALKABOUT family wish to thank:

...My editors: Rory Hurt—who took a mess and made it readable, and Anton Wishik—whose experience made WALKABOUT more enjoyable to read.

...Mike and Karen Dreiblatt—thanks for your brainwork.

...Jerry Marsh—whose workhorse efforts not only got this dream on a road to reality, but showed me how even I had thoughts and ideas that were limiting and needed re-evaluation.

...Cal Roedell—a colleague and more importantly, my friend.

...Karen Roedell—your and Cal's support is appreciated in more ways than you know.

...Mike Soiseth

...Lew Bartholomew

...Laura Campbell

These people are very much a part of this book. Without them, I'd still be rewriting, editing and dreaming.

Hey, Ron Scott—thanks for the support, conversation, advice and education. I value your friendship (and your talents as the best darn mechanic in Port Angeles!).

And, of course, WALKABOUT became that much more special with the friendship and hospitality of:

Pat Barnard
Gerry and Freddie Andrews
Anders and Nancy Edgerton
Nancy Bellanger and the Harrison Group Home
Katy Easton
Kleiner Group Home
Wayne Bretthauer
Rainbow Inn
John Phipps
Larry & Jane Zappone
Quilceda House Group Home
Jan Kohler
Crestview Group Home
Kurt & Lucille Ames
Jack & Jo Robertson
Circle S Motel
Davenport of Assembly of God
Pastor Cindy Rodkey and the Presbyterian Church of Reardon
First Baptist Church of Airway Heights
Pastor Neil Buckaloo and the Lutheran Church of Cheney
Pastor Brian Elster and the Lutheran Church of Sprague
Pastor Bob Lester and the Lutheran Church of Ritzville
Steve & Judy Schmitz
Pastor Stan Unseth and the Church of the Nazarene in
    Conell
Tom & Glenda Latimer
Pastor Dan Tourangeau of the First Congregational Church
Steve Hunter & Family
Pastor Bud Ludbetter and the Church of the Nazarene in
    White Salmon
Pastor David & Helen Zimmerman and the First Baptist
    Church of Stevenson
Pastor Belzer and the Church of the Nazarene in Washougal
Jim & Meg Hurst
Pastor Dennis and the Methodist Church of Battleground
Bruce & Alice Flannagan
Outward Bound Group Home
Pastor M. Ross and the Lutheran Church of Castle Rock

Pastor Starkey and the Assembly of God Church of Vador
Tony Olney and the Freedom House of Centralia
Pastor Burtis and the (Neighborhood) Christian Center of
    Tumwater
Don & Fay Holden
Tyee Hotel of Olympia
Assembly of God of McCleary
Cedar House Group Home of Montesano
Sue Hickman
Jan Cunningham
Pastor Gery West and the Quinalt Valley Chapel of Neilton
Roberta Nalley
Judy Ware
KONP Radio of Port Angeles

And, of course, the people of Port Angeles and the great state
of Washington.

INTRODUCTION

I guess you could say that I walked into Reggie Feckley's life, and he walked into mine.

He walked around his town of Port Angeles, Washington. Dixie, my German Shepherd, and I walked 3,000 miles across America.

Together we had little in common except this mutual use of our feet. But when we put our minds, and our feet, together we created a bond that grew stronger with every step. We shared an adventure—an inspiring and perspiring journey of development and discovery.

Reggie Feckley was born in 1946. He was born with brain damage that caused mental retardation and a speech defect. When he was a boy his father died and his mother had to go back to work. At that time, little was understood about disabilities such as Reggie's, and his mother was advised that the best thing she could do for Reggie was to place him out of harm's way. She was told that a person with his problems would need close attention and assistance for the rest of his life. Institutions and large foster care homes with other disabled people provided Reggie, and others like him, a safe place where he could live. Reggie was fed, clothed, bathed, and given all of the things he needed to live day to day. In fact, his needs were so carefully met, he hardly had to do anything for himself!

Most healthy people thought that because Reggie was "retarded" (what people with developmental delays or disabilities used to be called), he would never be able to take care of himself, live on his own, work at a job or learn very much of anything. Later, other people came into his life. People who believed Reggie was capable of learning how to do things for himself. They knew that he just needed the opportunity and the time and effort from some skilled, caring people. For a long time, some of those believers were considered dreamers and radicals.

In 1985, Mrs. Feckley moved Reggie closer to where she lived. The Lauridsen Group Home in Port Angeles, Washington, a city of over 17,000 on Washington State's Olympic Peninsula, was to be Reggie's new home.

The Lauridsen Group Home (for adults with developmental disabilities) is respected in Port Angeles, with programs to help integrate its tenants into the heartbeat of the town. Like many group homes, it doesn't have hundreds of residents but only a handful. Fewer tenants means the Lauridsen Group Home can provide more individual care and training, offering tenants the opportunity to maintain a higher, more normal, quality of life.

The Lauridsen Group Home, a relatively large facility with over 20 tenants, does its best to provide Reggie, and all clients, with the best quality of life possible. The programs stress growth and independence. Reggie was finally given the opportunity to do things for himself. He was finally given the chance to learn how to lead the life of an adult. It was a big challenge, but he was up to it.

Five individual apartments, in two separate buildings, make up Lauridsen Group Home. Reggie shared one apartment with four other men, including one man with whom he shared a bedroom. At his own pace, Reggie learned how to keep himself and his apartment clean and how to prepare his own meals. He proved he could get about town safely and was free to do so. He also held down a job. Reggie was a valued employee at New Broom Janitorial. Like all other people, Reggie aspired to have a happy life and be a valued member of his community.

Meanwhile, in the fall of 1988, Dixie and I were walking around Port Angeles looking for a place to live and a job. We had just spent over two years walking 3,000 miles from New Orleans to Neah Bay, Washington, a tiny native American community at the far end of the Olympic Peninsula. It was the adventure of a lifetime! But as we accepted the end of one journey, we were looking forward to creating the next. The fun part was that we just didn't know where the next step was actually going to take us.

We decided to stay awhile on the Olympic Peninsula, and headed for Port Angeles. Towering over the southern border of this beautiful town are the Olympic Mountains, the home of deer, Roosevelt Elk, black bears, marmots, and hordes of other wild animals. Plush forests support wildflowers that are not to be found anywhere else on the planet. North of Port Angeles is Victoria, British Columbia, Canada. The border between the two cities is the Strait of Juan de Fuca, patrolled by salmon, crab, oysters, millions of fish, seals, sea lions and even dolphins and whales.

Gliding overhead are bald eagles, ducks and sea gulls. Dixie and I had found a home!

When Dixie and I stumbled onto Lauridsen Group Home, I thought it was an apartment building. I asked if there were any vacancies, and was informed that it was a group home for people with developmental disabilities. As fate would have it, they were looking for a new counselor to live on the premises, and they asked if I was interested. It was a match made in heaven!

Once it was confirmed that Dixie and I would live there, we were introduced to many new friends. Reggie was introduced to me as a man who loved to walk as much as I did.

"I like to walk, too," he said to me, shaking my hand. I couldn't understand his words very well, but I got the general idea.

"Reggie spends many hours each day walking around town," I was told by Anita Weems, a veteran training counselor.

"Then I guess Dixie and I will have someone to walk with," I said. At that time I had no idea what possibilities were stirring.

Before I started working at the group home, I had only limited experience with people who had obvious physical or mental disabilities. But like most people, I had friends and relatives with some kind of disability. In fact, each one of us has differing abilities, talents and limitations. With most of us, the disability is hard to see and we don't concentrate on it. With others, the disability is so obvious that we overlook many of their talents.

When I first arrived, I wasn't sure what my new friends at the group home could or could not do, and that included Reggie. The first thing I came to understand was that of all the people I had met while traveling across America, never had I found people with more individual and unique personalities.

Each one of my new friends had different talents and different potential. There was Lee Arrowsmith, who could put jigsaw puzzles together in record time; Tracy Pittenger, who attracted the love and friendship of every animal; Jody Markham, the singer; Fred Cnockaert, the cook. And of course, there was Reggie Feckley, the walker.

Besides the things they were good at, I found that the bottom line was that each one is an individual. They aren't just bodies with disabilities or slow minds, but people with likes and dislikes and varying temperaments. Ricky is good-natured, Steve likes to read the newspaper, Mark aspires to enter college, and Rebecca enjoys coffee and cigarettes. Here was a group of people that wanted to enjoy life and to decide how best to do so. The bottom line was not the differences, but the similarities my new crowd shared with every other crowd of people I have encountered in my travels.

Working at the Lauridsen Group Home made me realize that it is my responsibility to notice the similarities, as well as the individual differences and abilities of each person I meet. Everyone, myself included, deserves that respect.

As my relationship with my new friends grew, I wanted to do something special with them. I wanted to share the good fortunes of my life with them, and I wanted to share their friendship and special qualities with people across America. I wanted to do something that would give us all the opportunity to have fun as well as grow as individuals.

With the following story, I hope all my friends everywhere will enjoy sharing in some of my wonderful experiences.

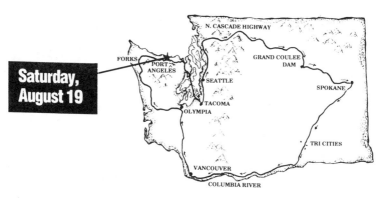

chapter 1

FIRST STEPS

Reggie Feckley clomped down the steps of the Lauridsen Group Home and out into the morning sunshine. He turned and waved. Janet and I waved back as we walked down to her office. He was going for a walk. We didn't know where he was going; he probably didn't, either. We just knew he was going to put a few miles on his shoe leather—and that he'd be back!

"Don't go too far," I called to Reggie as he walked away from the group home. He cocked his head and smiled. I was teasing him and he knew it. Soon enough he would go for a real long walk—long enough to last a lifetime.

"Tomorrow's the big day, right?" he called back. He didn't wait for us to respond. He knew the answer. "Get plenty of rest, Schlicky," he instructed my five-year-old German Shepherd.

Dixie, my dog, walked over to Reggie with her tail wagging. Born with a speech disorder, "Schlicky" was the way Reggie pronounced "Dixie." A year's friendship with Reggie taught me to understand what he was saying, even if it

1

was mumbled and slurred. Even though some people might describe his speech as mumbo-jumbo, Reggie worked words as well as he could, and I found that he had thoughts as important as anybody else's.

Reggie patted Dixie's head and then rubbed her favorite spot just above her tail-bone. She could handle affection like that all day. But when Dixie lost sight of me as I turned the corner of the building, she immediately left Reggie's satisfying hand and came to find me. Dixie was forever by my side! Reggie chuckled. "See you later, Schlicky." He turned toward the street, looked both ways, waited for a pickup truck to pass and crossed the boulevard.

It was a mile-long walk from the Lauridsen Group Home to the pier overlooking the Strait of Juan de Fuca, which serves as the city of Port Angeles' northern border. The two buildings that were home to over 20 adults, all with some degree of developmental disability, faded behind Reggie as he headed downtown. He had one more day to break in his new walking boots. Tomorrow's walking would be official—Sunday, August 20, would be the first day of WALKABOUT.

Hot dogs roasted over a campfire and a can of beans simmered beside the hot coals. With nothing to hear but the creaks and moans of grandfather trees swaying to the music of the Elwha River, Janet and I relaxed in our little slice of heaven on Earth. Janet and I often shared the beauty of this inspirational forest, and found that some of our best conversations developed in these peaceful surroundings. WALKABOUT was born in just this way on a chilly, starlit, winter night.

Janet Phipps and I met at the Lauridsen Group Home. A special education teacher, Janet was presently the program coordinator of the Lauridsen Group Home. Her job was to train the staff at Lauridsen how to teach adults with disabilities to live as independently as possible. "The group home tenants are not children," she explained the first day we met, "they are adults and need to be respected as such. Our job is to help them make good choices in their lives and see that they are given the opportunity to achieve them."

A few years earlier Janet decided to leave her home in Chicago. She had driven as far as she could until the Pacific Ocean got in her way. Like myself, Janet also loved the great outdoors, and together we spent many days hiking the trails of the nearby Olympic Mountains or sitting by the swiftly flowing Elwha River, enjoying a campfire under the twinkling stars. Although she was my boss, she soon became my best friend.

"Now this is the way to end a day of work at the group home," she said softly, watching the hot dogs turn from artificial pink to charcoal gray, or was it black? "When it's smokin' it's cooking, when it's flamin' it's done," pretty well summed up Janet's theory of campfire cuisine.

We were only fifteen miles from town, but it might as well have been a billion! The clear February evening rolled over Janet and I as we relaxed, alone in the campground. Even Dixie was in her own vision of paradise, frolicking though the woods to her heart's delight. She reveled in the life growing throughout the forest, and I could barely catch the sound of her I.D. tags jingling as she tore through the trees. Dixie and I had spent so much time together that I was tuned into that sound like a mother to her baby's coo.

"Nothing tastes better than a well-burned hot dog cooked under the stars!" Janet joked as she took her first bite. In the months to come this joke was repeated so often it became a WALKABOUT tradition. As I chomped down (or was it choked down?) one of her infamous burnt hot dogs (why, oh *why* do I always forget to cook my own food?), Janet and I started talking about the people at work. Janet had been working with people with developmental disabilities (called D.D.) for twelve years, and had a lot of experience. I asked her why she thought so few people realized how much our friends with disabilities were really capable of accomplishing.

"I think it's an old stereotype," she told me. "Most people see a few handicapped people that are not good at some things, and so they think all people with handicaps will never learn anything. They focus on what they can't do, not what they can."

"That's silly," I said. "Everyone is different!"

"Well, Steve, I know that and you know that, but it's hard to teach that to millions of other people," she sighed. "You know, not too long ago I met a woman and I told her what I did for a living. She said, 'Oh, how *wonderful* that you work with all those *wonderful*

people! It's so important to keep them all busy!' All I could think of
was that it sounded more like she was describing puppies, not
people. I got so disgusted with her. Our friends want to live a life,
not be kept 'busy.' And let's face it—they are not all 'wonderful!'
Some people with D.D. are likable and some aren't. They're all
just individuals."

"Did you tell her that?"

"Probably not as well as I should have," Janet said, more to
herself than to me. "I should have taught her a thing or two. We
spend a lot of time trying to teach the people we work with
important things. Maybe we need to spend some time teaching the
public a few important things, too. So many people just think of
our tenants as 'those poor retarded people.'"

"It makes me wonder which is worse, the disability or the lack
of faith people have in people with developmental disabilities."

"Yeah," Janet said, rather softly. "What's really weird is that
I've worked with many people whose own family and friends have
caused so many problems. I believe that's where a lot of it starts."

"What do you mean?" I asked.

Janet took a deep breath. I could see that she was trying to say
something just right. This whole subject was very dear to her and
yet it was also very touchy. I stared into the racing river until she
continued. "You see, Steve, some parents have a hard time accepting that their child has a disability. They don't seem to understand
that their child has a different learning process and/or physical
abilities. They have little patience with their developing child and
that slows the process even more. Heck, you've seen how it can
even affect behavior!" I knew it was difficult for Janet to be critical
of other people but she held strong, experienced opinions and it
was important to share them.

"Of course," she added, "there are many families who are
loving, caring, and sympathetic. Unfortunately, when they go too
far with that, they 'baby' the child forever. The person grows up
with hardly any expectations and develops few skills, little self-
esteem or self-reliance. Then we wonder why they continue to
need so much assistance...forever."

"That's interesting. Maybe the reason so many people refer to
our friends as 'those kids' is because that's the way they treat
them," I offered. "I find that strange because most of the folks are

older than me. And no one has referred to me as a kid since I was a teen-ager. I'd be offended if they did."

"I think that 'kid' thing is a good example of how nondisabled people create most of the differences seen as so obvious," remarked Janet.

"I bet if people had similar expectations of people with disabilities as those without, most of our friends at the group home would have been more independent years ago," I said. "They certainly would have had more opportunity to lead a normal life."

"I'd also argue that they wouldn't all have to be 'housed' with other disabled people who they may or may not like, having to share everything as if they were forever in sleep-away camp." Janet shook her head in disgust. She had discussed this situation much too often. It was a depressing conversation for her, but her comments were helpful. People learned quite a bit from her. Finally she looked at me and threw up her shoulders. "That's the way it is. So tomorrow we go back to the group home and do the best we can with the way it is." Janet picked up a pebble and tossed it towards a cedar tree. She missed and let out a sigh, revealing her frustration. "The community programs, the services, and the allotted money is better than it used to be but far from where I hope it will end." Suddenly she scrunched up her face and added, "You know, Steve, this is not really the place to talk about all this depressing stuff."

"Well, let's change all that!" I demanded, ever so naively.

"Good. Let's talk about something else."

"No. I mean let's change all the stuff we think needs changing." Obviously, I wasn't ready to change the subject. The vastness of the forest creates thoughts with no borders.

"Oh, sure. No problem. Let's just change the world." Janet looked at me and saw I wasn't kidding. "Seriously, Steve. Do you think it's easy to change the way people think?"

I didn't reply. I just raised my eyebrows and shrugged.

We added another log to the fire and watched as the flames rose toward the sky.

"Hey, I've got it, Janet. We need to find a good way to tell everyone that people with disabilities should be treated as equals. All we have to do is come up with an idea that will show what a person with a developmental disability is really capable of, if they are given the right support and opportunity! What do you think?"

"That sounds good to me," she replied softly, having heard people suggest that before.

"Well, you're the boss. Any ideas?"

"I've had plenty. But you want something new, glamorous, innovative, unique and fun, don't you?"

"You know me so well," I said with a smile and an innocent shrug of my shoulders.

"Yes, too well," she teased. "Well, let's see." She thought deeply for a moment and then said, "Nope. At the moment, I'm void of any worthwhile thoughts."

"Well then," I said, joining the thought process. "What are our assets?"

"Well, I have over 12 years of experience. That should count for something." She thought for a second and then added, "And you have long legs and a big mouth."

"That's true," I quietly agreed, wondering if I had just been insulted. We sat and thought for a few minutes (Janet with a slight smile), and stared into the designs made by the orange glow of the fire. The only sound was the crackling of the burning wood and the infinite rush of the river.

"I've got it!" I exclaimed. "What if we help one of our friends do a cross-country walk like Dixie and I did!" Dixie and I had spent more than two years walking over 3,000 miles from New Orleans, Louisiana, to the Northwest coast of Washington State. The walk had been a rite of passage that brought me into manhood. I thought a similar walk might prove to be just as life-changing for one of our friends.

"That's a great idea, Steve!" Janet exclaimed. Often I had dazzled her with tales of my adventures walking across a continent. "We can show that a person with D.D. can do the same thing any other person can do! If we walk along the roadways and through the towns like you and Dixie did, just think of how many people we can teach about people with developmental disabilities!"

Janet and I knew we were on to something big. We sat for a few minutes, turning a crazy idea into something fantastic. We got so excited about our great plan that we were spitting out ideas as fast as we spit out crisp pieces of wiener. Then another thought streaked across my mind like a shooting star across the night sky.

"Hey, you know what else, Jan? This year, 1989, is the one

hundredth anniversary of Washington becoming the 42nd state of the Union. We could walk around the state and be a part of the centennial celebrations."

"That's a great idea!" said Janet. "What a perfect time to walk around the State of Washington. We'll walk the state and talk to people about equal rights, free choice, self-determination and open opportunities for *all* people."

As we ate the food and burned all the firewood, Janet and I discussed all the things we would have to do to make this WALKABOUT a reality. "Of course, we ain't doin' nothin' if the big bosses don't think it's a good idea," Janet reminded me, with a wry smile. "Let's face it, Steve, this is kind of nuts!"

"Well, then our first step is to convince them that we know what we are talking about. And once we get going, I bet we could get a ton of publicity from the local newspapers and radio stations. I bet we can rally up enough support to help us get donations for all the gear we would need, too," I countered.

"I bet you're right," Janet said. It wasn't too difficult to get her thinking optimistically. The potential of this dream was so very real. "Of course, the $64,000 question is, who at the group home is going to want to walk even half the distance you and Dixie walked? After all, let's face it, they're only disabled, not crazy!" she chuckled. I laughed softly in agreement.

Janet and I thought about that for about two seconds and together we blurted, "Reggie!" We knew that even at age 43, Reggie Feckley would be the perfect person to make the walk.

"Steve, I know that Reggie loves to walk. In fact, the whole town knows it. But you're the expert; do you really think Reggie could walk eight or nine hours each day, maybe over a thousand miles around the whole state?!" Janet spoke softly, as if she was trying to contain her excitement for fear this dream could too easily be wild fantasy.

"I don't know," I replied honestly. "I just don't know. But if anyone should be the one to try, it's Reggie! Reggie deserves the chance. It shouldn't be any different than when Dixie and I left New Orleans. And look how it turned out for us. It was the greatest adventure of our lives!"

"True enough! It may be true that Reggie has certain limitations and it may take him a bit longer to learn things, but perhaps we have found a way to use one of his best skills. The most exciting part is that this kind of marathon walking is not a natural talent, but something he is going to have to work hard at, just like anyone else."

This day, like the day before and the day before that, Reggie walked around town like a minor character in the book of life. Not his book, of course, but the book of life written by society. As far as most people were concerned, Reggie was only "one of those guys who's always walking around town." Winter, spring, summer or fall, Reggie casually walked Port Angeles. Reggie was noticed by many, but was seldom paid much attention.

But tomorrow, the book of Reggie's life would open a new chapter. Reggie's walking would attract attention—a lot of attention—all around Washington.

Rocking his torso back and forth as if he were building momentum to thrust himself forward, Reggie walked and thought deeply about his upcoming journey. He walked with a smile, waving to the passing cars. He didn't know most of the people driving past but he liked to think that he was popular. "If you wave to people that you don't know, they'll think you're crazy," I once explained. But still, that was the way he chose to spend so many hours strolling through life. It was his life, it was his style. Perhaps he wanted to believe that he knew a lot of people and a lot of people knew him. Just like anyone else, Reggie yearned to be liked.

"Tomorrow I go for a big, big walk," Reggie said to himself as he walked down the street. Almost as an afterthought he added, "No problem!" Almost everything was "no problem" to Reggie. He may not have originated the phrase, but he *did* perfect it.

A car horn sounded and Reggie snapped out of his daydream. He waved first, then looked up. Passing by, waving hello from her van, was his boss from New Broom Janitorial Services. "Bye, Carol, see you next year," he shouted, making himself laugh. "No more work. Big, big walk!" Reggie rocked forward and kept on walking, talking and laughing out loud.

Reggie Feckley thought about his dreams and fantasies. "I want to live in my own house," he reminded himself as he strode past the many rows of houses. "I'll build it myself. Other people have houses. I can have a house, too. It'll be a house in the woods."

Reggie had never really learned how to put his dreams on a road to reality. All he had was the dream. Turning dreams into reality is something that is taught and learned. Unfortunately, it hasn't always been taught to people with developmental disabilities. "Why bother?" the old system believed, "What can they do with it anyway?" Could WALKABOUT turn that old belief around and put Reggie on the road to reality? A road that showed him that dreams could truly become real?

Reggie walked out onto the wooden pier, picked up a pebble and threw it over the rail. He watched the splash and then turned around and scanned the majestic Olympic peaks towering above the highest evergreens. He headed back uptown towards his good friend Shirley Knight's house. Shirley also worked at the group home and was the supervisor of Reggie's building. Shirley knew how anxious Reggie would be the night before WALKABOUT began, so she had invited him to spend Saturday night at her house. "I like that," he told her when she made the offer to fill his last night at home with movies, popcorn and ice cream.

Shirley was very impressed with Reggie's ambition and wanted to show it. "From step one until the very end of WALKABOUT, movies, popcorn, ice cream and big dinners will be the exception and not the rule," she explained to Reggie.

"No problem!" stated Reggie.

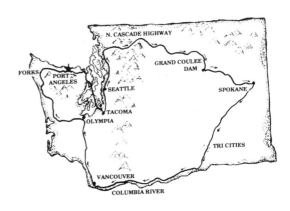

chapter 2

PLANNING, TRAINING and ANTICIPATING

A warm, overcast spring day, in the middle of April, was as good as any to map out the route for WALKABOUT. Reggie, Janet, and I sprawled over the Washington State map strewn across Janet's office floor. Confused by all the lines on the map, Reggie mostly listened to the ideas Janet and I came up with. He wasn't concerned about where we walked, just as long as we walked.

We sketched a route that we figured would be 1,300 walking miles around the state of Washington. We hoped to be back in our homes and our own beds within three months of our first steps.

"All we would have to do is average 14 miles a day, rain or shine," I explained after highlighting what appeared to be a good, walkable route.

"No problem." Reggie was very agreeable. He would get up every few minutes and pace. He was ready to go anytime.

Janet was skeptical. She had a better understanding of distance than Reggie. "I'm just glad that all I'm doing is driving the support vehicle," she said. She was happy to leave the walking up to the professionals. As support driver, Janet's main duty would include fund-raising and finding places for us to sleep at night. Hopefully, she would also be able to arrange for us to speak to groups of people about WALKABOUT on our route. "Fourteen miles each and every day?" she questioned, raising an eyebrow. "For three months? I don't think so."

"Would you believe...*12* miles a day for *four* months?" I asked, cracking a smile. Walking around the state with Reggie and Janet on WALKABOUT would be a world away from the trip Dixie and I took across America. It was impossible to judge exactly what each team member would realistically be able to accomplish for an extended period of time. Dixie and I usually walked about a thousand miles beginning in late spring, continuing through the summer into early autumn. For the winter, we did some fast talking and promised hard work to anyone willing to give us a chance at some new and interesting job. Then the following spring, we'd hit the road again, ending up "who knows where." WALKABOUT would be totally different from my cross-country trip, but it had two very important aspects in common. One, we'd be walking; and two, we didn't know what we were getting into. But just like when Dixie and I left New Orleans, Reggie, Janet, Dixie and I were determined to give WALKABOUT our best shot.

"I've been thinking," Janet said. "Since we'll be sharing a booth with the centennial people, maybe we should leave on the last day of the fair from the fairgrounds. We'll have hundreds of people right there for our 'blast-off'," she mused.

The local centennial commission of Port Angeles had sanctioned WALKABOUT as an official centennial event and allowed us to share a booth with them. We'd be able to meet more people, tell them about WALKABOUT and hopefully get a lot of support and donations. "We can advertise our blast-off as another fair event. The more people that get involved from the beginning, the more support we'll have behind us with every mile."

"Yeah," I said, running the idea through my head, "that works out well. That's late August, isn't it? If we leave Port Angeles at that time, we can beat the winter snowstorms before they hit the Cascade Mountains in the central part of the state, and we can miss the blistering summer heat of the desert in Eastern Washington. Then, by the time it gets cold in the east, we'll be back on the west side of the mountains where it's temperate." I've walked many miles in weather that was anything but perfect, and learned the hard way that showing respect to Mother Nature was always an important concern to successful long distance walking. One must walk with the weather, not against it. "You know, the more we think about all this, the better everything is coming together, almost naturally."

Janet looked at Reggie and asked, "Anything you want to add, Reg?" Reggie listened but wasn't very concerned about the details of the plan. He had no previous experience to compare to, but it was important to ask him anyway. After all, it was *his* walk.

"No problem," he said. "Let's go!"

"Then WALKABOUT begins on August 20th," Janet said triumphantly.

Through the rest of winter, all through the spring and most of the summer, we planned and we trained. I added extra mandatory miles to Reggie's daily strolls. Twice a week we found time to take long walks together, heading up the roads leading to the mountains. We worked up to five miles uphill and walked the same distance down. Sometimes we ran part of the way. "There are many different muscles in our legs, Reg," I explained. "Some muscles are used when we go uphill, some when we go down, and others are used when we walk on flat ground."

"I'm strong, Steve," he told me.

"I know, Reg, but we still have to get stronger. You've never trained for anything before, have you?"

"Nope," he said. "I'm already strong. Are you strong, Steve?"

"Pretty strong, Reg. But I have to get back into shape. I've been lazy this winter. No matter how much we train, and no matter how good we are at walking, WALKABOUT won't be easy. Once we get started, we are going to be walking over ten miles every day. Even when we're tired and bored, we're going to have to walk, walk, walk. It'll make these walks feel like a short stroll. You don't mind training, do you?"

"I like it," he always said. "I like to walk." He never hesitated when I asked him to train with me, but he wasn't convinced that he wasn't already strong enough to begin WALKABOUT at any moment. We had this conversation almost every time we took training walks together, but I didn't mind. It was all part of the process. We both had so much to learn.

"Is Schlicky strong, too?" Reggie asked. Reggie cared about Dixie. Dixie, like myself, developed friendships based on how her relationship with a person evolved. Because of the training sessions, Dixie was beginning to associate Reggie with walking and I could see that a foundation for a real friendship was forming.

"She's in training, too, Reg," I answered. "We played ball just yesterday." Although Dixie accompanied us on every walk, it wasn't her stamina I was concerned about. Every two or three days we played "chase the ball" on hard, rough asphalt pavement in the local school yard. My main concern was the pads on her feet. We had to toughen them up. "Hopefully her pads will be as tough as my unshaven face by the time we are ready to leave," I added.

"Ha, ha," cracked Reggie. "You should grow a beard, like me."

"Then everyone would get the two of us mixed up," I joked. Reggie joined me in laughter. We don't look anything alike.

Reggie is 6-feet-tall. He is slim, and with his long, skinny legs he seems even taller. His light brown hair is brushed back and you can see how his hairline has moved back with age. He sports a thick mustache all year long, and in the winter his full beard makes him pretty hairy. Then his broad beard covers the loose muscles of his face, although it can't hide a tenseness that Reggie sometimes shows around his eyes, forehead and lips. While planning WALKABOUT, we decided it would be easier to stay clean without hairy cheeks and a hairy chin. He wouldn't shave his beard off until summer, though. "I'll keep the mustache," he decided.

I am also six feet and slim, but I have a full head of black hair (yes, I know, there are plenty of gray strands, too) and I'm clean-shaven.

Dixie doesn't look anything like either one of us although she's hairy from the tip of her nose to the tip of her tail. She has no choice but to keep it that way! Shaving her light brown fur, no matter how hot it gets, would be like asking a person to walk naked in the glaring sun without sunscreen. It's best just to brush her often, preventing any unwanted extra fur from over-heating her. Of course, with her big ears, golden-orange eyes, powerful body

*Training in the
Olympic Mountains*

and intelligent, experienced face, Dixie was the most attractive of the future WALKABOUT walkers.

In the early evenings, while Reggie was at work, two outgoing, straightforward, "go-get'm" group home tenants, Jody Markham and Mary Miller, joined me as we went door to door and store to store asking for support from the townspeople. We raised enough money and gathered enough equipment to get WALKABOUT in motion. But getting someone to donate a van was a bit beyond the fantasy, so we decided to turn my big, tan, 4-wheel drive Isuzu Trooper into the WALKABOUT support vehicle.

As we patiently waited for summer to roll by, we trained, we collected donations, we fixed up the Trooper, and we got permission from all the people necessary to put WALKABOUT on the road.

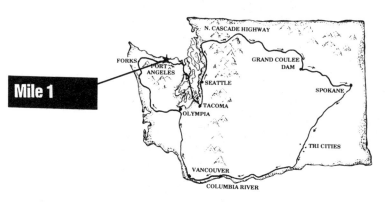

chapter 3

Sunday, AUGUST 20th

Waiting for August 20th to approach was like waiting for the turtle to cross the finish line. Months of training, planning and anticipating seemed like years, but finally, our day arrived.

I loaded the Trooper with clothing, gear, food, and other necessities, and that poor truck was jam-packed from dashboard to rear defroster. For the next few months, this motorized storage center was to be the home of three adults and one big dog. It had to carry everything we would need, including our support driver, and occasionally Reggie, Dixie and me.

It was Sunday morning and we were ready to walk! There was nothing left to do except wait until the official kick-off time. The official kick-off place for WALKABOUT was the entrance to the Clallam County Fairgrounds, on the western edge of Port Angeles. Janet knew that Reggie didn't like crowds, although soon enough he'd be surrounded by the biggest crowd of his life. Reggie decided to spend the morning relaxing at the group home.

I drove over to the fairgrounds early, to clean out our WALKABOUT space in the Washington State Centennial booth. The four-day fair was coming to a close and we were about to take our first steps. Janet stayed behind with Reggie. "Steve and Dixie are taking care of things at the fairgrounds. Why don't you go through your room and make sure you've packed everything you need," Janet suggested to Reggie.

"No problem," he answered Janet. He walked back to her office five minutes later. "I got everything."

"Great. Listen, I have to run to town and get a few last-minute things for myself. Why don't you relax here at the group home for a while, Reg," Janet suggested.

"No problem," answered Reggie.

"Don't go anywhere," Janet strongly reminded him. "And don't worry. We'll get you to the fairgrounds on time." This was one day Reggie didn't need to go on one of his treks around town!

"No problem. I'll stay here. Big, big walk, right?"

"That's right," said Janet. She laughed. Her nerves were as frazzled as a hen in a doghouse. I just couldn't imagine why. I mean, all we were doing was leaving our homes to live in an overgrown car as we walked around the twentieth largest state in the union for a few months. What was the big deal? It wasn't as if we were hot-air ballooning to Europe!

Actually, Janet's life wasn't going to change all that much for a few days. Rob Campbell, the administrator of the group home, had the honor of being the first WALKABOUT support driver. He earned that honor because he was the big boss at Lauridsen Group Home and he said he really would appreciate having the opportunity. I think he said something like, "If I don't go, then nobody goes," but don't quote me on that. Well, he is the boss, and also our good friend. We were thrilled with his support and enthusiasm. Rob would be our support driver from Port Angeles to the point where we walked off the Olympic Peninsula. Then Janet would join us full-time.

Hours dragged as I cleaned up the booth and moved all the WALKABOUT T-shirts, buttons and balloons into the support vehicle. Hopefully, we'd sell them when we got on the road, making money to buy food and gasoline. Although Rob would be our first support driver, Janet had promised to make sure that everything would be ready for him when he met us at the fairgrounds. With her own errands to take care of, she decided to ask one of her staff to bring Reggie to the fairgrounds for kick-off.

Finally, Janet arrived at the fairgrounds. She was nervous and all a-flutter. She had one last duty to accomplish and that was to get Reggie, Dixie and me together and ready to take that first step. An excited crowd of friends, co-workers, neighbors and well-wishers had gathered at the front gate. They had been invited to become official "WALKABOUTers" and were excited about escorting Reggie, Dixie and me on the first few miles across Port Angeles.

There was a glowing energy in the air as the crowd of people mulled around the front gate. The parade was ready to take off. WALKABOUT was only moments from walking into history. Local newspaper camerapeople were ready to catch it all on film. There was only one hitch. Only one thing missing. Not one of those people was from the group home! And Reggie was nowhere to be seen! Janet became frantic. She ran to the other entrances to check if the crowd from the group home misunderstood which gate we were going to start from. No one was anywhere! Back she ran to the centennial booth where Dixie and I were waiting to get started.

"Is Reggie here? Did I simply miss him?" she asked, huffing and puffing. There was more than just a hint of fear and frustration in her voice. "Have you seen anyone from the group home?" We hadn't even started yet and already 20 people were missing!

It was a fairly ridiculous concept. I thought she was kidding. "Nope. Nobody's here but Dixie and me and our backpacks. Hey, did we lose Reggie even before we left town?" I joked. From the look on her face, I guessed she wasn't kidding.

Janet ran off to search for Reggie without pausing to answer. Dixie and I followed her back to the main gate. The whereabouts of Reggie was important to WALKABOUT. After all, if he got lost before we even left, it was going to be one *longgggg* walk around the state!

Back at the gate we found that some of the staff and tenants from the group home had arrived. Janet frantically scanned the crowd. Where was Reggie!?!

"Has anyone seen Reggie?" Janet asked.

"I think I saw him walking around about a half-hour ago," someone said.

"Where?" she demanded.

"I dunno," came the answer.

"Melissa," Janet said to one of the staff, "have you seen Reggie?"

"Rob went to get him. He's still at the group home."

"Why didn't you bring him?" Janet asked her.

"He wouldn't get in the van when I told him to," explained Melissa. Janet sighed. "He said that you told him not to go anywhere," Melissa added.

Everyone had expected a glitch or two, but in our worst nightmares we never dreamed that Reggie would be left behind! Rob rushed to fulfill his first support duty by making a mad dash back to the group home to get Reggie.

Four o'clock, the official kick-off time, came—and went. The crowd anxiously waited for Rob to come back with Reggie. Finally, at 4:30, the soft murmuring of the restless crowd rose to a round of cheers and applause as Reggie and Rob arrived and joined Janet, Dixie and me in the heart of the crowd. Reggie looked around in amazement. "They like me?" he whispered in my ear. Yes, all these people were there for him! The throng of people swarmed in and covered us with last-minute hugs, good-byes, and best wishes. This was the moment we'd all been waiting for! Our dream was becoming reality.

After months of planning, we took our first WALKABOUT step. With hands clasped and raised high over our heads, Reggie, Dixie and I began what we hoped to be a 1,300-mile trek. We left the Clallam County Fairgrounds surrounded by dozens of friends. The parade of people moved through town at a festive pace, and everywhere there were balloons, smiling faces, and the basic, everyday, Western Washington clouds. Happy feet and happy walkers escorted their friends to the edge of town!

The three-block-long crowd drifted across Port Angeles like the fog rolling in from the Strait of Juan de Fuca. Reggie safely fell behind the mass of people and carried the rear, watching the parade of people ahead of him. Dixie and I were surrounded by the crowd. Yet, with all the people, only Reggie, Dixie and I stood out. We were the only ones wearing a backpack; the only ones who would need extra water, sweaters, socks, and snacks.

Alone in his thoughts, Reggie walked along looking at all the

Photo by Steve Breakstone

*The crowd went back to their
homes, but WALKABOUT walks on*

people that were there for him. "Teamwork!" he was thinking.
That was another of Reggie's favorite phrases.

About one-and-a-half hours after leaving the fairgrounds, we
arrived at McDonald's on the east edge of Port Angeles.
McDonald's graciously provided pop to all who had joined
WALKABOUT on the first leg of the journey. I collapsed on the grass
outside the restaurant, making it seem like the three miles we'd
just hiked was too much for me. But I didn't fool anyone! Reggie
drank his pop and was ready to go. There would be no stopping
him now!

Dixie was ready to go, too. All through town I'd had her on a
leash, but now she was ready to be free again. Neither one of us
enjoyed being tied to each other by a leash. Dixie knew the rules
of the road; she'd proved it over thousands of American miles.

It was time to say good-bye to our across-town escorts. They had their homes and families to get back to. Our home was back there, too, but we wouldn't be seeing it for a long time. "Our home is on the road now, Reg," I said. I knew that these three miles would not be like the next 1,297. From here on in it would be only two men and a dog.

"Big, big walk," he said. "Everyday we walk and camp out. Peace and quiet. I can't wait to get to the mountains."

The surface of a man is not a mystery. It is the inside that is interesting. Although I'd known Reggie Feckley for almost a year, I knew that I would now begin to see the growth of the "inner" man. I wondered how he would change. I began to wonder how I would change.

We were only a few miles out of town, but the big trip had begun! The clouds let go with drops of rain but there was no turning back. It would be months before we would see Port Angeles again. We had walked just a few miles beyond the city limits when the sprinkling rain became a serious shower and we called it a day. The first night was spent at our friend Pat Barnard's house, not far from where we stopped walking.

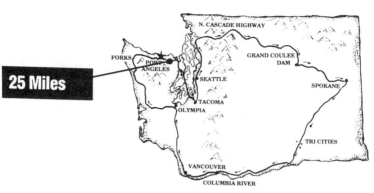

25 Miles

N. CASCADE HIGHWAY
FORKS
PORT ANGELES
GRAND COULEE DAM
SEATTLE
SPOKANE
TACOMA
OLYMPIA
TRI CITIES
VANCOUVER
COLUMBIA RIVER

chapter 4

The FIRST FEW DAYS

The first few days would be "break-in" days. All the experiences that Dixie and I had on our walk across America were history. It felt like we had to learn to walk all over again. We knew how to walk with each other; now we had to learn how to walk with Reggie.

Dixie led the way as we walked east on Highway 101, the only major road on the Olympic Peninsula. I walked a few feet behind Dixie's trotting legs and Reggie walked right on my heels, holding up the rear. Cars passed us as we passed homes and businesses and open pastures.

Dixie, with her dog-pack laying on her sides and buckled under her belly, was feeling good and strong. She proudly carried her own leash, biscuits and my rain gear. Her pack also served as a walking advertisement, because WALKABOUT was written in bright yellow on each side of her pack. I took as much pride and happiness in Dixie as a father feels for his daughter. In fact, that is how I have always felt about her. With cool weather and paws tingling with excitement,

21

Dixie could walk across a continent. She was born to walk!

"It'll seem like the same thing because we're walking again, Dix, but I know it's going to be very different." Even though people think I'm crazy for talking to Dixie like she's a person, we've always had a special bond and way of communicating since the day I adopted her.

Then I thought of the man walking behind me. From the moment Reggie agreed to WALKABOUT, our relationship really began to evolve. The bond was beginning to cement. Only time, and strides, would determine how strong it would become.

Like Dixie and me, Reggie was in good shape. But his real test was now beginning. Every day would be a long 10- to 15- mile walk. "As I've said before, Reg, sometimes the weather will be perfect. Sometimes the weather will be anything but perfect. Some days we'll have tons of energy. Some days our legs will feel like a ton of bricks."

"No problem. Big, big walk," he responded. That was the most important thing. Details and potential problems were not his concern. Maybe he was on to something. Maybe I worried too much. Of course, maybe it was good that at least one of us thought of these things! I may be an expert walker, but I am not an expert on life.

Although we had been talking about it for months, it was hard to tell if he had a serious understanding of what he was in for. Maybe it didn't matter. Maybe it would be *all* that mattered when he got tired, bored or missed his friends. Reggie was about to learn the meaning of the word "challenge." The walking wasn't just for fun anymore, it was now a responsibility. I had a challenge, too. I had to help Reggie accomplish his challenge.

We had been friends for almost a year, and yet Reggie and I had so much to learn about each other. The first thing Reggie learned about me is that I like to keep moving! I wanted to do nothing but walk until we were far away from Port Angeles. I feared this was all a dream and at any minute someone would say, "HA-HA, guys. Just kidding!" and drive us back home. Reggie also found I could go hours without speaking. That's just the way I am.

Reggie is just the way he is, too. A person's personality is a unique manifestation of how his experiences have affected him. Of course, Reggie's developmental disability and speech disorder, as well as the way people have reacted to those differences, are all part of his life experience. "I wonder how different I would be if I had gone through some of the challenges that Reggie has experienced," I thought to myself.

So many interesting thoughts were going through my head on this first day when, because of his constant interruption, I began to realize how much Reggie liked to chat. I also found out how much he repeated himself over and over and over and over. Maybe I should have realized this before, but the two-to-three hours during our training walks represented the longest span of time I had ever spent with him. I hadn't put two and two together. It had been easy to pass off. "Now I'll be with him 24 hours a day," I thought. "I bet this constant, repetitive chatting is how he learned to talk." I figured that because people had a hard time understanding him, he had to say things again and again. I don't know. Maybe he just didn't have much else to say. Either way, I saw that we both had to adjust to each other's habits.

"I like to walk, Steve," Reggie would say from two feet behind me. This was a familiar conversation.

"Me, too, Reg."

"I'm strong, right?" He asked. I was never sure if he had too much self-esteem or not enough. Was he convincing me or was he convincing himself?

"Yes, Reg, you are strong. And you're going to get stronger."

"Praise the Lord."

"Praise the Lord."

"Are you strong, Steve?"

"Yep, I'm strong, too."

"I'm strong, too. Right?"

"Yes, you are."

"Hallelujah!"

"Hallelujah."

"Praise the Lord!"

"Praise the Lord," I repeated back.

These two particular "Reggie-isms" invaded his conversation on a regular basis. Reggie appreciated the "Good Lord" or "Big Boss" but he repeated these phrases so much that I wasn't sure it was for spiritual reasons. He said it very clearly and he liked to say it...often!

I first believed that Reggie said things more than once to make sure that I had heard him. I tried repeating back to Reggie what he had said so he would know that I understood. He didn't take the hint. I told him that many people did not like to hear the same sentences over and over. New things took time and patience to learn. With over 1,300 miles to walk, I knew we had plenty of time to learn and practice. It was important to find a balance between accepting Reggie for who he was and hoping to teach him to say things only once.

We walked along and I wondered if this would be the typical conversation for the next three months. "I hope not," I prayed. I didn't appreciate my own skepticism. I stopped, turned and looked at Reggie. He smiled but I didn't say anything. Then he shrugged his shoulders. I smiled as I looked at his face. The usual sharp lines on his forehead, and the "crow's feet" growing from his eyes, were already more relaxed than I could ever remember. It was as if I was looking at him through a soft-focus lens.

As we walked we were reminded that you have to be ready for rain on the Olympic Peninsula at ANYTIME. August is usually warm and dry in Western Washington, the only month that sunshine can be counted upon. Or so we thought until reality hit us in the form of rain clouds. Rain fell on us as if someone was turning a sprinkler on and off. The light sprinkles didn't bother Reggie at all. He didn't even bother to put on his rain jacket. All Reggie cared about was the peace and quiet of life on the road. Even though we were just a few miles from home, he had no roommates to worry about and no staff asking him to clean his room, make his work-lunch, do his laundry, mop his floors, etc. Before him were just miles and miles and months and months to do what he loved best: walking.

"Reg, it's great to see you all excited. I don't want to be a bummer, but you *do* realize that it's not all going to be fun and games, don't you?" I felt I couldn't remind him of this enough. I knew from experience that sooner or later our legs would get tired. Or, more importantly, our minds would just get tired of walking. If he was prepared to expect it, he would be able to deal with it.

"No problem," he said.

"Well, I hope there are no problems, Reg," I said.

"We're going to walk and camp out. Walk the United States!"

"Not the United States, Reg." I reminded him. "Let's just start with the State of Washington."

"No problem. Big, big walk. I'm strong, right?"

Reggie liked the thought of walking across the United States, but that was quite a bit further than Janet and I had planned. For our first walk we agreed on staying in just one state. At least Janet and I agreed on it.

Of course, *where* we were walking wasn't as important as *how* we were walking.

"O.K., Reg, time for a test," I said to him. I didn't have to turn around to talk; he was right on my heels. "Which side of the road do we walk on?"

"We walk facing the cars so we can see them coming."

"Right! And what about the lines on the road?"

"You said to watch Dixie and see how she always walks on this side of the white line. Not this side," Reggie said as he jumped to the right of the solid white line that marks the edge of the roadway, "but this side," he said as he jumped back.

"And what if there is a sidewalk?" I continued, amused at the way he bounced back and forth while answering the question.

"Walk on it!" he answered triumphantly, raising his clenched hand. Reggie had passed the test!

"Good job, Reg."

"That's teamwork, right?"

"Right!"

"Hallelujah!"

The first full day of WALKABOUT continued to be exciting and full of surprises. A local Texaco station donated a tank of gas for the support car, and McDonald's in the neighboring town of Sequim had contributed a lunch which Rob brought back to us as we neared town. Even Dixie's efforts were rewarded with a 40-pound bag of dog food from the Clallam Co-op Hardware Store! Life was good on WALKABOUT!

Sequim is 17 miles east of Port Angeles and is its closest neighbor. By 5:30 P.M., just as we made it to the city limits, the sprinkle had become a downpour! We were soaked before we could get our rain jackets out of the backpacks. We had planned to camp at nearby Sequim Bay State Park, but we decided the idea of camping out in muddy puddles wasn't as fun as it sounded. Even

Reggie, who couldn't wait to sleep in a tent, knew we needed to find a different place to sleep.

"Not to worry, Reg! When we walked across America, Dixie and I learned that there are always alternatives."

"No problem," agreed Reggie. He wasn't worrying.

"If we can't find a dry place to stay in Sequim, we could always take the support car and go back home for a night." Reggie didn't say anything. His face went blank. I interpreted that as meaning he didn't like the idea. "Of course, if we can't deal with a little rain, we'll never make it around the whole state. Then again, this isn't just a little rain. It's raining cats and dogs!" Reggie shrugged his shoulders. "Something will pop up, I'm sure," I said with confidence.

"I want to sleep here!" Reggie said. I took that as being a good sign. Of course, at the moment, "here" was literally on the side of the road.

We met up with Rob and talked about possibilities as the rain continued to fall. He had an idea of finding a church that would put us up for the night, and off he went to find one. Reggie and I kept walking, discussing the possibility of sleeping in a church basement, when a man with a very happy face drove up beside us. Gerry Andrews, the man with the happy face, had seen Reggie, Dixie and me and had taken pity on us. He had met us at the fair, and had donated some money to our cause. Gerry was not only the Associate Pastor of the Sequim Presbyterian Church, he was also a man with a house and hot food and dry beds.

"Where are you guys spending the night?" he asked as he rolled down the window.

"Our support driver is checking out the Lutheran Church right now, and I'm sure they'll have a basement we can stay in," I told him.

Gerry wouldn't have any of that. "I got a better deal. How would you like to stay at my house? I'll even feed you dinner!"

Reggie and I looked at each other, then looked back at Gerry. "Show us the way!" we exclaimed.

"Great!" he exclaimed back. I wasn't sure who was more excited about the prospect of us sleeping in his home. He held on to his great big smile and gave us directions to his house. He drove off to tell his wife as Reggie, Dixie and I waited for Rob. When he arrived, we told him about our arrangements with Gerry. Rob had arranged for us to sleep in the church basement, but he liked our plans better. "And dinner too? Wow!" he said. Being invited to a friendly stranger's house for dinner was very new to Rob. Unfortunately he couldn't stay. The "sprinkles" in Port Angeles had caused a flood at the group home and "SuperRob" had been asked to fix it when he called to check in.

Rob dropped us off at Gerry's house. As Reggie and I were setting down our packs we overheard that Gerry's church was moving out of one building and putting everything into storage until the new church was built. On the Olympic Peninsula, rain never puts an end to plans. If it did, nothing would *ever* get done! People would never leave their homes, kids would never get fresh air, and moss-covered dogs would never be let inside the house. Being gracious guests, we insisted on earning our keep and innocently asked, "Can we help?" Little did we know what we were getting into!

Not long after walking 13 miles, Reggie and I were put to work in the biggest rainstorm to hit Sequim since Noah built himself an ark. Two pianos and three organs absolutely needed to be moved from the church basement just that night. Through narrow hallways and out finger-smashing doors, we hauled them up slippery staircases and into U-Haul trucks—all in the pouring rain. It felt really good (if soggy) to earn our keep.

"I'm strong, right, Steve?" asked Reggie, showing his muscle when we were all finished.

"Yes, that was hard work. You did good."

"I'm strong, right?"

"Yes, you are strong, Reg."

"You're strong, too?"

"Yes, me too. Thank you."

"Praise the Lord!" said Reggie.

"Praise the Lord."

"Praise the Lord," added Gerry, standing to the side, enjoying our conversation. Gerry smiled, ever so contented. I wondered if Gerry was considering it divine intervention that brought us together. We needed a good place to sleep and Gerry needed moving men. What an interesting possibility.

"Hallelujah," Reggie went on to say.

"Hallelujah."

"Hallelujah!"

Exhausted and dripping wet, we finally made it to Gerry's house for the evening. His wife, Freddie, made us a feast in appreciation for our hard work as moving men and WALKABOUTers. After getting to know each other over a very belly-filling spaghetti dinner, Gerry and Freddie showed us to our beds. We conked out right away and slept like babies. So went our first full day of WALKABOUT!

A much prettier day greeted us as the sun shone through the windows the next morning. The aroma of bacon, eggs, and toast got us out of bed, and our great breakfast prepared us to hit the road a-walkin'. "Today, Reg, we go beyond Sequim," I announced. *Now* this trip would finally get serious! Sequim was like the next-door neighbor to Port Angeles, and walking past Sequim was like walking off the block. "Now things get *really* exciting, Reg!" I added happily.

"Let's walk the United States!" he said, bouncing like a ball.

"Let's just start with the United State of Washington," I reminded him, hoping he would agree that was enough for now.

"No problem," consented Reggie. I thought so, too.

Reggie fell in line, walking right behind me as we hit the road. The 12 miles to the next "town" of Gardiner were lined with green trees and offered fantastic views of the Strait. It felt so "at home" to be back on the road. Even Dixie was ready to walk forever. Unfortunately, Reggie was beginning to poop out. This was only the second full day, and more often than I expected, Reggie asked me, "Can we take a rest, Steve?"

"We've been taking an awful lot of rests, Reg," I said more than once. "Walking is *work*, Reg. Not exactly like the work you do at your job for New Broom Janitorial, but it's still work. We can take rests, but we can't sit around all day. I was thinking, Reg, that most people wouldn't think walking is such an important talent, but we both know people that can't walk."

"Like Mark and Mike," remembered Reggie. Mike is a man that gets around in a wheelchair, and Mark has cerebral palsy. His right leg is shorter than his left leg and he can't walk very well. If he walks too much, he gets very tired and usually winds up on the ground.

"That's right. I bet they wish they could do this," I said.

"We're lucky," Reggie told me.

"I guess so. Maybe walking all by itself isn't so special, but the message you spread through walking is."

"Let's keep walking, we can rest later," Reg said with a burst of energy. Reggie didn't really need motivation to walk, he just needed to learn how to pace himself so that he could walk even farther.

"By pacing ourselves, we can walk a lot, get in our miles, and rest when we are tired. That way we'll always enjoy ourselves," I explained.

"I'll listen to you, Steve. You can teach me."

"You'll teach me things, too, Reg," I said, more to myself than to him. A good teacher also learns a lot from his students.

"I'm smart, right?" he asked. I didn't answer. I didn't think it was actually required. Reggie didn't ask again.

I was hoping to cover 15 miles that day, but I had to understand that if we walked only 12 miles at this part of the trip, that was O.K., too. Even though Reggie walked a lot at home, he never walked that much in one day. He had to learn to push himself a little harder, and I had to learn to be patient. I was confident we would work it out.

"When we get to a store can we buy some candy, Steve?"

"Sure, Reg, but remember, not too much. From now on we have to eat smart. We can't walk around Washington on Snickers bars." Reggie's affection for confection was well known. I was hoping that he would develop more of an interest in strange foods like apples, oranges and bananas. "Hey, Reg, did you know that juice and milk, especially chocolate milk, are almost as tasty as soda pop?"

"No problem," he said.

"Yeah," I thought. "We'll see about that." I was pretty sure that milk, especially the chocolate milk idea, could seduce him but I wasn't as confident in the alluring qualities of those other foods. Only time would tell if it would be a problem or not.

I convinced Reggie that we had enough walking to do without going out of our way to find a store that wasn't right beside the road. We walked until we came upon a store that practically blocked our path.

"Steve...?" pointed Reggie, ready to explode.

"Let's do it!" I said. Too late! Reggie was already inside.

Walking and stopping to buy candy...what more could Reggie dream of, I wondered? It made me happy to see him so happy, and we enjoyed a 30-minute candy bar/chocolate milk break. It wasn't a half-bad break at all and soon enough we were getting ready to get back in action.

"It's O.K. to take a break but we have walking to do," I said as we adjusted our packs. It was my job to keep us on track. Reggie looked re-energized and contentedly followed Dixie and me. Then, altogether too soon, I heard, "Steve, I want to rest."

"Again!" I wondered to myself. "He can't possibly be tired! Is he getting bored already? Great! This is going to be the shortest WALKABOUT in history." I imagined how foolish we would all look if he decided to turn around and just go home. "How many breaks is he going to ask for before I finally get the hint?"

I became upset and frustrated but kept it to myself. I hated thinking that I would have to constantly push him for 1,300 miles. Had I expected too much of a person with a developmental disability? Had I ignored his limitations? What *were* his limitations? It occurred to me that this very question could have been asked of anyone, disabled or otherwise. Then I thought of another question. "Hey, Reg, do you feel O.K.?" I asked.

"My feet hurt a little. I promise, I'll walk later."

"Your feet hurt, huh?" Of course! "Can I see them, please?" Reggie stopped walking, raised his right leg and pointed his boot towards me. I laughed. "No, I mean your naked feet."

Reggie and I walked over to some trees by the side of the road and he sat on a stump. I didn't notice any limp. He removed his boots and socks and I bent down to take a look. After the tears cleared from my now-clouded eyes, I saw them...BLISTERS!! All the pep talks in the world wouldn't fix blisters! Reggie's feet were reacting to their new life.

"Now I understand why you want to rest so much, Reg," I said.

"No problem," he replied.

"I don't agree. You use your feet when you walk, right?"

"Yup."

"And we're trying to walk the entire State of Washington?"

"Yup!"

"Then I believe we have a problem."

"You're right, Steve. I made a mistake. Everyone makes a mistake sometime," Reggie said as he shrugged his shoulders and flashed a smile that would make a con man proud.

"You're right about that, buddy," I said with a slight laugh. I removed my backpack, unzipped a side pocket and dug down to fetch out our first-aid kit. "Fortunately, I am ready for blister patrol," I said as I produced a long shiny sewing needle.

"Uh-oh," said Reggie, pulling his foot up his pant leg.

"Oh, be a man," I said, sterilizing the needle with alcohol. I knew Reggie well enough to know what to say to make him brave.

"I am a man, Steve. O.K., no problem," he said, handing back his foot.

I squatted down in front of him and placed his foot on my thigh. I held his foot in one hand and poured some alcohol on and around his blister.

"Ow!" Reggie flinched, reacting to the sting of the alcohol. Then I took the needle and poked. "YEOW!" he cried, trying to wiggle his foot from my hold.

"Oh, be a man."

"I am a man! It hurts!" he said, quite clearly.

"Oh, no it doesn't," I said, trying to convince him otherwise.

"Oh, yes it does."

"Just one more poke, hold still." I tightened my grip.

"OOOOWWW!"

"It's done. Let me just wipe it off and put a bandage on it." Ooze began to drain from the loose, flappy skin, and I allowed Reggie the privilege of cleaning his slime with a tissue. I'd already had enough fun.

"No more needles?" he asked, hesitantly.

"No more needles," I reassured him. And then I added, with a sly smile, "Until next time."

"I promise, I won't get any more blisters." Reggie said, quite determined. Reggie put his feet back together, ready to get away from me and the dreaded first-aid kit.

We might have slowed down some, but we weren't done in. No, it would take a lot more than soft feet to stop Reggie Feckley! Extra breaks, maybe. Less mileage, yes. But stop, HA! NO WAY!

"No problem," said Reggie as he bounced on his once-again

Blisters!

Photo by Steve Breakstone

happy feet. Dixie leaped up from her short rest, shook her body from her nose to the tip of her tail, and we were off. "Teamwork!" Reggie added, as we headed back to the road. With the destruction of Reggie's blister, we walked so well that by evening time we were close enough for Rob to drive us to the home of friends in the town of Chimacum.

The Edgerton family consists of Anders, Nancy, and their children, Sheffield and Sebastian. They live on a farm. They have cows and pigs and rabbits, a dog and a great big vegetable garden. Once again, we were treated to a feast. At this rate, we would walk 1,300 miles and gain weight! Even Dixie had a grand ol' time. She quickly made friends with the pigs. Dixie and the pigs ran up and down the pigpen fence, and between the barking and the oinking we couldn't tell who was having more fun!

Nancy and Anders gave us a tour of the farm and ended it by showing us where we were to sleep. Reggie was happy to know that people were nice enough to let us stay with them, but he was very frustrated. He couldn't wait to try out his tent. I guess we'd spent one too many nights indoors. Reggie just couldn't stand it any longer and asked, "Steve, can I sleep outside in my tent?"

"Believe me, Reg, later on we'll be sleeping out so much you'll be dreaming of a soft bed. We really should take advantage of sleeping on a bed in a house as much as we can."

Reggie didn't argue the point. Quietly, he said, "I like to camp."

Clearly, he was disappointed. Sometimes being an adult means having to accept disappointment. "Sure, Reg," came the words from my mouth. "Let's go set it up." Sometimes an adult can work around disappointment.

Reggie lifted his head. His eyes gleamed. That sight made my night! It was pure joy to see him so happy. He grabbed the tent and the poles from the support vehicle and looked around for a flat piece of ground. "Well, I guess it's you and the pigs tonight, Reg," I said. The only flat spot was right next to the pigsty. "You're going to wake up oinking."

"No problem," he joked, snorting through his nose. "I used to live on a farm." Reggie then proceeded to take the tent out of its stuff-sack and dump the poles on the ground. He stood there and looked down at them.

"Well, let's do it!" I said. I took one set of poles and began to fit them together. Reggie watched and attempted to do the same with the other set. He had a hard time figuring out how each end fit together but I let him try for a while. His face became contorted with confusion. The shadow of the barn overtook us as the sun lazily dropped below the horizon. Finally I said, "It's getting dark, Reg. Do you mind if I help?"

"I don't mind," he said handing the poles to me, "teamwork!" Although it contradicted his phrase, Reggie often liked to do things by himself, but this time he graciously accepted help. Together we connected the poles and I held the tent in place as he threaded them through the slots. We placed the fully formed tent over the ground cloth, and I showed Reggie where to pound in the tent stakes.

"Grab a rock," I said to Reggie, pointing to a bunch of stones laying by the fence, "and pound these stakes into the ground."

Reggie picked up a small boulder about the size of a basketball and quickly decided it was too big. He threw it back and exchanged it for a stone that was just a bit bigger than his fist. He pounded the stakes into the ground and together we attached the guy-lines that were connected to the tent. In no time the tent was tight and standing like a fortress. We grabbed his sleeping pad, sleeping bag and pillow out of the support car, unrolled, unstuffed and fluffed them and threw them inside the unzipped door flap. Reggie followed them into his new home and that was the last I saw of him.

"I'm a camping man now!" I heard him say through the wall of the tent.

"Don't you have to brush your teeth? Or go to the bathroom?"

"Good night, Steve. Good night, Schlicky. Good night, pigs. No oinking, tonight."

"Good night, Mr. Camping Man," I answered, laughing. "You are something else, Reggie Feckley," I said to myself as I walked back inside the house. Rob, Nancy and Anders were finishing up some cocoa when I came in. Soon after, Rob, Dixie and I headed to our beds. The three of us slept comfortably, but I believe Reggie slept with a smile.

Two more days of walking that tree-lined curvy road brought us to the Hood Canal Bridge. Rob parked the support vehicle and walked with us across the floating bridge.

"So this is what it's like for you guys," Rob said, his eyes cautiously watching the speeding cars passing right beside our legs.

The bridge was not made for walkers and there was no sidewalk to walk on. Skimming the surface of the canal, just above the white cresting waves, we carefully held close to the rail as the traffic raced by.

"Well, if we fall over, it's nice to know we won't fall too far," I said, teasing Rob.

"No problem," laughed Reggie. With 50 miles behind us, Reggie was fairly comfortable with the cars passing by so closely. We didn't like it but we were used to it. Rob looked as if he would have felt safer swimming across.

"This isn't fun!" Rob yelled, trying to be heard over the screaming traffic. "Maybe I should have said good-bye on the other side of the bridge."

Reggie and I just laughed. "It's good that you know the kind of life we WALKABOUTers are going through before you leave," I said. "This is not a 1,300 mile cakewalk."

"Shouldn't you put Dixie on a leash?" Rob questioned.

"It wouldn't be a bad idea with any other dog, but haven't you noticed how close she stays to my legs?" I asked him.

"All I notice is how close these cars are to *my* legs!"

Much to Rob's surprise, we made it to the other side without being smashed or splashed. It was time to say good-bye to the Olympic Peninsula and to Rob, as Janet had driven out to trade places with him. They recovered the support vehicle, exchanged car keys and we all hugged Rob good-bye.

"I'm very proud of all of you," Rob said before he drove off. He was our friend and my boss, and we couldn't have taken that first step without his support. "You are doing a great thing for the group home, yourselves and all your friends."

"Praise the Lord," Reggie said.

"Good-bye, guys."

"Good-bye, Rob."

Rob put the car into gear and drove off. Janet was now the official WALKABOUT support driver.

Another few walking miles put us right into Kitsap Memorial State Park. Although all the best spots were occupied when we arrived, we found a campsite just beside the bathroom. There were a few trees whose branches hung overhead but we were out in the open. Except for the trunks of those trees separating us from the next campsite, we had little privacy. But it became our home for the night and we helped each other set up the tents. We bought some firewood from the Ranger station and sat around the fire and cooked hamburgers. After dinner, Dixie went inside our tent and laid down on her foam pad. Quickly she drifted, like a log on a calm lake, into a deep sleep. Dogs usually sleep most of the day, and her awake cycle still wasn't quite used to our all-day walking schedule.

Reggie and I stayed up to share with Janet all the experiences we enjoyed during our first week. We told her about the rain, the blisters, the scenery, our new friends and even the food donations. We made everything sound so sensational she began to tingle with nervous excitement. She became so antsy about the thrills of WALKABOUT she tried to convince us to get walking again right then and there. Somehow we convinced her to settle for roasting a whole bag of marshmallows instead. It didn't quite quell her restlessness but it did keep her happy—or at least quiet. We had already walked over a dozen miles, it was dark and we weren't moving. She would just have to be patient and enjoy the anticipation (and the marshmallows) until we were ready to walk again. Even if Reggie and I were foolish enough to bow to Janet's whim, Dixie had made it quite clear that her walking day was long over.

Finally, after running out of stories and junk food, we followed Dixie's lead and went to sleep.

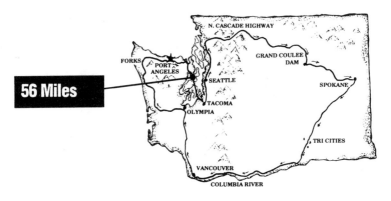

56 Miles

chapter 5

The FIRST CAMPOUTS

"Where's the cooler?" I called out. Janet had taken charge of the support vehicle, and already her messy style of "order" had me confused.

The support vehicle, my two-door Trooper, is long and narrow and tall. Usually, when it was just Dixie and me, I kept the back seat folded down. That way there was plenty of room to carry any thing we wanted, but mostly it gave Dixie a lot of space to enjoy a comfortable ride. For WALKABOUT we kept the back seat set up for Dixie and either Reggie or me when we were being driven to a place to sleep. Therefore we kept most of our gear stashed in the back cargo area. Somehow, Rob, Reggie and I managed to find space for three tents, sleeping bags, pads, pillows, assorted camping gear, clothing and toiletries, a 40-pound bag of dog food, a cooler of food, pots and pans, and a milk crate filled mostly with plates and utensils. We also had large plastic bags stuffed with WALKABOUT T-shirts, buttons and balloons, and a long folding table for Janet to set up "shop." The Trooper, crammed to the hilt, afforded no elbow space, and Rob could hardly see out the rear-view mirror. It was crowded but it was "home." We had everything we needed, but it was a good thing we didn't need anything more.

And then Janet replaced Rob. Once he removed all his personal stuff, Janet conveniently rearranged all the equipment, food and clothing we had so neatly arranged. Then she added her stuff. As a matter of fact, I think it was *all* her stuff! It was just about everything I had ever seen in her apartment! Janet enjoyed camping but didn't believe in "roughing it."

We decided to take the day off and sleep in, which was a real treat for Reggie, Dixie and me, although Janet couldn't wait to get on the road. Nevertheless, she slept late. I was the first one up that morning, and when I went to get my chocolate milk, I was in for a surprise!

"Hey, Reg," I asked him as he emerged from his orange tent, "have you seen the cooler?"

"Nope."

"Hey, Jan, where'd you put the cooler?" I called to her.

"Over by the picnic table," she replied.

"Oh no you didn't," I said.

"Oh yes I did."

"Well, I don't see it."

"Well, maybe you're not looking right."

"Do you think I'm looking wrong?"

"Well, that's where I left it."

"Janet?"

"Yes, Steve."

"It's GONE!!!"

"No. It can't be. Maybe it's just moved."

"All by itself?" I was disappointed. "I want my chocolate milk!"

But it *was* gone! Someone had quietly tiptoed into the campsite during the night and stolen our cooler. Dixie slept inside the tent with me, but I'd ignored her when she'd growled during the night. I thought she was just upset that some other campers were walking close to our tent on their way to a midnight "run to the bathroom." I shouldn't have doubted her! I should have let her do her job. I should have let her out of my tent, and if that wasn't enough "shoulds," I realized that I should have let her chase down the marauding burglars!

There was no use whining about the lost chocolate milk, but I did anyway. I wasn't too thrilled about losing the cheese, the jelly, the butter, the juice, the lettuce and the apples, either, but the chocolate milk was the worst! The only consolation was that we kept a crate in the support vehicle that served as a pantry for foods such as cereal, peanut butter, bread and canned vegetables. So that morning, breakfast consisted of instant oatmeal with no milk. We weren't terribly satisfied, but at least we weren't going to starve.

Reggie had walked away when I'd started whining. This was his first official camp-out and he didn't want to know about it being ruined. Until our cooler was stolen, Reggie was in camping heaven. He wasn't about to leave heaven so he just moved it to a different part of the campground until I got over the "tragedy."

It was a disappointing chocolate milk-less mini-breakfast, but we got by. We did our best to fill our bellies, and then Reggie and Janet headed to town in search of a car-top carrier (and more chocolate milk). With all Janet's luxury items, there was hardly room for Reggie, Dixie or me! We knew that the Costco Discount Warehouse was close by, and Reggie and Janet headed for it.

Before they left, we had unloaded the back of the car to make room for the carrier Reggie and Janet were to bring back. We scattered all our stuff about our campsite, and Dixie and I hung around the campsite with absolutely nothing to do but make sure slimy hoodlums didn't take our clothing, camp gear, cereal, peanut butter, etc. For two hours we watched our stuff just sit there. It was actually quite enjoyable. We waited patiently under a cozy cedar tree for our "family" to return "home." Soon enough, I heard them drive up.

"Guess what?" Janet cried, as she burst out of the support vehicle. "We were sitting outside Costco, waiting for it to open, and a very nosy but wonderful lady asked if we were in town for the local fair. I told her that Reggie was the star of WALKABOUT and we gave her a brochure and I explained what it was all about. I told her we were waiting for the store to open so we could buy a car-top carrier. I can't believe that I am a such a good talker but we impressed her so much with what we were doing, she told us that she had a car-top carrier at her house and we could have it for $25!"

"You're kidding!" I said, wondering if she was pulling my leg. Given the chance, Janet could pull until my legs detached themselves from my body. I believed her, though, when I caught the gleam in Janet's eyes. I knew that she dreaded talking to people she didn't know. One of Janet's biggest challenges would be asking perfect strangers to put us up for a night, or even worse, buy WALKABOUT T-shirts so that we could continue eating. She knew all along that those would be her responsibilities, but only now was the reality of it setting in. I could see that this first unexpected experience was a real confidence booster for her.

"We had to wait for her to finish shopping," Janet continued, talking so fast I thought she would burst, "so Reggie and I went in to see how much Costco charged for carriers. Would you believe they charge a hundred and twenty-five dollars!?"

"No problem!" cried Reggie, his pitch rising in excitement.

"That's great! Things are happening on WALKABOUT!" I said. "You know, I'm not even surprised that things like this happen. I've always believed that opportunity will come to you if you try to meet it halfway. I believe walking 1,300 miles qualifies as at least halfway!"

Janet agreed. "And we saved one hundred dollars!" She was bouncing up and down.

"We could buy chocolate milk every day!" said Reggie with a gleam in his eye.

"I'm beginning to love that man," I said to Janet, winking at Reggie.

We went to work right away. Janet spent the afternoon (dis)organizing our gear while Reggie and I wiped the carrier down and cleaned it up.

"Teamwork, right?" asked Reggie.

"At its finest," I answered.

The shining moment of the day was right after I painted "WALKABOUT" on all sides of the carrier. Reggie and I lifted the carrier to the roof of the car and Janet strapped it on.

"Lady, Gentleman, and Dog," I said, "I present to you...The Official WALKABOUT-Mobile!" We all cheered and looked at the WALKABOUT-Mobile from every angle. It brought tears to our eyes and lumps to our throats!

The next morning, Park Ranger Mike dropped by our campsite with good news. "I found a cooler out in the field yesterday. Did you folks lose one?" he asked. Ranger Mike, his official state park name tag announcing his moniker, walked straight and stiff, as if his shorts were all scrunched up. His uniform, including hat and tie, was so neat and sharp it gave the impression that he was an army general. He spoke softly and directly, with a slight hint of intimidation. It wasn't what he asked or how he asked it that made me feel like a child confessing a foolish mistake, it was how he created the illusion of unforgiving power.

"Yeah," I admitted, avoiding his eyes. "We were foolish and left our cooler out overnight." We had all but forgotten about the stolen cooler, not to mention my chocolate milk, until I remembered my disappointing breakfast. Not wanting to accept all the blame, I summoned the confidence to add, "I can't believe people would take anything at a campground, but somebody did. We lost our chocolate milk and all!"

"It was probably some kids from town," Ranger Mike told us. It sounded as if this was common and we should have been ready for it. "Had you reported it to me," he said with a quiet growl, "you could have had it back yesterday, and the little scamps that took it could be in jail right now."

"Really?" I said. "Boy, do I feel dumb!"

From under his broad-rimmed hat, Ranger Mike gave me a funny look, but all he said was, "Stop by the ranger station and you can pick it up." He pivoted and walked back to his Ranger-mobile.

"Great!" I said. "Hey, do you have the chocolate milk, too?" I asked before he drove off.

"Sorry. The scoundrels who stole the cooler ate the food, drank the chocolate milk and split. That's the way they work."

"Boy, oh boy. What's happening to America when even chocolate milk ain't safe?" I wondered.

Reggie, Janet and I discussed whether there was a special school where people went to become park rangers, but something inside told us not to ask when we walked over to recover our stolen property. We were afraid that if we started asking too many questions we'd get scolded for not having engraved our name on the cooler. Anyway, the permanent WALKABOUT team was all together, and the creation of the official WALKABOUT-Mobile was complete. So after a day of rest, we left Kitsap Park with a surge of energy. Reggie, Dixie and I had walked almost 15 miles, passing a few small urban towns, when Janet came to pick us up.

"Boy, you guys did some good walking today. Do you realize that you walked to probably the only place that has no campgrounds, no friends and no group homes?" said Janet. "You would have made my first real day a lot easier if you'd have walked ten miles less or fifteen miles more."

"Welcome to WALKABOUT," I said, smiling. "No one stopped by and offered their house to sleep in, did they?" she asked hopefully.

"Where are we going to sleep, Janet?" Reggie wondered.

Now it was my turn to say, "No problem, guys. Just like the old days, right Dixie?" I was remembering back to the many adventurously strange places we camped when we walked across America. I turned to Reggie and Janet and explained, "We'll just have to make up a good place to sleep." I thought for a moment. "We passed a baseball field back a couple of miles. I bet we could improvise something there."

Janet was pretty skeptical but didn't have any better ideas. This was very new to her. She didn't even have any opinions! Reggie, Dixie and I climbed into the WALKABOUT-Mobile and we went to check it out. On the far side of left-centerfield, beyond home-run territory, there were big mounds of dirt. I instructed Janet to park the WALKABOUT-Mobile so that it couldn't be seen from the road. She positioned it beyond the dirt mounds, beside a stand of tall evergreen trees.

"Will we get in trouble?" asked a concerned Reggie. It was an important thing to think about. We were in a town, not out in the country. Janet awaited my answer, too.

"If we are quiet, and clean up any mess we make, I think it will be O.K. We're not disturbing anybody. If someone comes and says we can't stay, we'll have to figure something else out. If we have to, we can go to a motel. That's what the emergency money is for. We're in my area of expertise now. Dixie and I have done things like this so many times. I'm confident there will be 'no problem.'"

"I want to sleep in a tent!" was Reggie's opinion.

"Me, too," added Janet. She was really getting into the swing of things.

"I want to have a campfire," she stated.

"Me, too," said Reggie.

We looked around to make sure the area was fire-safe. We also wanted to make sure we wouldn't be bothering any of the people that lived close to the field. Everything checked out, so we unloaded our gear, and Janet helped Reggie practice setting up our tents. I gathered some scrap wood by the trees, and Janet worked with Reggie to get the fire going.

"This is really camping out," said Reggie. "I love my sleeping bag," he told us.

"Have you ever camped out before, Reggie?" asked Janet. "I know you haven't since you've lived at the group home."

"When I was a little boy," he remembered.

"Was that when you lived at the institution or at the foster homes?" Janet was more aware of Reggie's background than I.

Reggie was quiet for a moment, thinking. Then he said, "Never at those places. When I was a little boy. Before my father died."

"That was a long time ago," I said. "No wonder you were so anxious to sleep out in the tent."

"I like camping out," he said.

"Me too, Reg," I added.

"Me three," said Janet.

Janet turned towards the fire pit we had made and began to set up a campfire. Reggie walked over to help. Janet looked up at him and showed Reggie how she used a little piece of paper and small twigs. "We don't use the big pieces of wood until after the fire gets going," she explained.

"No problem."

"And since we're having sandwiches and potato salad for supper, we can keep the fire pretty small. That way we won't even have much smoke, and no one will know that we are here."

"Or think the ballfield is on fire," I added, overhearing the lesson as I stood beside the trees.

"O.K.," Reggie said as he added small pieces of wood.

After a while, the fire was fine and burning contentedly. We just let it be and sat around, eating dinner and staring at the flames.

"You know, it was a campfire just like this when Steve and I came up with the idea of WALKABOUT," said Janet as she reflected on how this whole journey got started. "Of course, there would be no WALKABOUT if you didn't agree to do the walking," she said to Reggie. I remembered back to when Janet and I first talked to Reggie about our idea....

After Janet and I came up with the idea of WALKABOUT, and decided that Reggie would be the perfect candidate to make the walk, we had to actually ask him. Walking around a state is not something one can assume another would want to do. And if Reggie did turn the idea down, we weren't sure anybody else at the group home would want to give it a go.

I knew that it wouldn't all be fun, and parts of it would be hard work. The glory, though, would be phenomenal! I planned to discuss the bad as well as the exciting parts of the project when I asked Reggie if he wanted to try it. Unless Reggie understood everything that this walk involved, he wouldn't really be able to make his own choice. We wanted him to choose what he wanted to do, not just what Janet and I wanted him to do.

Reggie had never been given the opportunity to attempt such a big project. I was worried that Reggie might be too afraid to try something new. It's quite difficult to try to understand what goes on in the head of another man, disabled or otherwise. "I don't want to scare him off," I thought to myself. Just days after we came up with the idea of WALKABOUT, Janet and I were in the backyard of the group home when Reggie, walking around as usual, came over to say, "Hi."

"Hey, Reggie, we were just thinking about you. Janet and I came up with a fun idea for a project, and thought you might like to be a part of it."

"O.K."

"You haven't heard what the idea is yet! Let me tell you about it." I was excited and talking quickly. "We were thinking of going on a real long, long walk. It would take many months. We want to walk around Washington!"

"I like to walk."

"Understand now, this walking would be different from the walking you do around town. Every day you, Dixie and I would walk many miles. We would be walking all day, from morning to night. Sometimes it might be hot, sometimes it might be cold and sometimes it might rain on us."

"I like to have fun."

"Well, I guess that could be fun, Reg, but I want you to understand that this can be tiring as well as fun. And at the end of those tiring days you can't come home to your bed. Sometimes

Relaxing "at home" after a hard day

we'll stay with friends or even strangers. And if we can't find a bed, we will have to sleep outside in a tent. You'll be far from home. You might get real tired. And other than Janet, Dixie and me, you won't be able to see most of your friends for a long time. When we get up each morning, you'll have to start walking all over again."

"That's O.K. with me. I like to walk. I like to live in the woods."

"Reggie, you have to think about this very seriously. It can be fun but we'd be walking for a purpose. Our walk would be a way to help teach people all over the state about people with developmental disabilities. You would be an unofficial representative. We want to show everyone that people with developmental disabilities have the right to make their own decisions to do all kinds of things, and that they have the ability to do things if they are given the chance and have support.

"You can show the people of America what a person with a disability is capable of doing. You might even encourage other people with developmental disabilities to do some things they themselves didn't even believe they could ever accomplish."

"I like that," he said.

"Personally, I think the most important part is that you can introduce yourself as a person wanting to enjoy life and do a lot of different things. You can show that there are differences between all people. The things that make you different are of value and don't give others the right to treat you with any less respect. A lot of people just don't quite understand what that really means. But you have to decide if all that is O.K. with you. Many people will begin to talk about you. They will use you as an example. Do you think that you can handle all that? It will be a big responsibility."

"No problem!" answered Reggie. I had no idea if he totally understood all that I had said. "Will you walk, too, Janet?" he asked.

"No, Reg," answered Janet. "Only you, Steve and Dixie will walk. My job will be to drive the support car. I'll carry most of the food for us and Dixie, the camping equipment and extra clothing for all the different kinds of weather. I will also find us places to sleep at night. After you guys walk all day, I will pick you up and drive us to where we will sleep. Then each morning I'll drive you back to that exact same spot. There will be no cheating on WALKABOUT! Of course, it is dangerous walking right next to the road—in case of an emergency or an accident, we can climb into the car and go for help."

"That sounds good. I'm glad you are coming, Janet!" said Reggie beginning to dance where he stood. It was curious to see him become antsy with anticipation.

"Me, too," I added. "We would really miss her. Oh, there is another thing Janet will do while we walk all day long. She will sit outside grocery stores and sell WALKABOUT T-shirts and buttons to raise money so that we can keep eating."

"I like that," said Reggie, as he rubbed his belly. Reggie seemed ready to go.

I looked into Reggie's eyes and was certain that he meant what he said. It was the response I was hoping he would give. Then I looked at Janet and she looked at me. The look we gave each other communicated the exact same question: "Does Reggie really realize that WALKABOUT isn't only going to be 'fun and games' but also hard work?" Of course we were thrilled that he was immediately enthusiastic about the plan, but strangely enough, we reacted to what appeared to be his reflex answer by giving him reasons to turn the project down. "Reggie, don't you think you will miss your friends? Won't you be embarrassed by all the attention? You know, Reg, it can be boring to do nothing but walk all day long."

It's amazing how quickly even experienced counselors can fall into the role of "protector." It didn't appear to us that he had considered the pros and cons of such a project, and we felt a need to guide him into our definition of the proper steps of thought. We never expected that we'd have to convince him to go for a walk, but this was above and beyond any kind of walk Reggie could have ever dreamed.

Or was it? There I was, a lover of long distance walking, one minute hoping to convince a person to go for glory—and as soon as he unhesitatingly agreed, I tried to change his mind. Both Janet and I had to remind ourselves, more than once, that the bottom line of WALKABOUT was to get away from treating people with disabilities as naive children that had to be protected from anything dangerous or unpleasant. I wonder how many times it had been the fear of "nondisabled" people that prevented "disabled" people from doing what they wanted to do. The theme of WALKABOUT would be that all people deserve to have the opportunity to create as fulfilled a life as possible, based on their own choices, good and bad. Life is experience, positive and negative, and no one should be denied that. What an individual was willing to put into life was as much as he or she would get out. Advising a person is one thing, controlling is another.

Reggie didn't appear to us to have any concept of the hard work that WALKABOUT would really take, but then I ask, did Janet or I? Many circumstances would develop over the course of time that could make each of us easily regret such an undertaking. But there was always the other side of the coin.... We'd never know if we didn't try! The difference between those that do things and those that don't do things is this: those that do, DO, and those that don't, DON'T. First Janet and I, and then Reggie, saw an opportunity and were ready to grab it. It became as simple as that. We were aware that there would be many obstacles on the road ahead; it would be silly if our fears became one of them.

"I want to go," Reggie repeated. There was no doubt.

"Great!" I replied. Janet and I had finally put an end to our uncertainties. "I knew you'd go for it! Are you ready to get into shape and to train hard like the athletes we see on T.V.?" I asked.

"I'm ready. I'm already strong. Look at my muscles." Reggie bent his arm and showed me his right bicep. Then he said, "I'll go pack my suitcase," and took off like a coyote on the heels of a rabbit.

Janet and I laughed. "I think we have a little time to worry about packing, Reg," I called. It was too late. He was heading to his room to find his suitcase.

"I guess we have our answer," said Janet, thrilled to see Reggie so happy.

Janet and I continued to discuss whether Reggie understood exactly what the trip would be all about or how hard it could be. We didn't want Reggie to be unpleasantly surprised or get upset if WALKABOUT didn't turn out to be as much fun as he'd thought. We certainly didn't want him to quit two weeks after he started. These early concerns became one of our first WALKABOUT experiences.

I ended the conversation by sharing the following thought: "The only thing I am sure of is that Reggie has the same right to take this opportunity that Dixie and I did when we left New Orleans."

When I first thought about walking 3,000 miles from the Mississippi River in Louisiana to the Pacific Ocean in Washington, I didn't know what might happen. All I knew was that *anything* could happen.

But anything could happen anyplace. Why would any sane person choose to live out of a backpack and walk across a continent? I can only find the answer in my development. Maybe it was because my father went on many business trips and I wanted to travel just like dear ol' dad. I thought it was the most exciting part of his executive position. Add that to the influence of so many Jacques Cousteau and National Geographic safaris on television that showed me how all the world was so gloriously interconnected. People, at least this person, were supposed to be living and frolicking in the world of nature, not hiding from it in cities and office buildings. It all seemed so exciting; so natural. I remember that I used to wonder how an average person like me could have such experiences. Those people on television were very special. Those experiences were for special people, weren't they? I was just a middle class kid though, growing up in a middle class culture.

Kids like me grew up to be comfortable professionals and family men. I tucked my dreams away.

Although I grew up in and around New York City, my mother, sister, dog and I spent the summers in upstate New York's Catskill Mountains. Dad would join us at the Sun Ranch Bungalow Colony on the weekends, after his work week ended. This world of beauty was full of trees and deer, lakes and fish; it was green and mountainous, peaceful and beautiful. It was a far cry from The Bronx. It called out to me on levels I couldn't quite hear. Its music passed beyond the surface of my mind, attaching itself to the very core of my being. Maybe that is why I would sit for hours looking quietly out of the car window on those long trips back and forth between the city and country. I remember thinking, on a very subtle level, "Boy, I wish I could walk along all this incredible stuff instead of having everything come and go at 60 miles per hour. I just want to absorb all this glory." It was a decade or two later, while walking over the Colorado Rockies, that I finally realized that very little of my life was happenstance. Whether I was conscious of it or not, every step of my life was based on the trail I had laid down behind me. First I created the dreams and then I lived them out.

In my first twenty-two years of life I had gone on plenty of walks, but none very special. I never even considered walking the 20 mile walk-a-thons for cancer that were sponsored by local organizations. That was much too much, I thought. But when I did go for a walk, I would walk lost in thought, often with my eyes focused on the ground ahead of me. I would philosophize about the meaning of life, trying to understand the questions, let alone figuring out any answers. If there were any answers, how would they apply to my life? How would I *make* them apply to my life? I guess I was searching, although not only did I not realize what I was in search of, I wasn't even aware that I was searching for anything at all. As unaware of it as I was, the journey had begun long before I had taken step one.

Thinking has always led me to happiness and fulfillment. Education, in any and all its colors, nourishes that process. Growing up in New York City is an education in itself, and college, of course, is also a very special and important education. "But what would be next?" I began wondering about two years before I even knew if they would let me and my barely passing grades graduate.

"Will I go down to the city and find a job? Will I then get married and have kids? No," I told myself, contemplating the culture I was brought up in, "that path is not right for me. I still have so much to learn!"

My next classroom, I decided, was to be "on the road." Five months after graduating from Hofstra University, my best friends, Mike Dreiblatt and Karen Mottes, and I headed south in a Dodge Ram Van on a horseshoe journey of America that would ultimately take us to the exotic state of Alaska. We wanted to see the world, or at least the United States, closely and comfortably. We left New York and headed south. Fascinating places—from the heavenly Smokey Mountains to the alligator-filled Okefenokee Swamp— became "home" for a night as we camped out. We also slept in our van in the parking lots of McDonald's, Burger Kings and Wendy's in towns we had never heard of, nor can remember. Every day we learned more about America, other people, and ourselves. Two months and two thousand miles after we first put the van into gear, we found ourselves in New Orleans, Louisiana. As I said, anything could happen anyplace. However, more things happen when you go to different places.

As incredible as that trip was, we weren't fulfilled. We would hardly touch the gas pedal and we still rolled along no slower than 30 mph. Before we even pulled into New Orleans, Mike, Karen and I discussed that something was missing. We had a great time learning, doing and experiencing life on the backroads of America and yet it just wasn't enough. After a while it was like eating mounds of potato chips for dinner. It was fun but our bodies, and our minds, craved something much more substantial. We needed a food that would satiate our souls, keep us going and help us grow. Deep down I knew what had to be. Looking back I find it funny how I tried to ignore what I now understand was inevitable.

It took much convincing to psyche myself up for what would be the next step of my journey through life. In fact, Mike had to do a lot of good talking to get me to seriously consider walking across America. We had discussed it but I was very unenthusiastic about the idea. "Steve," Mike would say in a very persuasive, well thought-out opinion, "we'll still be going to Alaska. Except instead of riding in the van we'll walk to Seattle. When we get there we'll take a ferry to Alaska. Think about it, one of the best parts about this venture is that as soon as one adventure ends, we'll move right into another." Mike had always been a good talker, and made the plan sound like the whole-grain, unprocessed bread for which my body ached. Still, it took me a few days of hard thinking. To say that I knew he was simplifying the plan is an understatement. Karen, too, was not easily swayed. However, there was one important point I could not argue: what we had been doing was dissatisfying. It came down to the fact that I had no better alternative.

Finally I agreed and we began to plan this frightening operation together. We even got a puppy, Drake—a half Black Lab/half Irish Setter—to share the experience with us. It was Mike's first dog and there was an immediate bond. Ironically, it turned out that Mike and Karen (and Drake) decided that their path led to a different destination. Their journey led to some traveling in New Mexico and Colorado and then they headed back east to get married and raise a family in Vermont. As close as we still were, we knew it was time to go our separate ways. (However, that was only a physical separation, not a spiritual one.) This decision of theirs came in the middle of our training.

My first major setback hit before I even set out! I had to rethink this walk across America idea. Instead of being one of three people and one young dog setting out across country on foot, it would be just me! In one fell swoop I found myself without my team, destined to take on the world all by myself. Was that acceptable? Could I handle that, physically and mentally? I reached deep down to my core and searched for strength. What I found was that it was surrounded by layers of fear. It came down to deciding if I was ready to take life head on. I had always spouted that I believed a person needed to take risks and work at creating a good, happy life. Now I became aware that that philosophy was easy when one was supported by mom and dad. Was I prepared to put my money where my mouth was? Maybe. Did I have a better alternative? No. Was it time to walk across America? Yes, no, yes, no. Yes!! I was ready. It was time. It was my destiny!

Walking across America would finally become the means for me to bring together all the things I loved. It was travel and nature, a direction in life, a challenge, an education, walking and thinking. Thinking, the simple act of running ideas and thoughts through my head, is an activity I enjoy as much as another might enjoy playing chess. Sometimes it's fun to contemplate philosophies on life, other times it's exciting to come up with plans and figuring out how to execute them. Thinking is my spiritual guide. The one thing I was certain of, in a plan of uncertainty, was that I would have plenty of time to think.

For some time I tried to close my ears to this personal call of the wild—but ultimately, I couldn't deny it. Walking across America called to my heart, not my ears. It was difficult to understand what my senses were relaying to my mind. I wasn't sure what was out there that I was looking for, what exactly I needed. All I knew was that I was hungry and this was the only food that would sustain me. I accepted my solitary destiny, and with the decision finally made, I put myself into full gear.

The first thing I did was go to the library and get books about other people who had undertaken similar adventures. I learned a lot from their successes and even more from their failures. I knew I had to get my mind as well as my body into shape, and I also needed good equipment. So I shopped around and bought the best backpack, sleeping bag, tent, boots, and other equipment I could afford. Then every other day I went to the Sheraton Hotel in downtown New Orleans and ran up and down all fifty flights of stairs! Twice! I also worked my way up to an eight-mile run every two days!

Also during that time, I went to the local animal shelter and looked for the perfect dog. My new companion would have to be my friend as well as my protector. For three weeks I met all the dogs that came and went at the shelter, but none of them was just right. Most of them were just too small. None sparked that special chemistry. I kept looking. Finally, I was introduced to Dixie, a female German Shepherd. She was only nine months old, and skinny from weeks of living in a cage, but I could tell she would become just the perfect size to walk across America with a backpack of her own. I remember asking her through the bars of her cell, "Do you want to stay in this lonely cage, or do you want to walk across America with me?" When she started to whine I let her out of the cage. When she jumped all over me I knew I had my answer. Since then, Dixie and I have become family, like father and daughter.

Even with all that training and all our plans, Dixie and I knew only one thing for sure—we had no idea what we were in for! We had a lot to learn as we walked, and the only way to learn would be to get on the road! We couldn't imagine how hot it would get in Texas, how cold it could be in Idaho, how much it could rain in Washington, or how lonely, discouraged and desperate we would feel at any given mile in America. We couldn't predict that Dixie would get run over by a farm truck or stepped on by a frightened horse in Kansas. On the other hand, how could we have guessed that we'd have the opportunity to work on a real American farm or wrangle a 70-year-old cowboy's herd of horses in the mountains of Colorado, or that Dixie would be named the Meaty Bones® and Jerky Treats® National Poster Dog? We had never dreamed how many wonderful people would take us in when we most needed a friend, encouraging us to keep going with their friendship and hospitality, but keep going we did—until we reached Neah Bay, the most northwest corner of the United States at Cape Flattery, Washington.

Just when we thought our walking was over, just when we figured we couldn't get beyond the insurmountable obstacle they call the edge of a continent, we met another friend to keep us going—Reggie Feckley.

Perhaps Reggie had a call similar to the one I had heard for so long. It was as if he was dressed for a party he instinctively knew was taking place yet had no means to get there. For so long he was waiting at the door, waiting for something to allow him to get on the path. Finally, after nervously pacing for more years than he could remember, his carriage had arrived in the form of a backpack, hiking boots and new friends. Reggie was on his way! We would go together.

Lost in our thoughts, we stared into the flames of the flickering ballfield campfire. Silently, we each were remembering back to the steps that had brought us to this unconventional campsite. We stared into the flames until they burned down to glimmering embers and it was time to get some sleep. We got some water out of the WALKABOUT-Mobile and drowned what was left of the fire. We went to sleep in our tents, excited about the days and miles to come.

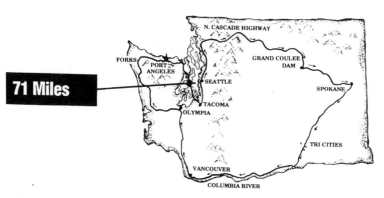

71 Miles

chapter 6

LIFE on the ROAD

We continued our walk along the highway. The trees we passed were slowly exchanged for buildings of businesses. They weren't as inspiring. The pavement expanded as the highway widened. It wasn't as peaceful. With every step, our quiet surroundings slowly shriveled away. Towns were felt before we even reached them, and the mass of cars began to grow. We knew peace and quiet would only be restored after we walked beyond the major cities of the upcoming Puget Sound. We had to work hard to ignore the noise.

"You said you used to live on a farm, Reg?" I asked. Reggie had mentioned it when we were with the Edgertons, and the noticeable absence of open fields was what made me think of it.

"Yep," he said. "I liked that!"

"When was that?"

"When Mom married Uncle Dick." Reggie's father had died when he was a pre-teen. His mother remarried years later.

"Was that before or after you lived in the institution?" I asked. I began to realize how little I really knew about Reggie. Most of what I knew about Reggie was the scant information that was in his files. At the group home, he didn't talk about his past very often. Little by little, WALKABOUT brought up memories that had been stored away.

"After the school," he said, thinking back. I knew that the school was the institution. After his father died, Reggie's mother had to get a job. At his age, and with his disability, he was too young to stay by himself. This was back in the 1950s, and his mother was advised to enroll him in an institution. He lived there for about ten years, until he was in his twenties.

"Then what?" I asked.

"I lived on the farm with Mom and Uncle Dick." Uncle Dick was how Reggie referred to his stepfather.

"Did you live there a long time?"

"No. Uncle Dick died. When you go, you go," Reggie explained. "It's up to the Good Lord."

"That's true, I guess. Did you like Uncle Dick?"

"Yup."

"Did you cry?"

"Yup. I miss him. We all go sometime, right? Up to the Good Lord," Reggie repeated, looking up at the sunny sky. "He's in heaven now, not the other place. Praise the Lord!"

"Did you live on the farm after Uncle Dick died?"

"I went to a big home."

"Why?" I asked.

Reggie shrugged. He didn't give me an answer. Later, Janet explained a little more of Reggie's background for me. She had been told that when he came out of the institution, he was a little hard to control. He had a bad temper and he was always looking over his shoulder, with a sudden jerk, as if someone was after him. No one was sure what happened to cause him to be that way or to make him so nervous. Reggie's mother had once told Janet that she found a big foster-care home for people with disabilities and she moved Reggie there after Dick died. "I love Reggie very much, but I thought that the foster home was better than living with me," his mother had explained.

The cars passed by, unnoticed by us as we walked and talked. I found Reggie's life fascinating. It was so different from mine. I had one home and one family. There were millions of people where I grew up in New York, but at least I had my own bedroom! I couldn't possibly imagine what it was like to move around or live in an institution with hundreds of strangers. I didn't get the impression that Reggie loved living in all those places with all those people. He often mentioned how much he loved his mother, Uncle Dick and his brother.

Just then Janet drove up and stopped. Behind her was another car. Shirley had driven out to visit us. "I wanted to come see you before you got to Tacoma," she said, taking turns hugging each of us. "I can't believe how far you have already walked!"

"I'm a good walker," said Reggie, as he hugged Shirley. "I'm having fun. I'm a camping man now!" He was so proud.

"I'm so happy for you, Reggie," she said.

Shirley, resting her head on Reggie's shoulder, got her first good look at the inside of the WALKABOUT-Mobile when Janet opened the back door. She let go of Reggie and walked right up to the car, staring. "You guys are living out of that thing?" she asked incredulously.

"No problem," answered Reggie. As far as Reggie was concerned, it wouldn't have mattered if the WALKABOUT-Mobile had been a golf cart.

Even with the carrier, the WALKABOUT-Mobile was stuffed to the gills. It was bulging at its sides. There was just barely enough room for all the gear and the extra things we thought were absolutely necessary. Janet, especially Janet, had brought more things from home than I had expected, realized, or even cared to think about. Clearly we all would have to sacrifice some of our things— especially Janet. "The theory behind camping is not how much stuff you need," I had tried to explain, mostly in vain, "it's learning how much stuff you *don't* need." I had pointed out that she really didn't *need* her entire wardrobe, shoes, a box of books, her knitting bags, or her typewriter. Janet thought she needed these things to keep from getting homesick, but she listened to my opinion and tried to understand.

"If and when Shirley comes out for a visit, I'll find some things to send back with her," Janet had promised. She turned her head and I thought I caught her smiling ever so slyly. She would probably ask her good friend Shirley *not* to come.

"She'll just spend *my* portion of the food money on telephone calls," I thought to myself. "Reggie and I will send some things back, too," I pledged to Janet. "Right, Reg?"

"Right." We confused Reggie with our banter, but he played diplomat with the best of 'em.

Shirley did come out, though, and we were all happy to see our friend. Her perspective on our new life gave us a different point of view. She just stared at the WALKABOUT-Mobile, amazed at what she saw. "Not too long ago, three people and one dog lived in three separate apartments. Now the four of you are living out of a car! I can't imagine how much your life has changed in the last couple of weeks."

"*ALL* OF IT HAS CHANGED!" Janet cried, finally breaking down. We all turned to her. "I miss my friends. I miss the other tenants. I miss my office. I miss television. I miss my shower. I miss my living room. I miss my bed. I miss…"

"Whoa! Slow down, Janet. Try not to dwell on all the things you don't have anymore," Shirley advised. "You're going to make yourself crazy!"

"…my normal life!" Janet took a deep breath and calmed down. Shirley took her hands. I turned to Reggie and we shrugged our shoulders and shook our heads. Until Shirley had made that statement, I don't think Janet had realized how quickly her life had been turned upside down. Of course, maybe I was the one who didn't realize it. Janet was proving that she was very well aware of the differences and had thought about it in detail.

Shirley gave Janet a good, long hug and tried to calm her down. I thought Janet was mostly kidding. At least, I hoped so. Reggie was very confused. He didn't quite understand if Janet was really upset or not, either.

Shirley went to her car and brought some homemade food over to the WALKABOUT-Mobile. She told us all to relax, and she made us lunch. With the multi-colored spectacle of passing cars, and the variety of odors from their exhaust, the highway offered us quite an original place for a picnic.

"Life on the road," I said out loud, knowing what everyone was thinking. It was exciting and special in a very strange sort of way.

"I feel like I am having a true WALKABOUT experience," Shirley stated. "This is pretty weird, but just too much fun."

I laughed as I got up and walked over to the WALKABOUT-

Our happy (WALKABOUT) homemaker, Janet Phipps

Mobile for a second helping of lunch. Then I saw something that made my eyes bulge.

"More pillows!?!" I cried, trying to keep my eyes from leaving my head. "Lawn chairs!" I turned to Janet, eyes squinted and glaring. "No wonder you so easily agreed to get rid of some stuff. You had Shirley bring out things to replace them. Janet," I said directly, "it's time you learned what 'roughing it' means. This is life on the road! Shirley, you will kindly take those extra pillows and lounge chairs home with you," I demanded. I started tossing things left and right. "We just don't have the room!"

"Oh, of course, we do," claimed Janet, making light of my hysteria.

"Well, it seems that with all this extra stuff, there's only room inside for one person, and maybe Dixie," I said. "Where is the other person supposed to ride?" I demanded. Janet said nothing, but looked at me and then focused in on the car-top carrier. "I don't think so," I said, wondering if she seriously thought I wouldn't mind riding on the roof. There was a good chance she was very serious!

Yes, it's true. I did become a bit cranky. But I soon calmed down enough to enjoy the rest of our visit with Shirley, even if it wasn't until she drove off with the offending items safely tucked into *her* car that I breathed a little easier. Janet's eyes were teary, but she accepted her new temporary life.

"I'm sorry that I got a little carried away before, Janet," I said as I gave her a hug. "I really don't see how we could carry all that stuff, and I strongly believe that in a few more days you'll get used to it. Reggie and I did."

"I understand," she said, hugging me back. "I guess you're right. For all the time we planned WALKABOUT and during all the months that I have been so excited about it, I didn't think about what it would really be like. It's not an easy way to live. I'm sure I'll get used to it."

As I hugged Janet, I noticed Reggie standing beside the WALKABOUT-Mobile. He had a strange look on his face, holding his own hands, like an uninvited guest listening to a loud discussion between his hosts. He wasn't sure if we were fighting or not. I pointed it out to Janet.

"I hope we didn't scare you, Reggie," reassured Janet. "We're not really upset with each other. We just sort of had a difference of opinions."

Reggie gave a half-smile. "You're still friends, right?"

"Of course!" I said. "We're hugging each other, aren't we?"

"Hallelujah. No problem!" He gave a full smile, his eyes lit up and he said, "Are you ready to walk some more, Steve?"

"I guess so. Janet, we'll meet you up the road at about six o'clock."

"You know, Steve, sometimes it feels like we're married. You're my best friend and all that, but I never wanted to *marry* you."

"I wouldn't touch that with a ten-foot guardrail," I said, clutching my heart.

Reggie pointed at us and just cracked up. "Are you two going to make babies?" he laughed. I ran over to him, grabbed him and threw a few fake punches. Dixie jumped up, her two front paws hitting my back. Reggie pulled away, laughing hysterically, grabbed his pack and said, "Let's go, Schlicky!" Reggie turned toward the highway and off he went. Dixie followed a few steps, but then turned and waited until I adjusted her pack. We then joined Reggie and headed up the road. Janet, still laughing, took off in the WALKABOUT-Mobile.

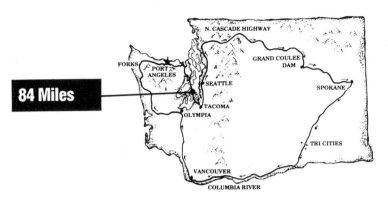

84 Miles

chapter 7

NEW FRIENDS

"HONK! HONK!" came the sound of a familiar horn. In normal life, honking horns often meant "watch out," or "get out of the way!" But this was WALKABOUT! Drivers sped by but often "beeped," smiled and waved, giving us an encouraging pat on the back for our efforts.

"Hey, they know us!" Reggie always exclaimed as he waved back.

"If they don't yet, they will soon," I told him. No longer did passing cars think him crazy for waving even if they didn't know each other personally. Of course, they may have thought him nuts for trying to walk around Washington, but we didn't bother to stop them and ask!

"Honk, Honk!" repeated the familiar horn. Reggie and I, and even Dixie, recognized the distinctive alto pitch of the WALKABOUT-Mobile's horn. To our ears it was the sound of comforting music. Janet had pulled over on the other side of the road behind us. We waited for a lull in the traffic and hurried across.

"Hey! Guess what?" Janet said with passion. "Tonight we get a roof, a bed *and* a hot shower! Sponge baths work for awhile but believe me, we need a shower! You've almost made it to Port Orchard," she continued. She was speaking so fast she could hardly breathe. "I called a group home there and we're all set up!"

"That's great!" I said. "What do you mean we *need* a shower— oh, never mind, I know what you mean."

"We also get to meet new people. The idea of WALKABOUT is to share our ideas, right?" This was the first time Janet made a connection to stay with strangers on WALKABOUT. "What do you think about staying with new people, Reg?"

"No problem," he replied. The look on his face showed otherwise, indicating his uncertainty. Reggie was shy and didn't really like crowds. He knew that a group home meant there would be a lot of people. On the other hand, WALKABOUT was an opportunity to change and grow. Maybe these opportunities would help Reggie enjoy meeting new friends.

"This is what WALKABOUT's all about, Reg. WALKABOUT is not only walking, it's a project to raise awareness about nice people like you…to teach others about all the things that people with disabilities can do." I wondered if his reluctance to be with strangers or crowds might cause him to put an end to WALKABOUT one day. It was an uncomfortable thought.

Janet drove us into Port Orchard and, following the instructions she had been given, quickly found the group home. It was the last house on a residential street filled with your typical American middle-class homes. There was still plenty of daylight and the neighborhood was alive. Dogs were barking, children were playing ball and riding bikes, a woman was painting her mailbox, and an elderly man tended to his rose bush.

The group home looked like any other house on the street, although the wing with the bedrooms was longer than most houses. There was no one outside or on the front lawn so we got out of the WALKABOUT-Mobile, put Dixie on a leash, and walked to the door. Just as Janet was about to ring the bell, the door swung open and we were greeted by a half-dozen smiling faces inviting us inside. Our excited new friends welcomed us, and questions came from all directions, including the large living room where some people were still watching television. Opposite the living room was an extra kitchen which I immediately noticed, thanks to the two people creating the aroma that wafted up my nose and settled in my belly.

"What a great welcome, huh, Reg?" I said as I turned my head. "Reg?" I thought he was right behind me. I thought wrong. I took a few steps back and looked out the door. Reggie caught my eyes searching for him.

"I'm going to walk around for a little while," he explained before I said a word.

I was about to remind him that our new friends wanted to meet him and might think it was rude if he didn't come in, but Janet tapped me on the shoulder and suggested that I didn't pressure him. "Sooner or later he'll come in on his own," she said. "He's nervous. Let's not pressure him. I'm sure the folks inside will understand." Janet was right on both accounts, and Reggie finally came in when we told him that dinner was served. For Reggie, hunger pangs were more intense than shy pangs.

Dinner conversation with the friendly staff of the Port Orchard group home reminded us that this was also a chance to *learn* from others, too.

"You mean you've helped your tenants buy their own homes?" I asked as my eyes bulged open in surprise. Janet and I had never even considered that possibility!

"Sure. Why not? Some even own their own businesses!" said Bob. He was program coordinator for the Port Orchard Group Home.

"Wow, that's great! I can't believe we haven't even thought of that!" said Janet, showing how impressed she was. "Where'd you get the money?"

"The staff got together and came up with ideas. One of the things we did, and the easiest way to get money for a small business, was to have Bingo games and invite our neighbors to play. They had fun, and we made some money. That got the ball rolling, one thing led to another, and we were in business, so to speak. With some of the profits from the first business we started, we were able to start another. The rest is history."

Janet and I were amazed. We had never thought of that before. The liveliness of Bob's speech conveyed excitement about his programs; the pride of what he, his staff and the tenants had accomplished.

"We asked the tenants which ones wanted to own a business, and asked them to think about what types of things they might like to do," Bob went on to explain. "Now, one lady makes sandwiches and has a lunch cart down at City Hall, and one man bought vending machines that sell pens and disposable lighters."

"We even have a man who grows the best tasting alfalfa sprouts in town and sells them to a local grocery store," added Amy, another staff member.

Bob and his staff made Janet and I realize that we had been underestimating Reggie, and ourselves!

The counselors and tenants at the Port Orchard Group Home were well aware of the great things *all* people were capable of accomplishing, but they also understood how difficult it was to turn ideas into reality. They wanted to know how Reggie, Janet and I got WALKABOUT started. Now it was our turn to impress them.

"WALKABOUT is a great idea, but what did the people down at the Division of Developmental Disabilities think about it?" Bob asked.

The Division of Developmental Disabilities, or D.D.D., is one part of the Washington State Department of Social and Health Services. Washington State developed this department to help people with special needs. D.D.D. is specifically designed to make sure that people with developmental disabilities receive the support they need to live and work as independently as possible. They help people with disabilities find the best places for them to live, and the best jobs available for them.

"When Janet and I first told the people at D.D.D. about WALKABOUT, they were very interested, but quite concerned about Reggie's welfare," I explained. "They asked questions like, 'Will he still have his job when he gets back? Have you thought about his safety? What if he changes his mind and decides not to finish? Is Reggie being exploited because of his disability?'"

Janet explained, "We had the same concerns, too, and had already thought about them. When they asked, we were ready with the answers."

"We explained to the D.D.D. that Karen Higgens, Reggie's boss at New Broom Janitorial, had not only agreed to save his job until he got back, but had decided to continue to pay him while he was on WALKABOUT. Karen felt that this type of walking was also working. Reggie would be working hard!" Janet said.

"And in regards to the safety factor," I added, "Dixie and I are experts in safely walking long distances."

"And what *will* you do if Reggie doesn't want to continue walking all the way around Washington?" asked one of the counselors at the group home. "I'm sure I would have second thoughts as soon as the temperature went above 85° or I had to walk all day in the rain."

Before I answered that question, I turned to Reggie and asked, "Do you want to do this, Reg?"

"Yep!" he answered. No one doubted his statement.

"That's the first and most important question and answer, but he has the right to change his mind. Of course, if he decided to quit, I would find out why he wanted to stop, as I would with any friend. Then we would discuss the importance of his decision. If he wanted to stop, even after thinking about all the good points and bad points, then that would be fine. Ultimately, it would be his choice. This walk is about everyone's right of free choice."

"And we don't think we are exploiting Reggie," Janet added, "because he wants to do this. Reggie has a lot to gain. He is getting the chance to improve his own life. That's not exploitation. That's opportunity and adventure!"

"I like to walk," said Reggie, slowly coming out of his shy shell. I was proud to see him speak his own mind in front of strangers. "I'm having fun!"

Our new friends in Port Orchard told us they liked what they heard. "I guess the people at D.D.D. liked what they heard, too, and that's why you're here!" Bob chimed in.

After a great night's sleep, we woke up, had breakfast, and were given an enthusiastic send-off that got us back on the road. Reggie, Dixie and I put 13 noisy miles behind us before Janet came to pick us up at about 5:00 P.M. We were feeling energetic, though, and wanted to keep on walking. We invited Janet to see what WALKABOUT was like from a walker's eye view. She parked the WALKABOUT-Mobile in a safe place and walked with us.

We were getting closer to the busy city of Tacoma and the traffic was mounting. Travelers were speeding to and from their homes and businesses, and the constant roar of the cars was deafening. Reggie, Dixie and I didn't like the loud chatter of the freeway but we had gotten used to it. Janet, on the other hand, began to get a different taste of WALKABOUT.

"WHAT?" I asked.

"I SAID IT'S NOISY OUT HERE!" Janet repeated.

"YEAH, I KNOW. IT'S A REAL NICE DAY."

"NO. I SAID, 'IT'S NOISY OUT HERE!'"

"OH. WELL, IT GETS WORSE THE CLOSER WE GET TO TACOMA."

"Uh-oh," said Reggie.

"WHAT?" asked Janet and I.

"UH-OH," repeated Reggie. "LOOK," he said, pointing in front of us.

A state policewoman pulled over and turned on her flashing lights. "Pitter-pat" pounded our hearts. "We're being silly, we aren't doing anything wrong," I thought. "PITTER-PAT," thumped our hearts. We stopped and waited for her to pull up closer.

"Uh-oh" we all groaned, as we stood our ground.

"If she's going to tell us we have to find another road to walk on, it's going to be days before we get to Tacoma," I said to my co-walkers.

The State Trooper opened the door of her patrol car, stood up and adjusted her hat over her short-cropped brown hair. The policewoman's youthful face contrasted most interestingly with the way she wore her tailored blue uniform. It gave off an aura of secure confidence. She offered the impression that she could handle *any* situation she might encounter. Just as I was watching the officer walk towards us, our four-legged protector ran ahead to check "the stranger" out. That had been her job when it was just the two of us coming across America. "Dixie!" I yelled, stopping her in a flash. It made the officer nervous to have a German Shepherd run towards her and it made me nervous when the officer moved her hand towards her pistol. I didn't want to see how the officer was trained to react to an encounter with a big charging dog.

"She was just coming to say 'Hi,'" I reassured the officer.

"Oh, I'm sure," she responded with a sincere smile. "How are you folks doing?" In my mind her bright smile altered her whole appearance from threatening soldier to friendly neighbor. However, I figured we must have been doing something wrong or she wouldn't have stopped us.

"No problem—Pretty good—Peachy," answered Reggie, I and Janet.

"Good," said the officer. "I hate to tell you this, but you folks can't hitchhike on this road."

"We're not hitchhiking, officer," I explained, "we're WALKABOUT!"

"You're whatabout?" she asked. Before I could answer, Reggie pulled from his pack a WALKABOUT brochure, which explained the who, what and whys of our project. The officer took it from Reggie's hand and began to read. We just stood there waiting for her to say something. She finally looked up toward Reggie and said, "You're Reggie?"

"Yup," he said proudly.

"And you think you'll be able to walk around Washington?" she asked.

"No problem," answered Reggie.

I'm sure the officer believed him but she did seem amazed. I don't know if it was because it was a tremendous undertaking or because he was disabled. "I'm very impressed," she finally responded, looking at Reggie and slightly cocking her head as if she didn't understand what she was looking at. I wondered if she would be the first person we met on WALKABOUT that we were able to convince that people with disabilities really can do things for themselves. Some people knew it already, but others had yet to learn it. "I'm sure you'll do great, Reggie. Good luck."

"Since we're just walking, is it alright if we stay on this highway?" asked Janet.

"Sure. But be careful. Stay as far to the side as you can. And walk in single file. There's a lot of traffic." The officer headed back to her patrol car with the brochure in her hand.

"Believe me, we know," Janet said as three 18-wheelers thundered by.

Police officers often made Reggie nervous, but he felt really good about the way the policewoman had asked him questions. "I want to be a cop someday," he told us as we continued down the highway.

Photo by Steve Breakstone

**Dixie's favorite new friends
always walked on all fours**

What were we to say? After a moment Janet said, "There are a lot of tests to pass, but it's O.K. by us if it's O.K. with the police."

"I'd be a good cop," said Reggie. He thought for a second and then asked, "Am I too old to be a cop?"

"Probably, Reg," answered Janet. Reggie didn't respond.

We walked a bit further, and then Janet found a good place to cross the road so she could head back for the WALKABOUT-Mobile. Reggie, Dixie and I kept going until Janet met up with us again. We piled into the WALKABOUT-Mobile, headed to a nearby county park, and called it a day.

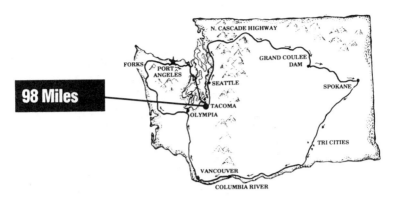

chapter 8

INTERVIEWS, BRIDGES, MAPS and TACOMA

"Hey, Reg," I called, breaking the silence of our pace, "Look over there!" I pointed down the road. In front of us, about a hundred yards ahead, was a man with a tremendous camera. It was bigger than a bread box. Reggie looked, not understanding where I was pointing. "Straight ahead!" I instructed. "The guy with the camera!"

"Hey, we'll be famous! I'm a good actor," Reggie preened.

"I'll bet you are, Reg, but let's keep walking. I bet he wants a picture of us at our best." We walked toward the photographer with smiles as big as Seattle. "This is what WALKABOUT's all about, Reg. Now, everyone is going to know about you."

"Hey, I like that!"

Stares, "beeping" horns of passing cars, interviews and the occasional reporter/photographer were all part of the deal. Dixie and I had gotten used to a lot of publicity when we walked across America, especially when Dixie became the 1988 National Poster Dog. Now, it was Reggie Feckley's turn to be in the limelight.

The newspaperman snapped pictures until we were ten feet in front of him. "Hi," he said.

"HI!" said Reggie and I. Dixie ran ahead, nose at the ready. The photographer held out his hand for Dixie to sniff. Then she allowed him to rub her chin, letting me know that all was well.

"Great dog," he said. "And you must be Reggie Feckley?"

Reggie shook his hand and said something that neither one of us could understand.

"Yes, and I'm Steve Breakstone. This is Dixie. Nice to meet you."

"Nice to meet you, too. I got a call at the newspaper office from Janet Phipps. She told me all about you and I'm quite impressed. How far have you walked so far, Reggie?"

"Mumble, mumble," was Reggie's reply.

I was surprised by Reggie's lack of clarity and I quickly took up the slack. "Over 90 miles so far. But we only have about 1,210 miles to go."

"Oh, that's it, huh?" laughed the reporter, catching on to my sarcastic joke. We walked over to the side of the road and sat down on the grass as he took out a note pad.

"What do you think so far, Reggie?"

"Mumble, mumble," Reggie said again.

I covered for Reggie and told the WALKABOUT story to the reporter. Reggie walked away. He laid down under a nearby tree and the next thing I knew his eyes were closed and his breath was heavy, sounding like a light snore. This was Reggie's first interview on the road and he fell asleep!

I explained to the reporter that Reggie was terribly nervous. He had never before had an opportunity to talk to a reporter. "Unfortunately, when Reggie gets nervous, his thoughts become a bit jumbled and his speech becomes quite difficult to understand." Reading the reporter's face, I added, "I hope you don't think that he doesn't even know what he is doing."

"I'm sure that's not the case," said the reporter. He was very kind but I wasn't convinced that he believed me. I had the feeling that the reporter believed Reggie to be the "stereotypical retard" doing what he was told, without having the ability to think about it. He glanced over toward Reggie and sympathetically said, "I guess that's one way to deal with nervousness."

I finished the interview and when the reporter got up to leave, Reggie awoke. When the reporter held out his hand, Reggie shook it limply.

"Good-bye, Reggie. Good luck!" said the reporter.

"Thank you. Good bye," said Reggie, almost clearly.

The reporter walked back to his car after telling us that our picture and story would be in the paper in a couple of days.

"You were a little nervous, weren't you?" I asked my companion. He shrugged. I think he thought I was mad at him. "That's O.K., Reg. As long as you do the walking, I'll do the talking. How's that sound?"

"That's teamwork! Right?"

"Right!" I said. "I'll tell you what. After we get to a place where the traffic isn't so loud, we'll practice answering questions. I'll make believe I'm a reporter asking you questions."

"I like that," he agreed. "You're an actor, too, Steve."

"Yep. I even have a degree in acting from college," I told him.

"You're a good actor, right?"

"One of the best, Reg. At least that's what I tell everyone."

"I'm a good actor, too. Right?" he asked.

"I don't know Reg. I've never seen you act."

"I'm a good actor," he said convincingly.

"And don't forget, Reg, when you shake a person's hand, do it firmly. Not too hard, and not too soft, just like we practiced. It shows character."

"No problem, Steve. I make mistake. I'll remember next time. Let's practice," he said, holding out his hand. I shook his hand and squeezed. Reggie squeezed back with equal pressure.

I smiled and said, "Perfect!"

"No problem. That's teamwork!"

We were back in action and hit the road. A breeze picked up and I wondered if it came from the massive amount of cars flying past. Then I smelled salt water.

We came around a curve in the road, and above some tree tops

Reggie noticed the top half of two towers. "There's the bridge!" said Reggie, pointing to the Tacoma Narrows Bridge. "No problem, right?"

"Pretty exciting, huh, Reg? Soon we'll be in the big, bustling city of Tacoma," I said, as if I couldn't wait to get there. I had mixed feelings, though. I've lived in cities and I've walked through cities and I have finally decided that I just don't care for really big cities at all. "I hope you don't mind even more traffic, bad smells, lots of stop lights and brain-rattling noise, Reg."

"No problem. I like the city." Of course, the city is exciting if you have never spent much time in one. The institution that Reggie lived in was in a city, but the residents had not been allowed to go off the grounds without supervision. It was feared that a person with Reggie's kind of disability would make him susceptible to all kinds of dangers: would they get hit by a car, would they get mugged, would clerks in stores take too much money for a purchased item? With these considerations, the caretakers in charge of the institution decided that it would be best for the residents, for their own good, to be "protected" from all these hazards. I grew up in a city and that reasoning appeared to be valid.

Wait a second! Those are concerns that anyone has to consider when they live in a city. I, myself, had to learn how to be aware and take care of myself when I was growing up in New York City. Through adult guidance and experience I was able to live quite safely and happily. It certainly beat never leaving my apartment building for fear that something bad might happen. That's no way to live! So what is the difference between Reggie and myself? I was taught to be aware of danger, and I was surrounded by people who had faith in me and respected my right to make my own decisions as I grew into adulthood. Reggie had been denied those opportunities. When I looked beyond the surface of the decision to protect Reggie, I began to wonder if it was the city that had really been "protecting" itself from the residents of the institution.

"Of course," I said, continuing my conversation with Reggie, "hitting the 'big city' gives us a chance to see a lot of people and have a lot of people see us. Showing ourselves off to people is very important to WALKABOUT."

"Maybe we'll be on T.V.," hoped Reggie. "And then we'll be

in the mountains, right?" The mountains were his number one priority.

"As long as we keep walking, we'll get there," I assured him.

"After the city, Steve?"

"After the city, Reg. It won't be soon enough, will it? I thought you liked the city."

"I like the city," he answered.

We pushed on and the traffic got heavier. Reggie was right behind me, and even Dixie walked closer to my legs. She, too, had an opinion about the cities. She shared many of my thoughts (surprise, surprise), and I knew the big city didn't thrill her, either. She knew she had to be extra careful on the busy streets so she walked right next to me. Like a good father, I kept a watchful eye on her. Dixie preferred to walk on country roads that offered the scents of cows and horses and pigs, not city streets filled with the stench of too many cars. In Tacoma, we would smell only exhaust.

We walked onto the Tacoma Narrows Bridge and immediately enjoyed the adventure of seeing the expanse of water below us. We felt pretty safe though, because this famous bridge has been hangin' around since 1950. Of course, the *first* Tacoma Narrows Bridge (nicknamed "Galloping Gerti" because of the way the wind made it sway) was built in the same spot and had crashed 190 feet to the water below! On November 7, 1941, just one short year after "Galloping Gerti" opened, 40-mile-per-hour winds huffed and puffed until they blew the bridge down. The bridge builders learned so much from that failure that the one they rebuilt (the one we had to cross) is still standing. "This is one of the best suspension bridges in the world!" I told Reg.

"Good!!" Reggie declared.

The Tacoma Narrows Bridge spans the Tacoma Narrows Waterway for over a mile. Step by step we walked further and further onto the bridge, and higher and higher over the water. The further out we walked, the higher we rose, higher and higher until it seemed like we were miles above Puget Sound! The bridge shook mightily as cars and trucks thundered across. It shook so hard that Reggie and I had to hold onto the rail, and even Dixie crouched down and walked slow. Would it shake us over the rail? Maybe. Would it collapse for a second time? Probably not. Would WALKABOUT come to a splashy end? Possibly! It was frightening and exciting all at the same time. Then, halfway across, we saw a sight that made us forget our fears.

"Hey, look Reg! There's Mt. Rainier." Watching over us through the bridge towers was the snow-capped peak of the highest point in Washington. "How inspiring!" I softly said, awestruck. We stopped and stared. "The peak of Mt. Rainier is 14,410 feet above sea level, Reg!" I finally said. "It remains one of the most beautiful natural monuments of this great state!"

"That's really big, Steve," agreed Reggie. He looked up at the peak and down at the water. I could swear I saw him tighten his grip on the rail.

"It sure is, Reg."

"You're smart, right, Steve?"

"I am when I read the signs on the side of the road, Reg."

We continued walking and I looked up at Mt. Ranier again. "You know, Reg," I said, "with views like this we could walk forever!"

"No problem!" confirmed my comrade as he matched me stride for stride.

Unfortunately, that wonderful sight was the last glory we had for many days. We came to the other side of the bridge and stepped into...Tacoma!

Tacoma didn't do us any wrong, but the closer we got to the inner city, the more I was reminded of what it was like to look for something in my mother's old junk closet. First of all, Tacoma is an old city that has grown and grown and if you don't know your way around, you are bound to get lost! Second, while individual people and certain buildings are attractive and interesting to look at, when you pack them all together in an endless string, the pretty colors tend to blend and everything becomes one ugly shade of gray.

Then there were the streets, the highways, the alleys and the *map.* Unfortunately, they did not agree! As we walked on the freeway beyond the bridge, I began to notice that we had somehow missed the exit we were instructed to head for. A busy, city freeway is *not* a good place to walk, and we all wanted to get off it as quickly as possible! Dixie walked right under me for safety, and even Reggie was only a stride behind. The traffic had been racing worse than ever, and the shoulder was almost non-existent. I had a sinking feeling that we were in the wrong place but with few street signs it was impossible to get our bearings. There were no stores on the freeway where we could ask directions, and no one was going to pull over and offer assistance. Reggie assumed I knew where I was going, and I was embarrassed to admit that I didn't. "HELP!" I cried into the wind.

By chance, as we were walking over an overpass, I happened to notice the name of the street below us. It was the street we were supposed to be on! According to the map, the place we were standing on just didn't exist. But there we were!

"Well, Reggie, strangely enough, I believe that Sprague Avenue is right underneath us. It's not supposed to be there, but there it is. According to my calculations, and if I got Janet's directions right, Sprague Avenue is the road that takes us downtown. If we go past it, who knows where we will end up! If we ever plan to see Janet again, we'd better get onto Sprague right away."

"Oh-uh," muttered Reggie, not any less confused or concerned.

I was expecting him to say, "No problem!" But Reggie, like Dixie and myself, has always been quite fond of Janet, and we all certainly wanted to see her again. Also, we were both aware that Janet carried almost all of our food.

We turned to get onto Sprague Avenue, but there was no freeway exit ramp! The only way to get off the highway and onto Sprague Avenue was to climb down a steep embankment separating the two roads, then haul ourselves over a ten-foot fence.

"Think you can climb over that fence, Reg?" I asked him as I calculated the possibilities of his ability to conquer the steel fortress. The fence just stood there, as if it were a mountain daring us to scale its sheer cliff.

"No problem," said an inexperienced but confident Reggie. Once again, I made a mountain out of a molehill as I underestimated his self-confidence in such matters. "Can Schlicky climb it?" he wondered. Now that was a serious concern.

"Hmmmm. Good question, Reg. Well, let's see." I pondered the situation and then said, "Maybe if you go over first, then I can pick her up, hand her to you, and you can help her over the rest of the way," I suggested.

It didn't look like it was going to be easy but we decided to give it a try. Although Reggie was steady on his feet on firm ground, climbing a fence was a different story. There was a support pillar made from a concrete slab that held the fence in place, and the first thing Reggie did was step up onto it. Then I explained to him how to put his hands and feet through the open squares of the chain-link fence and pull himself up a little at a time. "Now throw your right leg over the top bar, stick it back in the fence on the other side, and then bring your other foot over," I yelled as he got to the top. The roar of the passing cars made coaching especially difficult, but he understood, and after a few minutes he was standing on the pillar on the other side of the fence. "Now comes the hard part, Reg," I told him.

"No problem!" he said. Reggie found this all very exciting. Dixie didn't, though. She was well aware that her turn was next.

I took off my backpack and unhitched Dixie's. I climbed onto the pillar and handed the two packs over to Reggie. Then I jumped down and turned to Dixie. An 80-pound German Shepherd is too big to pick up very often, and Dixie definitely did not like the idea. Not even by her "father!" (Kids!) I asked her to jump onto the pillar and she had no problem with that. No problem, that is, until I climbed up and joined her on the narrow slab.

"This is it, Dix. You ready, Reg?"

"Ready, Steve. Don't worry, Schlicky, I'll catch you on this side," said a reassuring "Uncle" Reggie.

Still, Dixie didn't look very happy. She couldn't put her paws through the links of the fence so I had no choice but to pick her up. Her eyes opened wide, her forehead wrinkled and she flattened her pointy ears back against her head. Those were all the signs that told me she was nervous. My big, brave German Shepherd was acting like a scared little puppy! Her shaking legs and kicking feet didn't make me too happy either. With a grunt and a groan from me, and a whine from her, I lifted Dixie up and over the fence to the waiting arms of her good buddy, Reggie. Dixie laid across Reggie's forearms waiting to be let down but just then Reggie's right foot slipped off the pillar. From my side of the fence I could do nothing but gasp. It's amazing how much terror your mind can imagine in just a quick moment of time, but Reggie, through reflex, instinct, or quick thinking, I didn't care which, quickly thrust his body toward the fence. Dixie let out a loud huff as she was smashed into the fence, but it was worth it as Reggie was able to grab hold and secure his footing. "Man and Dog Tumble Into Traffic on Highway" would not have been a very happy WALKABOUT newspaper headline! Of course, the publicity would have been tremendous, but that would have been the end of the story...and my two best friends. Fortunately, Reggie got his footing and let Dixie jump down. She ran around in circles, happy to be on all fours again. I let out a sigh of relief.

The "Great Wall of Tacoma" was not to be outdone. There was one more climber to go. With Reggie and Dixie watching and waiting, I began to scale this unrelenting barrier. I climbed to the top bar and just as I threw my front leg over I caught my pant leg in the only jag of sharp metal on the entire fence. I guess it was pretty funny, and decided to join Reggie in laughter and accept my pants being the only casualty. It could have been worse. I could have had my jeans ripped from my body and been forced to walk through Tacoma in my undershorts. That would have stopped a few cars! Probably a police car. Finally, I jumped down, still fully clothed, and joined my companions. We put our packs back on and we were back in action! "That's teamwork!" as Reggie would say. After another couple of miles of uncertain roads, we found our way to where we were supposed to meet Janet. The three of us were definitely ready to walk out of Tacoma!

"Hey, Steve, here comes Janet!" Reg called out.

"What a relief!" I replied. When Janet drove up, my anxiety caught up with me, and I whined that this was the first time we had been on course all day. "We never found the exit we wanted way back when we first got into Tacoma, and it's been scary ever since," I said to Janet as Reggie, Dixie and I hugged her. As it turned out, her day hadn't been any easier than ours.

"First I tried to find the best streets for you to walk on through Tacoma," she said. "In no time, I was hopelessly lost. Every road I drove on was a hill that went up & up, and then every turn I made brought me back to the same place. Imagine my surprise when I found myself at sea-level, again and again."

"I'm glad you found us," said Reggie.

"Thank you. But let me tell you, it was pure luck. I'm not even sure how I got to this spot or how I found you."

"Praise the Lord!" said Reggie, quite appropriately.

"Praise the Lord," agreed Janet, as Dixie jumped up and surprised Janet with a lick right square on the lips. "Yuck! She licked my tongue!"

"That only means she loves you," I explained.

"Ain't love grand!" she said sarcastically. "I love you, too, Dixie," she said and bent over to give Dixie a kiss on the head.

It was a strange and tiring WALKABOUT day. I wasn't surprised at all when Reggie changed the subject and asked Janet, "Did you find us a place to sleep tonight?" After what we had been experiencing, it was understood that there would be no camping out in the City of Tacoma!

Luckily, after many phone calls earlier in the afternoon, Janet had found us a place to spend the night in a Tacoma group home. She made the arrangements and got directions over the phone, so it shouldn't have been a shock to us when we got lost again, but it was! Ninety minutes later, after 23 wrong turns and 47 traffic lights, we found the group home. When we arrived, our new friends raised our spirits with a hero's welcome.

Ten tenants and three staff shook our hands and escorted us right to the dinner table. After we were served a much-needed meat loaf dinner, and after we answered a million questions, we went to relax in the living room to watch T.V. with some of our hosts. Others excused themselves and went to their bedrooms. Reggie sat for just a few minutes before turning to Janet and me. "I'm going for a walk, O.K.?"

"You're going for a walk?" said Janet, not believing what she heard. Then she turned to me and said, "Have you noticed that after a long day I like to sit and relax, and you like to take a long, hot shower, but Reggie wants to go for a walk?"

"I guess that should tell you something," I answered. "He's amazing, isn't he?"

Janet raised her eyebrows and shook her head. She turned back to Reggie and asked, "After a day like today, where could you possibly want to go?"

"I want to walk around the stores." He was referring to a nice, large shopping center right outside the front door of the group home. In fact, the group home was basically built in the back parking lot of the shopping center. It certainly wouldn't have been my first choice for a good place to build a home of any kind. I wondered who could have possibly thought that anyone would chose to live in such a place. I wondered if someone thought it didn't matter because the occupants would have disabilities. Did someone think that a person with a disability wouldn't mind having a parking lot as a front yard and the shopping public as neighbors? That thought made me angry. On the other hand, considering the day we all had, the group home was a welcome haven, and for all I cared at that moment, it could have been located in a toxic land-fill!

While Reggie went for his walk, I attempted to shower the grime of Tacoma off my body in the "boys" bathroom. I figured that I would need all the hot water in the city to do a really good job, but I cut my shower short when someone came in to use the toilet. I grumbled, for the second time, that there was no lock on the door. It appeared to me that the bathroom had been purposely designed so that it could accommodate more than one person at a time. Personally, I prefer complete privacy in the bathroom of my home, but then I remembered that I wasn't in my home. I was in other people's home. Still, I wondered if the tenants minded that they couldn't use their bathroom without being interrupted. Maybe they didn't mind. Maybe they did. Maybe I was just tired and cranky.

I put on my best smile, came out of the bathroom—a lot sooner than I had originally hoped—and noticed that Janet had a look of worry on her face. She had just hung up the phone after enjoying a long talk with a friend from home, but she wasn't smiling. It had just occurred to her that Reggie had not yet returned from his walk.

"You know, Steve, I probably shouldn't even worry about it, but considering the luck we all had today, I think we should go out and look for him."

"Janet," I said, still drying my hair, "the shopping center is not even across the street. Reggie's pretty smart; I'm sure he's fine. Let's wait a little longer. I'd rather walk through Tacoma on my tongue than leave this building right now."

"Hmmmm," thought Janet. She was either wondering about Reggie or entertaining a mental image of me walking on my tongue. I didn't inquire.

We sat there for about five minutes, letting our imaginations fly. It gave us the chance to visualize all the possible experiences an inexperienced man could find in a strange city. We were both well aware how easy it was to get lost.

"Let's go find him," we both said at the same time. I quickly clamped my mouth shut before Janet could make plans for my tongue.

We scanned the parking lot and there was no sign of him. It was a big lot but it was late in the evening and there were only a few cars scattered about. No Reggie. At six feet tall, and with his very special "rock and stroll" method of casual walking, Reggie would have stood out. We saw no Reggie. "Do you know if he had any money on him?" Janet asked me.

"I'm sure he had at least a dollar or two."

"Let's go check the stores," Janet suggested. "Maybe he wanted to buy a candy bar for dessert. There are only two stores that are still open. I'll check out the Albertson's Supermarket and you look in that giant Ernst Hardware Store."

I went into the store and looked around. No Reggie. I went from one end of the store to the other, looking up every aisle. No Reggie. I looked again. No Reggie. "Have you seen a tall man with a mustache that may have appeared to be a bit confused?" I asked the check-out clerk at the front of the store.

"Nope," came the answer.

"Hmmmm, surely Janet found him," I thought to myself.

I left the store and headed for Albertson's. Unfortunately, all I saw was Janet heading towards me with her hands up in the air. This wasn't good. "You don't suppose our worst nightmare is becoming reality," I said to her when we were close enough.

"You get the car. I'm calling the police," Janet said tensely. I guess she did suppose the worst.

Janet ran back to the building and called 9-1-1. The dispatcher said she would send a squad car. I took the WALKABOUT-Mobile and drove up and down the streets. I figured that I could cover more ground driving than walking. The way I figured it, there were only about a billion stores, buildings, alleys, streets, etc., that he could have been in. "Or maybe somebody..." I stopped the thought dead in its tracks.

Worrying makes time go *soooo* slow! Back and forth I drove, looking this way and that.

"Reggie!" As I glanced back at the shopping center I saw him, casually crossing the parking lot, walking back to the group home.

"Reggie!" I shouted through the window as I sped over. "Good grief, man. Where have you been? Did you get lost?"

"I went to get some candy. I told you and Janet." He sure seemed calm.

"You were gone for a long time. Janet and I got worried. We looked in every store for you."

"I couldn't find what I wanted in the stores around here, so I had to go to another store. A nice man helped me cross the street. I bought candy for you and Janet, too."

"Well, but, well, don't, uh, don't do that again!" was all I could sputter. "I was nervous!" What could I say? He hadn't done anything wrong, and he'd been careful. He knew exactly what he was doing. Perhaps Janet and I had overreacted. In fact, it appeared as if Reggie was better at finding his way around Tacoma than either one of us! Maybe it was time to let Reggie find the best roads to walk on!

Reggie hopped into the WALKABOUT-Mobile and we drove the 400 feet back to the group home. Janet had a gigantic look of relief on her face when she saw Reggie. She immediately called the police and told them "We found him, safe and sound. Case closed. Thanks anyway!" Then she turned to Reggie and he told her the same thing he had told me. She didn't know what to say either, so she said, "Well, but, well, don't, uh, don't do that again! I was nervous!"

"I'm sorry," he said sincerely. He was afraid we were really mad at him. "I make mistake. Everyone makes mistakes." He gave a smile, trying to diffuse our tension.

"That's true," said Janet, "but the only real mistake you made was that you went further and were gone longer than we expected. Next time just let us know so we don't worry. We care about you."

"O.K. That's a deal. That's teamwork, right?"

Back at the group home, we settled down and laughed at our suspenseful experience. One of the counselors who tried to help us find Reggie shared his opinion on preventing such scary misunderstandings.

"I think we should build a big home out in the country." Scott was very friendly, very sympathetic, and very sure of himself.

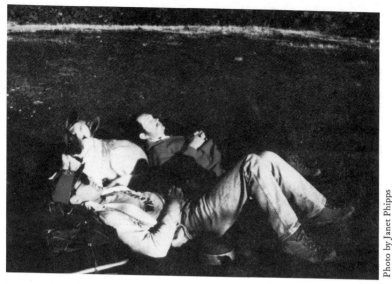

Photo by Janet Phipps

*The easiest way to deal with
misguided maps through big cities*

"Maybe an apartment house, with a workshop next door. That way we wouldn't have to worry about this kind of thing happening. We could keep our people safe and not have to worry about them."

Janet listened to his thoughts, and respected his opinion as it was from the goodness of his heart, but she felt compelled to share her differing viewpoint. "I disagree," said Janet. "The only thing that really happened tonight was that we showed a lack of faith in Reggie.

"In my opinion, Reggie is doing this walk to show people that he is capable of doing all sorts of things by himself. He doesn't need to be sent away. He wants to learn how to be a part of his town. Sure, it's a little scary at times, but that's what being an adult is all about. People *need* to make mistakes. We all learn from mistakes. If Reggie lived in a place where he couldn't make mistakes, he would never learn anything. Besides, he's a man, not a child, and the choice should be up to him."

The next day Reggie, Dixie and I walked out of Tacoma and through the maze of streets towards the suburbs of Seattle. It was still busy with people and cars, but we did a little better job following the map. We only got misplaced twice!

Janet decided to play it safe and spent the day in one place. She found a grocery store and set up a small table and sold WALKABOUT T-shirts and buttons at the entrance.

"Today I met one of the most interesting people of the whole trip," Janet told us when she met up with us at the end of the day. We could see her excitement tingling through her body. "He said he really admired Reggie."

"He likes me?" asked Reggie.

"He doesn't know you, but he certainly respects what you are doing. The man, no, I mean *really* cute man, walked over and wanted to know what WALKABOUT was." Janet was talking as quickly as a chattering songbird. "I told him all about Reggie walking around the state and showing that everyone is good at something if you give them the chance. He said he really liked the concept of WALKABOUT.

"Then he told me that four years ago both his hands were smashed in an accident. He showed me his hands and they were mostly twisted and mangled. He didn't even have all of his fingers. 'You can't imagine how many people don't want to hire me,' he explained, 'because they don't think I'm able to do very much. You know what I like about your project?' he went on, 'I like how it stresses people's ABILITIES, not their DISabilities. Reggie and I are a lot alike. In fact, the only real difference is that Reggie has had his problem his whole life, while I am still a rookie.'"

"He's a smart man," added Reggie.

"Yes, I agree," I said. "I'm happy to see that you're having interesting WALKABOUT experiences, too, Janet. I bet it's even getting easier to live without all your STUFF!" She playfully smacked me in the arm and we all laughed.

We piled into the WALKABOUT-Mobile and Janet drove us to our "home" for the night. She didn't say a word the whole way there. That man had really made an impression on her.

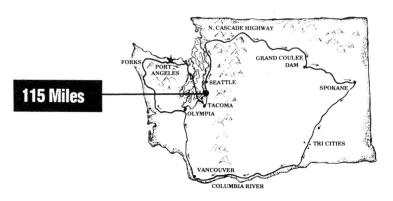

chapter 9

WHERE'S REGGIE?

You know you are in the middle of an adventure when something happens while you are doing nothing!

The WALKABOUT team decided to take a much-needed day off. We were in the town of Burien, which lies between Tacoma and Seattle, and Janet's friend Wayne had kindly let us rest in his apartment. Janet and I were relaxing in front of the T.V. when Reggie went out into the courtyard to smoke one of his occasional cigars. After half an hour or so, Janet decided to go talk with him. She found his chair empty and he was nowhere in sight. "Gone again," she thought. Janet walked through the pool area to see if he was there, and then she walked over to the front gate to see if he was out in the parking lot by the WALKABOUT-Mobile. As she approached the gate, Janet caught a whiff of cigar smoke.

"Reggie! Are you out here?"

"No problem."

Interestingly enough, the police officer standing beside Reggie disagreed. So did the building's manager. Reggie was not able to make either the lady or the policeman understand who he was or what he was doing there.

"I'm walking the United States," he tried to explain. The officer and the manager didn't understand what Reggie was talking about. Indeed, it did seem like quite a fairy tale.

Reggie had left his wallet with his identification back in the apartment, and therefore the officer didn't know who Reggie was or where he lived. The cop then decided to ask the police station to call every group home in the area. After a while, they had finally contacted the Lauridsen Group Home way back in Port Angeles. The staff at Lauridsen told the police who Reggie was, but even the staff didn't know why Reggie was at this building. The officer was just putting Reggie into his squad car, ready to drive him all the way back home, when Janet walked out. The cop was very relieved to see her. So was the manager. Now they both had someone else to yell at.

"Who are you?"

"Why didn't Wayne tell me he had company?"

"What did you let him come outside for?"

"Wayne shouldn't have strange friends stay over!"

"We don't allow this sort of thing around here!"

Janet was surprised at their rudeness. All Reggie was doing was walking around smoking a cigar. Sure, cigar smoking isn't a pleasant habit, but it isn't illegal!

"Did he do something wrong?" Janet asked.

"No, but we don't allow this sort of thing around here."

Janet and Reggie walked back towards the apartment.

"Come on, Reggie," Janet said.

"No problem!" Reggie answered.

They never figured out what made the officer and the manager so angry. Was it because Reggie was hard to understand? Or because he was different? Who knows?

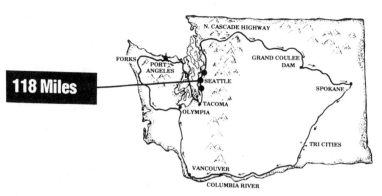

118 Miles

chapter 10

WHERE ARE WE?

"This has been a nightmare!" screamed our frustrated support driver. Janet was determined to put an end to a very annoying WALKABOUT day. We had been slowly making our way from Burien to Seattle.

"Perhaps the four of us just don't belong in big cities," I answered.

"We're not doing too well in the big towns between the big cities, either," hissed Janet, clenching her teeth. She had been searching for roads that looked like a good route for Reggie, Dixie and I to walk. She would figure the best routes and then drive back and tell us how to get to them. Reggie, Dixie and I would walk where we were told. "Let me give you some words of wisdom," she offered, with desperation in her voice. "Never try to trail-blaze during rush-hour!"

"Bad day at the office, dear?" I asked, trying to cheer her up. I quickly learned that the only thing that made Janet feel better was getting the frustration of city driving off her chest.

"It took hours just to get through the traffic lights! Then I figured out I was going the wrong way. So I had to turn around, go back through the lights, and go on to some more lights. Then I figured out I was lost again so it was back through the same lights, etc., etc., blah, blah, blah."

"Lucky for you there are only three possible ways to get lost at most traffic lights," I said, trying to be funny.

"Please don't interrupt me while I'm raging!" said Janet. "Anyway, finally, I couldn't take it anymore. I knew you wanted to keep going until six o'clock this evening, but for the life of me I couldn't predict with any accuracy which route would be safest for you. So, I decided that I'd come back and find you and we'd just call it a day." She sighed deeply.

"Actually, we were just getting into a good rhythm and we'd like to walk another mile or two, right Reg? The more we walk, the faster we get out of here."

"NO!" cried Janet, grabbing both our arms.

"Well, how 'bout just a few more blocks, then?"

"If you move another *inch* I'll run you down with the car!"

"Steve," said Reggie, "let's not walk anymore."

"Good thinking," I muttered as we climbed dutifully into the car.

"She'd run us over?" Reggie whispered.

I leaned over to his ear, almost sure Janet could hear me anyway, and said, "If I was so sure she wouldn't, do you think I would have climbed into the car so quickly?" Reggie looked at me and shrugged his shoulders. I gave him a wink. He gave a quick laugh.

Janet hit the gas and we headed off in search of the group home that was going to be our home for the night.

A calming night's sleep had Janet rosy-cheeked and ready for action. By mid-afternoon of the next day she had found a route that led us around Lake Washington through Seattle's eastern suburbs, right into the northern suburbs.

It was a busy road, with sidewalks to walk on to keep us safe from the congested traffic. People drove back and forth, occasionally parking with intentions of buying things or selling them. We walked by convenience stores, dance studios, medical offices, clothing stores and anyplace else where people could spend money. We walked, stopped, waited for the zillionth electric sign to change from the "WAIT" to the picture of the person in motion, and then we walked some more. I tried to tune out the unpleasant car sounds and sirens and horns, and tried to key in on the shuffle of Reggie's boots and jingle of Dixie's I.D. tags as they walked behind me.

"Soon we'll be in the mountains, right, Steve?" Reggie asked from behind. Although the sidewalks were wide, we still walked in single file—me, Dixie, and then Reggie.

"If we keep up a good walking pace, we should be out of the city lickity-split," I said, trying to motivate both of us.

"Too many lights, Steve."

"I know. Isn't it annoying? Too much traffic means too many lights."

"I don't like the city anymore. I want to camp out."

"We'll be out of it pretty soon."

"Praise the Lord!" Reggie said.

"Hallelujah," I replied. "But I guess we have to take the bad with the good. Sometimes we have to walk on busy streets right in the center of the big ol' city, and sometimes we get to walk along peaceful, scenic, tree-lined highways." There was a bright side, however. We had recently given two more interviews. Reggie hadn't been as nervous, but he still left most of the talking to me. He appreciated that reporters came out to talk with us. "Since we are in the city," I added, "it would be nice to think that all the people that pass us by have read about us in the newspapers and know what and why we are doing what we are doing."

"They know me!" Reggie stated. That thought always cheered him up.

"Someday, everybody is going to know you, Reggie."

"I like that," he said, smiling and waving to the passing cars.

"Of course, two guys walking with backpacks isn't too unusual in a city, but I bet not too many of them have a dog with a backpack."

"Schlicky's famous, too," Reggie said, bending down to give her a kiss on the head.

Just then a car without a muffler roared by. Reggie covered his ears and said, "I like the woods. I like the peace and quiet."

"Me, too. Take heart, every step we take is a step closer to the the Cascade Mountains."

"Hallelujah!"

"Hallelujah!" I said back. I laughed. Sometimes it was the most appropriate word in the world. Reggie and I had talked about his saying some things too many times, like "Hallelujah!" or "Praise the Lord!" after every sentence. Of course, breaking old habits is never easy, but I could see (and hear) that he was really catching on to new ideas.

A few days earlier I finally decided to share my thoughts with him about what was annoying to me. "I don't mean to sound insulting, Reg, but it's not really appropriate to say 'Praise the Lord' or 'Hallelujah' after every single sentence. You have to learn to use it at just the right time. Otherwise it doesn't mean anything."

"No problem," he answered, trying to understand that being respected as an adult means more than just being over 18 years of age. "No problem," on the other hand, was so distinctly Reggie that I couldn't even imagine suggesting he quit saying that.

Conversations were always a great way of diverting our attention from the stop-and-go walking we were forced to endure. The cars became a blur. Most people stared at us as we passed them. Some stopped us to say hello, to ask where we were headed, and to pet Dixie. Children pointed at us through the windows of storefronts. Who knows how many people had read about us in the newspapers? Cars honked, calling to us—or perhaps to a driver who slowed down to look at the people and dog they had read about. Normally we would appreciate the attention, but deep down we just wanted to keep walking until we were back into the country. Sometimes we were lucky and we'd hit a stride and just move along, each of us in our own world, thinking our own thoughts.

After one such section of quiet walking, I realized that I didn't hear Dixie's jingle anymore. I turned to see where she was. I noticed that Reggie wasn't behind me either. I looked down the street, and about forty yards back Dixie stood outside the door of a candy store. She stood there, her body facing the door, orange eyes staring at me, a wrinkle of concern in her forehead.

Just then Reggie came out of the store, holding two candy bars. Dixie ran back to me, wagging her tail, followed by her buddy.

"Schlicky loves her Uncle Reggie!" Reggie said to me as he continued to walk.

They had known each other for a long time before WALKABOUT, but they'd never spent much time together. Now Dixie, who'd always kept a sharp eye on me, was looking out for Reggie, too.

I laughed. So did Reggie. Dixie, with her mouth open, tongue slightly laying over her front teeth, looked as if she was smiling, too.

"One candy bar for me, and one for you, Steve, " he said, placing it in my open hand and looking at my face. I smiled, approvingly. "Teamwork!" he added. "And a little piece for Schlicky!"

Reggie was showing me that he was really learning. A few days earlier, we had talked about keeping fit. It had been a hot day and when we'd taken a break, Reggie had gone into a store. He bought a quart of chocolate milk and three candy bars. For days, Janet had given us a snack in our lunch or a goody for our packs, but Reggie had some of his own money and there was no reason he couldn't buy his own. With all the stores we passed in the city, it was just too much to resist.

We had stopped by a convenience store and he went in for a snack. When he came out, I looked at his loot and said, "You know, Reg, you've been talking about buying candy, chocolate milk, soda pop and cigars much too often. I think you've gone overboard." I didn't really expect him to eat all that junk at one time, but still I added, "If you're not careful and if you don't take care of yourself, you won't be able to finish this trip."

"No problem." I wasn't exactly sure what that meant at the time. I watched in amazement as he ate and drank every last bit of the sugary junk he had bought. Advice from me had passed him right by, just like the traffic.

"Reg," I said, after he downed his whole bag of goodies, "I can't believe you drank and ate the whole thing! That much junk food and sugar is really tough on your entire system!"

"No problem," Reg assured me. But sure enough, there was a problem.

After the usual amount of break time, I turned and said, "O.K., Reg, break's over. Let's go."

Dixie popped up immediately. Reggie stood up, and grabbed

his pack and put his arms through the shoulder straps. Then he stopped abruptly, took it off and sat down. "I, I can't walk. I don't feel so good. I got a headache, Steve."

"Yeah, I bet you do," I said, frowning. He was too sick to care how annoyed I was. We sat around for another hour, Reggie holding his belly, napping. I sat next to him, very disappointed.

Finally, I woke him up and we talked about the importance of not consuming too much sugar at one time. "Basically, Reg, you have to learn to drink a little less chocolate milk. And for goodness sakes, eat only one candy bar at a time!"

Reggie had to learn the hard way, but he impressed me with his progress. I hoped that he only needed one experience of eating so much sugar that he actually got ill. I realized that everybody does it sooner or later, and I wasn't mad at him. I remembered that I'd learned the same lesson during my first long walk. I recalled taking too much advantage of "all-you-can-eat" dinners in Louisiana's cafes. Hours would pass before my belly would allow the rest of my body to get up and walk. Back then only Dixie was with me, and she didn't get mad. I figured Reggie deserved the same respect. At least the first time, anyway.

I thanked Reggie for the single candy bar that he had just bought for each of us, and commended his self control. We walked on as we unwrapped our goody and dove into the sweet snack.

"Look, Steve," he said as he held up his wrapper, "I don't throw it on the ground, I put it in my pocket. I'm a good cop!" Reggie saluted me and we continued on.

We put towns such as Renton, Bellevue and Kirkland behind us. Seattle and its suburbs slowly became a memory. Each stride was a step further from the city. The cars still zipped past, the drivers taking care of their business while we slowly took care of ours. The sidewalk had come to an end, and the road was now called Highway 522. Luckily, the side shoulder gave us plenty of room for safety. Dixie walked right beside my legs, and Reggie was right behind me.

"Hey, Steve, Labor Day is coming soon, right?" Reggie asked. Conversation just sort of popped up at anytime on WALKABOUT.

"Yes, it is," I said. I wasn't even aware that he even knew about the holiday.

"And then kids go back to school, right?" he asked.

"That's right, Reg. Hey, that's very good! Where did you hear about that?"

"My brain told me."

"That's great. Hey, look, Reg," I said, changing the subject, "we'll be on a quiet road in no time flat." I pointed to the "city limits" sign as we entered Bothell, which we both knew was the last crowded town we'd have to contend with. The commuters and the trucks would head towards the Interstate, but WALKABOUT would wind its way north on peaceful Highway 9.

"Look, Steve," Reggie said, pointing up the road. He noticed how the four-lane road narrowed to two lanes, one for each direction of traffic. Concrete pillars, steel fencing and a couple of bulldozers crowded a section of road under an overpass.

Sounding like a soldier leading a charge, I said, "Looks like we'll have to battle our way through."

"I'm strong," Reggie said. "Are you strong, Steve?"

"Yup."

"You too, Schlicky?"

Dixie looked up when Reggie said her name, but I added a "Woof!" as if Dixie had said, "Yup!"

"Hey," I said, speaking as me, "see that sign with an arrow on the other side of the construction?"

"I see it," Reggie said, raising his hand to point in the same direction I was pointing.

"That means that we'll find Highway 9 somewhere in that direction after we get through the overpass. We're almost outta here!" I exclaimed, clenching my fist and hitting the air.

"Hallelujah," Reggie said once again, quite appropriately.

We patiently crept closer to the road that would relieve us from these past days and miles of less-than-pleasurable walking. The stress and strain of city walking had tightened up our minds and our muscles. Even Reggie's after-dinner walks had become less frequent. After cleaning up his plate he would take a nap. He'd get up only to get ready for bed.

I assumed that the lack of road workers meant that it was their lunchtime. There wasn't even one flagperson directing traffic. We were on our own. The side shoulder got dangerously narrow. The shadow of the overpass began to close in around us. We concentrated on the sight of where we couldn't wait to be, but no matter how hard we tried we couldn't ignore our feelings that the world was closing in on us. Already the speeding cars caused a breeze that made our T-shirts shake like a flag in the wind. Dixie's fur was ruffling. Our clothing and hair absorbed exhaust fumes like a vacuum sucks up dusty cobwebs in a haunted house. Cars were passing us by, much too close for comfort. It was bound to get worse.

"Maybe we should walk on the other side," I said to Reggie, pointing to the other side of the road where the shoulder appeared to be just a bit wider. Reggie awaited my decision as he acknowledged my leadership in this area. "It's a rough choice. I hate walking with the traffic coming at us from behind. We can't see what's happening. We have to rely, totally, on the drivers seeing us. Yet on this side we have an unrelenting stream of cars to the right of our body, and concrete and steel to our left." For the sake of someone's safety, certainly not ours, there was that fence that would leave us only three feet of space to walk. Should a car come too close for comfort, we would never be able to jump the thick wall of stone nor have the time to climb the steel barrier that rose many feet above it. "It's not much to go on," I said, coming to a decision that was definitely debatable, "but at least on this side we can see the cars coming at us. At least we can keep some of our fate in our hands. But remember, there will be no escape," I joked in a low, brooding voice, "from that 'Fence of Doom.'"

Reggie laughed deep from his chest, kidding around as if he were Count Dracula in a science-fiction movie. He was all heart!

He made me laugh, but I wasn't happy. "We've forged through rough city-walking since we came close to Tacoma. I think we can handle one more hurdle to earn the honor of walking on a nice country road, Reg. We can do it."

"No problem," Reggie replied as he took up the slack and walked on my heels. He suggested that I take hold of Dixie's collar to keep her as close to me as possible. I heeded his advice.

It really wasn't so bad...until we were actually under the overpass. Claustrophobia set in as the mass of automobiles came straight towards us. We tried to melt into the concrete barrier, but still it was like playing in traffic. There was only one way to go and that was forward. The thought of the safe haven of Highway 9 inspired us to move ahead as quickly as possible.

"PSSSSSST," was the sound that caught our attention. With the threat of death only inches from the three of us, our senses sensed the need to be extra alert. When the strange sound caught my ears, my head turned to see three teen-agers in a car. Only by instinct did we duck as the freshly opened beer can zoomed towards our heads.

"GEE WHIZ!" is actually a little less harsh then the words I really screamed, but they get the point across. The can crashed into the fence above my head with a vibration that echoed through my skull. Beer splattered all over Dixie and me, just narrowly missing Reggie.

"Hey!" Reggie yelled, looking back at the car. Only two seconds had passed, but the car was long gone. I stood in shock. Dixie, too, had been taken by surprise and the fur on her back rose as it did whenever she sensed danger.

I said nothing and took a deep breath.

"I'm a cop! They should go to jail!" Reggie yelled, looking back.

"I wish you were a cop. That was really stupid. And really mean, too," I said, quite disgusted.

Reggie untied my bandana from the frame of my pack and handed it to me so that I could wipe myself dry. Cars continued to zoom past, and I quickly realized that we had to get out of there.

We came to Highway 9 and finally rested in some shade. There were noticeably fewer cars. Janet came driving up, and we told her that we'd been attacked with a "Budweiser grenade."

"What's a Budweiser grenade?" Janet asked. She had certainly never heard of one before, because I had just made up the name.

I began to lay out the story for her, and her face changed from its usual rosy smile to one of disgust and amazement.

"Oh, my gosh!" she gasped. "That's terrible! Are you all right?"

"Yeah, it missed us by a few feet, but we got treated to a beer shower. What fun," I groaned sarcastically.

Janet was disgusted. "I can't believe people can be that stupid. Or that mean!"

"You know," I said as I washed and refreshed myself with clean water from the WALKABOUT-Mobile, "Dixie and I have walked over 3,300 miles together and that's the worst thing that has ever happened during our travels. The nasty people may be louder than the nice people, but there are definitely a lot less of the nasty kind. A hundred to one, there are a lot more nice people. They are the ones I really remember."

That was our final farewell to Seattle. The big cities were behind us and we headed toward the mighty Cascade Mountains!

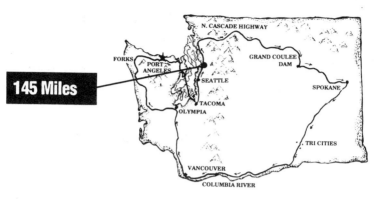

chapter 11

The BALLOON

On Highway 9 we continued north. Every time we looked back we saw the unique outline of Seattle's famous Space Needle and the rest of the "Emerald City's" skyline, an inspirational silhouette that faded with every step.

We appreciated the peace of the countryside and enjoyed the bright sunshine spilling over us. The miles passed quickly; our day went gliding by. Towards evening Janet gave a beep of the horn as she drove past. She would pick us up after we finished our 14th mile. As we neared the WALKABOUT-Mobile, Janet pointed to some people inflating a giant, rainbow-colored hot air balloon. As we walked closer, my adventuresome spirit instantly went into high gear. "That looks like nothing but fun!" I thought. "Maybe we could get a ride! And just think of the publicity!" I could see it now: "Washington Walker Takes to the Air" the headlines would read. I couldn't wait to get over there to talk to the balloonists!

The balloonists were full of admiration for

Up, up and ...
"no way, Steve"

Photo by Janet Phipps

Reggie, and they thought WALKABOUT was a wonderful project. They also thought giving us a balloon ride was a great idea.

The partly-inflated balloon was floating towards the sky as the passenger basket stayed anchored to the ground. "No way," Reggie said nervously, staring at the rising balloon. His plans did not include leaving Mother Earth.

"It would be great publicity for all of us," I pleaded with him.

"Schlicky would be scared," he said.

"She doesn't have to go. Just you and me. The publicity could help us get a lot of donations, Reg."

"Schlicky would bite us," said Reggie, making up any excuse to avoid the balloon.

"Think of all the chocolate milk we could buy." No reply. "Reggie, pleeeeze," I begged.

"I don't think so," he said quickly. A half hour later, our conversation had not changed. Reggie didn't like the idea, and I wasn't getting very far in my attempts to convince him otherwise. Reggie wanted to keep both feet planted firmly on the State of Washington, and wanted absolutely nothing to do with the balloon that was reaching for the heavens. Since it was a package deal, I had a sinking feeling I was about to miss my big chance.

Reggie walked back to the car and I turned to Janet and said, "I don't think even making him feel guilty about turning down this golden opportunity is having any effect."

"Nope," she said flatly. "And you've pouted long enough. That's not working either. Give it up, Steve. You'll get over it."

"No. I don't think I will. I'm going to be upset forever," I said, sticking out my lower lip.

"Don't forget," Janet reminded me, "Reggie has been spreading the word that people with developmental disabilities have the right to make their own choices. Today, you have to accept Reggie's choice *not* to take advantage of this opportunity."

I looked at her and said nothing. She was absolutely right. We walked back to the WALKABOUT-Mobile and loaded up.

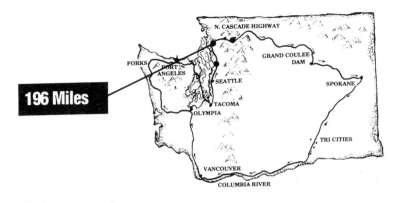

196 Miles

chapter 12

MOTIVATIONS

"Next stop, Quilceda House," Janet cried as we piled into the WALKABOUT-Mobile. Progress had been swift along the peaceful country roads, as we made our way north along Puget Sound. Soon we'd turn east to the mountains, leaving civilization behind. "By the way," Janet added, "Quilceda House will be our last group home for quite a while."

"I want to camp out," said Reggie. Through the cities, Reggie understood that we had to find group homes or friends to spend the night with. One does not camp out in urban parks! So far, each day we'd had home-cooked meals, refreshing showers, soft beds and a roof. Comfortable? Yes. Adventuresome? Hardly. "I miss the woods," he added. "I like the peace and quiet."

"Well, we'll do plenty of camping soon," explained Janet. "After tonight, there are no more group homes that I know of until we reach Spokane," she added, referring to the city clear on the other side of the state.

"That's only about three or four hundred miles," I said, casually. "No problem. Right, Reg?"

Reggie smiled at me and quizzically said, "No problem?"

Our new friends at Quilceda House made us feel at home right away. They fed us dinner, talked with us and tucked us into bed. At breakfast, a Quilceda House tenant named Marilyn volunteered to go along and help out.

Marilyn looked to Janet and asked, "Is there something I can help you with?" Marilyn was short, round, and full of cheer. She had Down's Syndrome and was living at Quilceda House. She spoke with a stammer, but it wasn't difficult to understand her. "I'm a real good helper. There's lots of things I could do. I like to help. Can I help?"

"Sure," said Janet, sensing Marilyn's enthusiasm. "Reggie, Steve and Dixie have each other all day long, but I'm alone most of the day. I'd love to have company! You can help me raise some money by selling Walkabout T-shirts and buttons outside of a grocery store. You can help explain WALKABOUT to shoppers going in and out of the store."

"Good," said Marilyn. "I like to talk to people. I can talk and never get tired. What should I say to the people? How much do the shirts cost? When do we leave? This is going to be fun! Does this mean I'm a WALKABOUTer, too? Can I wear my new WALKABOUT shirt?" Janet quickly understood that an afternoon with Marilyn would not be awkwardly quiet or lack conversation!

Janet and Marilyn dropped Reggie, Dixie and me off in the same place where we had stopped the evening before. We walked north on Highway 9, heading for Highway 20—the road that would lead us into the Cascade Mountains. Highway 20 is lined with small towns, many picturesque farms and the occasional stream. Fields of hay and pastures full of cows spread before us. We were within peaceful beauty, encompassed by a growing radiant heat.

The gray clouds that had covered Seattle had dissipated as soon as we walked into the country. For the first two days we had been so happy to be out of the city that we hadn't noticed the sweat soaking our shirts, but after enjoying a semi-cool morning, the noon sun poured heat over us like a bucket of blazing steam, slowing our steps. While leafy shade trees dotted the countryside here and there, not enough of them were growing beside the road!

"I don't get it, Reg. I don't know if it's spring or fall." I wiped the back of my hand along my sweaty forehead. Reggie was using his bandana to wipe his whole face. "This is September, for heaven's sake! The leaves are changing colors and starting to fall off the trees, yet it gets hotter with each passing day," I complained. "That's just not the way it's supposed to be."

"Soon we'll be in the mountains," responded Reggie. I wasn't sure if he was asking me, telling me, or just doing a lot of wishful thinking.

"If it's not one challenge, it's another," I said. "I'll tell you, it was rough walking through the city but at least it was overcast and cool. I guess we should feel lucky that it wasn't hot, too."

"It's up to the good Lord," rationalized Reggie.

"Yes, perhaps you're right. Maybe it's all part of His master plan," I said. "Boy, I sure hope it's a good plan." We cursed the heat, but we had to use these wide-open country miles to make up for lost time—you know, the city and all.

We kept on walking. The sun and stifling air melted our stamina like a candy bar in a hot car. "Time for a break, Steve?" Reggie would ask. Sometimes it was and sometimes it wasn't. Sometimes he just stopped walking. Dixie always agreed with Reggie. I took the hint. I had no choice.

I was trying to keep on the schedule that we had made up. We were not averaging 14 miles a day, and I was uncomfortable with that. It was still early in the trip and we could be recalled at any time. The staff at the group home missed Janet and me, and New Broom Janitorial needed Reggie. If it didn't look like we were getting the job done in a respectable amount of time....

The road changed from smooth black-top to a gravel base. Reggie and I had thick-soled boots that protected our feet, but the pebbles stung Dixie's foot pads. They quickly turned from shiny black to an angry bright red. She began to limp. She was sore!

The morning air, filled with all those luscious country smells of pasture animals, had called to Dixie, and she couldn't resist running this way and that, taking it all in. For a while she ignored the pain of her aching feet. She didn't consider how all that extra mileage would hurt her feet; pacing was beyond her understanding. When she was having this kind of fun, it was impossible to slow her down. By afternoon, the heat zapped her energy, and the rough road and pebbled shoulder had caused her pads to throb. She spent the rest of the day limping a few feet behind me, tongue hanging from her mouth. The hard walking had been taking its toll on Dixie, too. The noticeable lack of bounce in her steps made me realize how badly this heat was affecting my usually energetic walking pal.

I sighed. Walking in this heat just wasn't fun for poor Dixie. When she hurt, I hurt. Unfortunately, there wasn't very much we could do for her. We couldn't just sit in the sun and wait for her to heal. I knew she'd be more comfortable as soon as the road became smooth again, and experience told me that sooner or later we'd hit smooth road again. For Dixie's sake, we all prayed it would be sooner!

In the meantime, we had to push on. "It's easy to walk when the weather is cool and our bodies feel strong," I said to both Dixie and Reggie (and to myself), "but the only way we are going to make it around the whole state is to keep going, even when we're hurting. Right now we're hurting."

"Is Schlicky hurt real bad?" asked Reggie. He was quite concerned.

I stopped and looked down at her. "I don't think she's too bad, but I can only guess." I walked on and Dixie continued, slowly limping along by my side. With many thousands of miles behind us, I knew that Dixie would be by my side until she fell over dead. I stopped again to look down at her pads. "If I see that she is in too much pain, we can always let Dixie ride with Janet for a few days. I really hate the thought of that, though. I can't imagine walking without her. It would be like removing one of my legs."

"She'll be O.K., right?" Reg asked.

I looked at Reggie's sympathetic eyes. "Yes," I said. "I'm sure she will be. Besides, I know Dixie well enough to know that she'll just park herself when she's had enough."

We were shuffling along, depressed and discouraged. This was no way to WALKABOUT! "It would be great if Dixie could speak English and tell us exactly how she feels, but she can't. We've walked 3,500 miles together, some of them with power and some with pain. Let's put her boots on and see if they help."

Reggie laughed as I strapped Dixie's boots onto her feet. The boots, donated by Sporting Dog Specialties in New York, were a simple yet ingenious strip of leather, tied to her legs with leather laces. Her side toes stuck out of the sides of the boots, and her two middle toenails fit through special holes punched in the leather, keeping the boot in place. "She looks funny," Reggie giggled.

"I think she looks cute," I said.

"I feel silly," I could almost hear Dixie think. The look on her face confirmed my thought. "I love my backpack, but these boots are for the cats. The things I do for this man..."

"O.K., dog," I said to Dixie, "stop complaining."

"Her back feet, too?" Reggie asked. I had only booted her two front feet.

"No, I don't think so, Reg. She needs her two back feet for power. The front feet are only for steering. Besides, we'll be lucky if she doesn't kick those two off."

Our three pairs of boots plopped rhythmically along the graveled road. Dixie, as usual, accepted her fate, and chose to wear her boots—with or without pride. Each step brought us closer to the mountains, and we balanced the grueling miles with sporadic breaks. An occasional stream drifted beside the road, and the only cool thing to do was to sit, relax for a while and rinse our arms, legs, face and head in the cool water. Dixie would walk clear in, boots and all, right up to her belly. She would take a long drink, and let the water soak into her fur.

It was a glorious feeling—at least temporarily. The cooling effects of the water evaporated the moment we got back on the hot, graveled highway. We walked without words. Walking just wasn't fun. It was HOT!

"SWING LOW, SWEET CHARIOT...DA-DA, DA-DA-DA-DA-DAA" sang a voice, low-pitched, as if it was coming from out of thin air. It was difficult to understand all the words but I captured the rhythm. "Swing Low, Sweet Chariot...DA-DA, DA-DA-DA-DA-DA." It was coming from behind me. "Swing Low, Sweet Chariot..."

I turned around, and there was Reggie singing to inspire us! I broke into hysterics. "That was just too funny, Reg. What a way to fight the heat!" Reggie could be quite an inspiration when he wanted to be.

"Swing Low, Sweet Chariot," he continued, and I joined in.

Along the highway walked a dog and two backpackers singing the
old soulful hymn. I'm sure it was quite a sight. I could see Dixie's
step become even livelier as she tuned in to our mood.

"Where did you ever learn that?" I finally asked.

"At work," he said.

"You sang this at New Broom Janitorial?!? I never realized
how demanding mopping floors could be."

"No. My other job," he explained. I turned around, walking
backwards on the narrow shoulder, so as not to break up our
rhythm.

"What else have you done?" I never knew he had any other
jobs.

"I worked in a workshop."

"Where was that?"

"Big School."

"What did you do in the workshop?" I asked.

"Put things together. Take things apart. I didn't like it. I got
mad. I didn't want to do it," Reggie explained. I knew that many
sheltered workshops, especially many that had been connected to
institutional care, had their "employees" put things together, just
to take them apart again. The idea, from what I understood, was to
teach them how to work and give them something to do. Perhaps
good intentions, but did it lack insight? I can imagine how boring
and frustrating a "job" like that could be for anyone.

"You got mad? What happened?" I inquired.

"I quit," Reggie said, throwing down his hands. "I walked
away."

"I can understand that," I said sympathetically. "At least you
learned a song." I found Reggie's past history so interesting, and I
was glad he talked about the things he used to do. Conversation
livened us up so much that we didn't even care about the heat, and
we passed some shade trees without thinking to stop and rest.

"Did you have any other jobs?" I asked.

"I was a janitor. I liked that better."

"You mean at New Broom."

"No, before that."

"When was that? Where was that?"

Reggie shrugged. "I don't know."

"Was that in one of the other places that you lived?"

"Yup," Reggie said quietly.

"And now you like being a janitor?"

"I like it," he said softly. He then raised his voice and added, "I want to work in a woodshop, too. Work with wires. I want to fix things."

"That would be great, Reg. Maybe some day you can. Who knows?"

"That's what I want to do! Up to the Good Lord."

"Maybe. But it's up to you, too." I said. "Right now you are taking the walk of a lifetime. With every step we take on WALKABOUT, we are learning and proving that if a person wants something badly enough, he or she has to work *very* hard for it. I can't make any promises about a new job when we get back home, but we can surely work on it. I'll be glad to help, but the bottom line is that it's up to you. Accomplishing that new dream and goal will take hard work and determination. In a way, it will be like walking around Washington."

"I'm a good worker. I like that," Reggie quickly responded. He pondered my words and then, as if to double check, he asked, "No problem, right?"

I shrugged my shoulders and said, "We'll see, Reg." I didn't pull any punches with Reggie. I'd always support his dreams, but I couldn't *earn* him a new job in the community any more than I would walk around Washington *for* him.

I respected Reggie's hopes and dreams but at the same time I had to balance his abilities (those apparent to me, those I was unaware of and those he had the potential to develop) and the opportunities that existed in our community. In one sense he had to consider himself lucky to have a job at all. It shouldn't be a question of luck, of course, it was a right, but considering how people like Reggie had been thought of in the past and the respect that had been given...

Let's see, how would I feel about it? If being a janitor was my only available option, I would probably accept it rather than not having a job at all. Sometimes you take what you can get. However, I would never relish the thought that I would have to clean toilets for the rest of my life. I wondered if Reggie had similar thoughts. Isn't that what he just told me? Once again, I became aware of another similarity. It's amazing I had ever accepted the thought that just because a person had certain disabilities, he would have less ambition.

A very ugly thought flashed across my mind. "You know, Reg, there may be a problem. I've been saying that it's up to you, but that's not completely true. There are other factors that have to be considered. For instance, even if you are a good worker, some employers might be afraid to hire you because you have a developmental disability. There are those that just don't understand people like you. Some people are scared of you and others just think you will never be able to do anything or offer anything of value. They don't want people like you involved with their business." A look of hopelessness came over Reggie's face. It was very sad to tell somebody that they may not be able to do things in life only because other people wouldn't give them a chance. It's a disgusting reality. Enough to depress a person so much that he wouldn't even bother trying to work hard if he felt it would never make a difference. What a hopeless feeling came over the both of us.

Just then, just as we needed a little encouragement, perhaps through the actions of our thoughtful spirit guide, a truck came barreling by and shook the road. It jolted my brain out of that unproductive groove and back on the track to the future. "Hey, Reg," I said enthusiastically, "that's why we're walking. Some day everyone will know who you are and no longer will they be frightened."

"No problem," he added, confidently. We both got back on the right path of thinking; ready to take on the world! We talked about the meaning of WALKABOUT until we drifted into our own thoughts.

The heat didn't let up as quickly as our conversation, but as the miles wore on, the sun drifted behind us. Early evening rolled around and finally the WALKABOUT-Mobile drove up from behind.

"This lady *loves* to talk," Janet told us, referring to Marilyn, who was in the front seat. "And she's the best saleslady this side of the Pecos. We made enough money to buy food for a week!"

"Hey, Marilyn, what are you still doing here? I thought I saw the last of you," I kidded her. Marilyn could tell I was teasing her, and she smacked my arm. "Well, I can see you've already spent much too much time with Janet," I quipped, referring to the arm punch.

Marilyn laughed as Janet reached over and hit me, too. "I'm going to have dinner with you at Jan's house," Marilyn said. "I get to spend even more time with you."

"Jan invited us to spend the night at her house," explained Janet. Jan, whom we had met the night before, was one of the counselors at the group home where Marilyn lived. "Jan said she would be happy to drive Marilyn back home after dinner."

"That's right," said Marilyn. "But right now I want to tell you about everything Janet and I did today!" This she proceeded to do, beginning the epic from the minute they had dropped us off in the morning and recounting every detail right up to the minute they had driven up behind us. Marilyn's narrative began the instant we got into the WALKABOUT-Mobile, and didn't end until we drove up Jan's driveway. It was a fascinating earful.

A quick moment later, as we stepped from the car, we were overwhelmed with a fantastic *noseful*. "I'm hungry," claimed Reggie, rubbing his stomach.

"Wow!" said Janet as soon as she walked in the front door. The table was set with salad, fried chicken, mashed potatoes, corn, and warm dinner rolls. Then, all of a sudden, she had a change of heart. A look of apprehension overcame Janet's face. She stared at the table, inhaled deeply and then let out an even deeper sigh. "Uh-oh," she said. "I'm going to be in big trouble."

"Why?" asked Jan, worriedly. Her face became blank. She was probably thinking that we had stopped to eat on the way home.

"Yes, why?" I also asked. My question, though, was laced with quite a bit of friendly sarcasm. I knew Janet well enough to immediately understand her concern.

"Because," explained Janet, "after a feast like this, prepared by a person who really knows how to cook, it's hard to get these guys to eat what I make!" She shot both Reggie and me a look that would have spoiled our appetites if the food hadn't been right there in front of us.

"I guess tonight we stuff our faces," I said, smiling at Reggie.

"That's right. And tomorrow," Janet threatened, "when I serve my dinner, you guys will *eat it or starve!*"

"We'll eat, we'll eat," promised Reggie, giggling.

"He's so smart," Janet said, rubbing Reggie's back.

"But look what he's being forced to learn," I teased. Janet

didn't say a word. She just picked up a roll and threw it at me and it bounced off my head and onto the floor. Jan, Marilyn and Reggie broke into hysterical fits of giggling. Dixie, right beside me, enjoyed a quick snack.

As usual, the main topic of conversation was WALKABOUT. Jan and Marilyn asked us about "walking so far for so long."

"I like to walk," answered Reggie.

"Oh yeah? Even in this heat?" I said, giving Reggie a wink.

"No problem."

"Hmmmm," I hummed, wondering if Reggie was just trying to be macho. I decided to take his lead, though. We were in a cool house, feeding our faces, entertaining our hosts. This wasn't the time to whine—it was the time to impress. On the other hand, if we did it right, we could do both at the same time.

"The last few days have been scenic, but *hot*," I explained.

"Yeah, I bought eggs for lunch one day and we fried them on the pavement!" quipped Janet.

"Good joke!" laughed Reggie. Then he looked over and asked me, quite seriously, "Right?" I just shrugged my shoulders. He stopped laughing real quick, scrunched his forehead in deep thought, trying to remember back.

Then I laughed and so did Jan, Marilyn and Janet. "You're just giving me a bad time," Reggie said, laughing, but still not quite certain.

I slapped him on the back, then continued my story. "We're all glad to be back in the country again, but it seems that no matter where we are, there is always a challenge. The challenge now is the heat. We like to look at the bright side, though. Soon there will be more trees, which means more shade. It's fascinating that the closer we get to the mountains, the faster the land changes."

"How can land change?" Jan asked."Doesn't it stay the same?"

"Well, as the miles go by, the scenery changes. In the last couple of weeks we've gone from walking on roads that had trees everywhere to roads with no trees anywhere. Now we are seeing more trees again.

"Then, of course, there are the mountains! Not only are they beautiful, but they are fascinating. It's incredible to think that the mighty Cascades were formed by bubbling volcanoes, and the valleys were formed by huge masses of moving ice floes or glaciers.

Today we walked through a valley that was carved out by a glacier thousands and thousands of years ago. I think that's really neat."

"How do you know all that?" asked Marilyn. "I wish I knew all that."

"Well, now you know it. We stop to read each and every historical notice placed on the side of the road. I figure that if someone is going to take the time to put them up, I have an obligation to read them."

"I can't wait to be in the mountains," said Reggie, breaking back into the conversation. "Soon we'll be in the mountains, right?"

"Yup. The heat stinks!" I stated.

"On an adventure like this, there is a lot of pleasure, but *definitely* some pain," Janet added, ever so inspirationally.

"Sure, that's easy for you to say. The WALKABOUT-Mobile's got air-conditioning." This time I ducked and the flying dinner roll hit a kitchen cupboard.

"But we're strong! Right, Steve?" Reggie said, after laughing quite heartily.

"Right, Reg!" I answered, happy to have the subject of the conversation changed. "A little heat is not going to stop us!"

"Schlicky's still strong, too. Right?"

We all looked down at Dixie, lying on the cool kitchen floor. She had downed the second dinner roll, and was now out for the count. She opened her eyes when she heard her name, but she didn't raise her head.

"Actually," said Jan, "it looks like there is pain for Dixie, too. She sure looks tired."

"Does Dixie like to walk?" asked Marilyn.

"When the weather is cool and the roads are safe and the land is wide open, she loves it! However, I'm not so sure she likes to walk so far every day on the hot days. Reggie and I feel the same way. We're all doing the best we can. When her feet hurt, or the road is hot or has a lot of loose gravel, we put her boots on to protect her pads.

"Unfortunately, the roughness of the road we've been on has made her feet very sore and she has a bit of a limp. I've been very worried about Dixie. I've put her boots on and they help a little, but they rub on her knuckles and create other sores. She can only wear the boots for a short time. I really hate it when she's suffering. I force myself to remember that we've had these problems on every long walk we've had, and just had to learn to deal with them. Sometimes we just have to push on."

We were all looking down at Dixie. She wasn't moving a muscle. Then, when she realized we were all looking at her, she wagged her tail, ever so slightly. She knew how pitiful she looked and she was soaking it up. Or so I believed.

"All I can do is keep an eye on her, make the best decisions I can and hope for the best. Dixie is an important part of the WALKABOUT team. I don't want to stop her from doing the best she can, just like Reggie and me. Dixie is great motivation for her "Uncle Reggie" when he gets tired. She always inspires me, too."

"You know," said Jan, looking up at Reggie and leaving Dixie to her rest, "speaking of inspiration, I've been inspired, too. I've been working with disabled people for years and I wonder if I have been caught in a rut. We need people like you, Reggie, to remind us how much we *all* can do—to push us to continue to grow. I'm very proud to meet you. I'm honored to have you at my table." She looked deeply into Reggie's eyes, seeing the man within the man. Reggie cocked his head and smiled, humbly.

"Me, too," added Marilyn. She pulled her chair away from the table and walked over to Reggie. "I wish I could do what you're doing." She held out her hand.

"Thank you. I like to walk. It's easy," he said, shaking her hand. For a man with little experience with many different people, the friendly, well-mannered person that was Reggie Feckley greatly impressed Janet and me. He was a natural gentleman!

I was about to respond to Marilyn's comment about walking, but Jan spoke first. "The point of Reggie's walk, Marilyn, is to inspire people like you and me. It's not just walking around the state that's important, it's showing people that he can do anything he puts his mind to. He has faith in himself. Like you, Reggie has the right to try and work to accomplish things. Luckily, he is surrounded by people who have faith in him, too, and together they are making a dream become a reality. Our goal now is to find out what things you would like to do, and then maybe together we can find a way to make those things possible for you."

"I had fun today with Janet. I want to sell things to people."

"Believe me, she could do it," said Janet. Marilyn was more comfortable talking to strangers than Janet had ever been.

"Then that's what you have to start working on," said Jan. "Maybe you can get a job in a store. Thank you, Reggie. You are such an inspiration!"

"Thank you," said Reggie, shaking Jan's hand.

"On Wednesday we'll be in the mountains!" Reggie stated with certainty. Highway 9 had finally intersected with Highway 20, and we were now heading east. Reggie just couldn't wait to get into the Cascades! The thought of tree-lined highways was very exciting. As the number of trees along the road continued to grow, we knew it meant that we were closer to the mountains.

It was still depressingly hot, and we were taking a lot of rests. If the attraction of the mountains hadn't been so alluring, I knew it would be way past Wednesday before we got there. Reggie couldn't wait to do some mountain camping, and I had to keep reminding him of how much we had to walk to make sure we covered enough miles every day.

"Time for a break, Steve?" Reggie asked, every 45 minutes or so. Sometimes he didn't give me much choice and we'd just sit down on the grass right on the side of the road. If we were lucky, we'd find a place out of the sun, sometimes even settling for the shade of a small bush. Cars would pass by, now and again, so we still had to keep on our toes, so to speak.

The more breaks we took, the shorter the breaks became. As the official time keeper, I made it my job to finally say, "Ready to go?"

"Ready to go?" was one of Dixie's favorite phrases and she always popped right up, even if she was in the middle of a real good snooze. Reggie, too, would usually follow my lead. Usually, that is.

"Nope. Just stay right here. Leave in the morning from here," he stated, as I attempted to end one break.

I thought to myself, "Had I pushed Reggie too much?" It really was hot! A good leader should know when to lead and when to lay back. Maybe I had not found the balance for which I had been so desperately searching. I still felt that WALKABOUT was in its infancy, because although we'd come an awfully long way, we still had a lot longer to go. Maybe Reggie was losing interest. If he couldn't even push through the mountains he'd been dreaming of, I knew we'd never make another thousand miles. Not in this decade, anyway.

"You want to sleep right here on the side of the road?" I was trying to show Reggie that we couldn't stay there. If nothing else, we'd have to walk to a safer location. Reggie didn't always want to listen to me *or* my advice. I had seen Reggie's stubborn streak before, and just now I wasn't in the mood to see it again. Even when it was hot, it was easier for me to just keep walking. Motivating Reggie after each one of our frequent breaks was beginning to wear out my patience.

"Yep! Right here!" he answered, determined not to budge.

"Right there? You're going to sleep right there?"

"No problem!"

"Right there?"

Reggie didn't say a word. He just stared at me, looking quite serious.

Then, a quick beat later, "Just giving you a bad time!" he said, bouncing up. "Ha, Ha, Ha. I'm in a good mood. Let's walk!"

Reggie walked on, leaving me with my mouth hanging wide open. "Now *he's* learning how to tease *me*," I said to Dixie. "I'll never get any peace," I sighed. I tightened up the waist strap on my pack and followed the laughing man on towards the mountains.

Our pace never really got going, but at least we were moving. We were moving faster than zero miles per hour, but not by much. We shuffled along, Dixie in slow motion (for her), Reggie ten feet behind. For twenty-five minutes we walked, averaging only 2 miles per hour, but we walked.

"Schlicky's hurt, Steve. She's limping real bad. We better take a break."

I looked down at Dixie as she walked beside me. She was doing about as well as the rest of us—breathing hard, walking slow, and just too darn hot. She wasn't limping too much, nor was she wearing her boots, because the road had become a bit smoother then it had been.

"Dixie's O.K., Reg. She's just going to have to tough it out," I said firmly. Dixie's feet had become Reggie's most convenient excuse for taking another break. I didn't think he was teasing again, although I was learning that with Reggie I couldn't be sure. I have

The mountains are back there — somewhere

been accused of taking things a bit too seriously, but there are times when I'm right on target.

"Don't forget, Reg, there are people counting on us and we can't just sit down every time we get tired. When we spent the whole day and night at the state park a couple of days ago, we talked about pushing ourselves a bit harder when we got back on the road. Even Dixie has to understand this. We have to find the balance between resting ourselves and pacing ourselves. We've built up our legs. Now we have to build up our minds."

"Harvey would do it, right?" Reggie asked.

"Well, yes," I said. Harvey was Reggie's friend from home. "He's pretty tough. I'm sure he would."

"And Rob Campbell?"

"Rob would definitely do it, Reg."

"And my roommate, Ricky?"

"Yep."

"O.K.! I'm strong, right?"

"Yes, you're strong, Reg."

"You're strong, too. Right, Steve?"

"Yes, I'm strong, too."

"You too, Schlicky?"

"Woof!" I said for her.

"O.K! We're strong!" Reggie said, accepting that I answered for Dixie. "Let's go!" And off he went.

I took notice of how Reggie motivated himself by thinking about what other people could do. Reggie and I had some obvious things in common, such as walking and enjoying the woods, but we had our differences, too. I had spent much of my life trying to be different from others, to become a distinct individual and to decide for myself what was best for me. Yet, Reggie was a man who had felt (and been told) that he was very different from most people. He had been trying very hard to prove that he could be just like anyone else. There was no right or wrong, better or worse; there were just interesting differences.

Reggie found that this trip was harder than he'd expected. Yet, for all my pep talks and all the inspiration Dixie provided, Reggie's greatest motivation came from deep within himself.

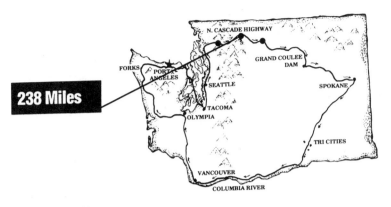

chapter 13

THE CASCADES

The road to North Cascades National Park follows the Skagit River for over 50 miles. As Reggie, Dixie and I walked under the hot morning sun, the invitingly refreshing Skagit became something of a tease, always just a bit too far off the road, or too far down a steep incline. It was rough walking, but we knew that it would be cooler as we got up in the mountains. Finally, the river met up with the road, beckoning to us from across the baking blacktop. It gave Reggie ideas.

"Look, Steve, the river runs right by the road. Can we fish?"

"Only if we use your string bean body as a fishing pole," I said. (Ha! I got him back!) "We don't have any fishing gear, Reg. But that river sure looks refreshing, doesn't it? Hey, let's go cool ourselves off!"

"Good idea!" said Reggie, and we turned off the road and headed toward the river.

Dixie and I had walked along many rivers like this one. It had been a while, but Dixie remembered how wonderful clean, cold, river water felt, and she splashed right in. She didn't even wait until I took off her pack! She took a big, long, slurpy drink. Reggie and I took off our packs, boots and socks, and followed Dixie's lead. After the sizzling blacktop, the icy water, born of melting glaciers, felt intoxicating on our hot and tired feet. This mighty river, glistening in the bright sun and bouncing over rocks, caused a tingle through our entire bodies as it skimmed across our legs. Reggie and I bent down and splashed ourselves silly. We were determined to send all the sweat and road dust on our bodies out to the Pacific Ocean!

When our feet finally became as refreshed as possible (and before they actually went numb!) we headed over to the grassy bank of the river. Reggie and I stretched out in the warm sunshine. For a change, the sharp rays of the sun felt good. On the other hand, Dixie, forever in her fur coat, found a cool, shady spot in the soft sand under a tree.

"Time for a snack, Steve?" asked Reggie.

"Definitely time for a snack, Reg!"

Reggie reached into his pack for two mostly melted candy bars, one for him and one for me. In my pack, I found some crisp apple slices that Janet had wrapped for us. Even Dixie had some beef jerky snacks in her pack. Off the highway and stretched out on the banks of the invigorating Skagit River, Reggie, Dixie and I enjoyed a perfect WALKABOUT moment. Talk about paradise!

Two hours later—still too soon—it became time to pull on our socks, strap up our boots, hitch up the packs and get back to walking. Away from the cooling effects of the Skagit, the sweltering sun again began to beat on us.

"Pretty nice day," said Reggie.

"Yeah, I guess you're right. Especially if you like it *hot*!" I said. "I think the sun is affecting your mind, Reg."

"It's Indian Summer."

"Sounds about right to me. I hadn't thought about that. Maybe this is just a heat wave and will pass," I hoped.

"Hi!" Reggie responded.

"Hi?" I questioned, wondering why he said that.

As we'd resumed our slow and sweaty progress towards the high country, a man had caught up with us from behind. His neck was red from the sun but his balding head was covered by a baseball cap, not unlike Reggie's or mine. His sweat-soaked shirt showed that he, too, had undertaken quite a hike. He sported a friendly country smile and responded to Reggie's greeting with a "Howdy. How ya doin'?"

"I'm Reggie Feckley," said my companion. Reggie quickly took off his pack, unzipped it and grabbed out a WALKABOUT brochure. The shy and insecure man who'd started WALKABOUT with me had been left in the dust, many miles behind.

"I'm Steve Breakstone and this is Dixie," I said, introducing myself and my dog.

The man stopped to talk and carefully studied our brochure. He looked at the map with the dotted trail showing our route around the state. He whistled in amazement, looked at Reggie and asked, "You've walked here all the way from Port Angeles?"

"I'm a good walker," Reggie said proudly.

"You still got a long way to go," he said. If I had to guess, I'd say the man was a bit skeptical, but definitely impressed!

"No problem," said Reggie.

"Well, I live down the road a bit and I walk six or so miles almost every other day. But I don't think I'd ever be ready to walk around the whole state. Good luck. I'm sure you'll make it." He turned to continue his pace.

"By the way," I asked, before he took too many steps, "since you live around here, do you think you can do something about this heat?" I assumed he realized I was mostly kidding about having any control over the situation.

"Be patient," he said quite simply. "I usually wait until about 1:00 in the afternoon to get the wind to blow and cool things off." Without a pack and with only a couple of his six miles left to walk, the man was way ahead of us in no time. That was the last we ever saw of him.

An hour went by, with the heat making another break sound better by the moment. Then a breeze began to stir. I looked at my watch, and what do you know? It was one o'clock! The man obviously had some connections! A lovely fresh mountain breeze came sweeping up the valley and cooled us off in no time.

We walked until Janet came by with lunch. After downing a couple of sandwiches and some fruit, we resumed our day's walk, the inspirational breeze at our backs. Refreshed, we walked through the valley all the way to where the road began its rise up the mountain. Janet had set up camp at Rockport State Park, a few miles back, and a good night's sleep would have us ready for mountain hiking!

The next morning, we began our climb. The road wound its way up into the Cascades. The river was on one side of the road and rough rocky walls bordered the other. In some places tunnels had been blasted through parts of the mountain so the road could get through. "We'll be coming around the mountain when we come," Reggie and I sang as we walked through the dark passages. Dixie howled along. We joked that the echo would start a rock slide or an avalanche.

By now the WALKABOUT team had camped out about eight times. Most of our campouts had been in small state or county parks. Reggie had loved sleeping outdoors in his tent at our previous campsites, but now he wanted to be in the mountains "like a real woodsman."

At each campsite, Janet had helped Reggie practice setting up his own tent, cooking on a camp stove and keeping safely warm by a fire. It was camping out, alright, but it wasn't quite camping in the place that Reggie had in mind. "Soon we'll be in the *mountains*," he'd blurt out every now and then.

We walked strong and far, landing right smack into the middle of real Cascade Mountain territory! We found a great camping spot on the shore of Lake Diablo, surrounded by glorious mountain peaks and majestic trees. If you closed your eyes and imagined your deepest, sweetest insight to what being in the heart of the mountains would be, that was where we were. It was another perfect WALKABOUT moment.

"Well, Reg, what do you think we should have for dinner on our first night camping in the mountains?"

"Hot dogs!" he exclaimed, showing that he had been planning this moment for a long, long time.

Janet had left to go back to Port Angeles for a few days and had been replaced by our friend, Judy Ware. Janet had trained Judy well, and she was well prepared. As Judy took a package of dogs out of the cooler for our dinner, Reggie walked off to gather the firewood. Dixie and I relaxed, listening to the soft breeze flow through the tree tops. We watched lazily as Judy fed half our buns to the ducks and geese in the lake.

"Hey!" I called, coming out of a daydream, "That's our dinner! How many miles did *they* walk!?!" Judy turned her head, smiled and waved her hand at me. Then she tossed more bread to the birds. "What's that supposed to mean?" I asked.

Judy turned completely around and said, "Janet told me to just smile when you get obnoxious. And to ignore you." Zip. Another bun became airborne and was gobbled up just as it hit the water. This must be Janet's revenge for the extra pillows and lounge chair controversy.

Tent set-up was a before-dinner priority, so when Reggie returned we all went to work. Judy had her tent all set up, and she went to set the dinner table. Reggie began to work on his tent, and I pitched the small tent that Dixie and I slept in. Then I moved over to get the fire started. Janet usually set up all the tents before we finished walking, but sometimes she waited for Reggie so that he could practice. Today, Judy, Reggie and I agreed that it was time for him to "solo."

Reggie pulled the tent from the stuff sack and laid out all the poles. The poles had to be put together, and although it took Reggie a while to do it, he did just fine. I kept my distance.

After the short poles were connected into four long, straight poles, they had to be placed through the sleeves of the tent in order to be used as the support frame. Reggie was doing just great until the poles began to fall apart while they were being threaded through the sleeves. He tried it again, but he was getting quite frustrated, and was soon grumbling to himself. Now, I've known many a camper to yell at a tent (tents have a very strange sense of humor, but they say that it's all in good fun), so I didn't think too much of Reggie's mumbling. I didn't think Reg would mind if I offered my assistance at this time, and he accepted it. I didn't take over, I only supported the tent for him while he attached the poles. Then I held out the guy lines that kept the tent in place on the ground as Reggie pounded the stakes into the forest floor.

"Here's your pillow, your sleeping bag and your pad," I called to Reggie, as I threw the items near his tent door. "You know what do to?"

"No problem," he answered. He grabbed them, took them

inside and for ten minutes all I saw were the tent walls shaking as he made up his "house."

Finally he came out, and we all roasted wieners over the campfire as Judy heated up some beans on her campstove. We wound up cutting the dogs into bite-size pieces and mixing them with the beans. Luckily (?) Judy had brought some hearty (?) rice cakes to serve as make-shift bread with dinner. (Somehow I know Janet just had to have something to do with that but I had no proof.) I fed Dixie some of her own hard kibbled dinner and gave her a hot dog and some beans for dessert. I offered her a rice cake but just as I did so she decided she was stuffed and went to lay down.

Reggie didn't say much. Every so often he would get up and just wander around camp. He sat on a boulder by the lake. "I like this," was about all he would say. The fact that he didn't say much wasn't important. I knew Reggie well enough to read his face. It said, "I am a man doing exactly what I love." The lines on his face had softened since we had taken Step One. The tenseness and jerkiness of his movements had relaxed. Contentment and happiness encompassed him. Sometimes I felt that I pushed Reggie to walk more in a day than he would have preferred, yet I knew that at this very moment he was loving his life more than ever.

After our traditional camp dinner of beans and wieners, we drifted off to our tents, feeling at one with nature. Lulled to sleep by the "hoot, hoot" of the owls in the trees, we all knew life couldn't be better. Our first night in the Cascades was a true wilderness experience.

Cool mountain air kept us in our sleeping bags until the sun rose over the ridge and warmed us up as the dawn rolled into morning. Then, with energy to burn and motivated to move, we ate a quick breakfast, shouldered our packs and grabbed a ride to the day's starting point. As Judy drove back to camp, Reggie, Dixie and I headed the other way, even further into deep mountain wilderness. We had a lot of steep uphill walking to do before we would make it over the Rainy Pass Summit at 4,855 feet. Then we'd have to head down into a mountain valley—who knows how far?—and then back up again and over Washington Pass. Our strides would then have to get us 5,477 feet above sea level! The hard work never seemed to end!

Reggie enjoying a quiet, happy moment

Sometimes hard work makes for the greatest of pleasures. We were thrilled to be in the mountains. It was so beautiful! Even Dixie was feeling great, running all over the place. There were a lot of neat things for her to check out as she ran through the trees and shrubs beside the road. Sometimes I think she just limped in the hot weather so we would take more roadside breaks! Maybe Reggie and Dixie were becoming better friends than I thought. Or maybe the smells from a lot of different mountain animals made her forget her sore feet. I was sure glad when she didn't see the bear run across the road two hundred yards further up.

"You didn't see that bear, did you, Dixie?" I called to her. She ignored me. She was in her own world. If she had seen it, Dixie's instinct might have caused her to check it out. "Don't forget, bears are one animal no one should ever get close to! Bears are pretty tough. Are you listening, Dixie?" She looked back for a split second and then went back to smelling and looking at every single thing that moved, including the buzzing bees and the cloud puffs. Nothing gave me more pleasure than to see Dixie enjoy herself in the woods. She knew the rules and she knew what she was doing.

After so many days of walking in the heat, the cool mountain air was such a relief! In fact, it was too much of a relief—it was actually starting to get a bit chilly when we stopped to rest. Now, that's not a complaint, mind you, but an observation. Walking was a lot easier now that we were surrounded by all that peaceful mountain beauty, with nice cool breezes at our backs. The heat was behind us, and all of us enjoyed the peace and quiet of the Cascades. Especially Reggie.

"Time for a break?" Reggie still asked, quite a bit more often than I would have expected. I chalked it up to his desire to stay in the mountains forever. The less walking we did, the longer we'd be in the mountains. We enjoyed a few extra breaks, but now he got up and kept walking when I reminded him it was time to move on. Nevertheless, I noticed I had to slow my pace way down for fear of leaving Reggie in the dust.

"You're walking pretty slow, Reg," I commented. I was hoping he'd pick up the pace.

"I like the peace and quiet, Steve," he said softly.

"You are O.K., aren't you.?" I asked.

"I'm O.K.," was all he said. I looked at him, but I just wasn't convinced. He didn't look A-O.K. to me. I could tell something was wrong.

"Do your feet hurt?"

"Nope. I just like it here." He didn't even smile as he said it.

"Are you sure?" I asked. Even though I knew we'd both built up plenty of calluses on our feet, I asked, "Why don't we look at your feet and see if you've developed some more blisters?"

"I don't have blisters. I promise." He kept on walking, which made me think that maybe he had at least one. On the other hand, the last few times I had looked at his feet, they had looked as pretty as mine (that's walking man's jargon, meaning "in good shape"). Usually, though, once the feet develop calluses, blisters no longer form.

"Hey, Reg, if you *do* have blisters, it really is best to pop them. A little quick pain now is much better than a lot of pain with every step."

"My feet are fine," he snarled. "You looked at them yesterday. We can keep walking."

I had guessed that he'd do some of his best walking of the whole trip in the mountains. I had thought I'd have a hard time slowing him down, but obviously, I was wrong. "Maybe Reggie doesn't want to go any further than the mountains," I thought to myself. By one o'clock we'd walked only six short miles. "This is where Reggie wanted to be all along. Why should he continue walking if it will only take him out of the mountains? Is this where WALKABOUT takes its last step?" I worried. My imagination was running amuck.

Judy drove by with lunch, but Reggie said, "I got a headache, Steve. No more walking today."

"I thought you said you were fine. Why didn't you tell me?" I demanded. "I thought you didn't want to be on WALKABOUT anymore."

Reggie shrugged. "I like to walk," Reggie said. "I just have a headache today."

I sighed. "O.K., Reg. I guess we'll have to call it a day. We'll just have to work harder tomorrow, if you're feeling better." We piled into the WALKABOUT-Mobile and headed back to camp. I was so confused. Why didn't he tell me he was sick earlier? Was he really sick? Or was it something else? I was so frustrated that I didn't quite know what was on his mind.

We got back to camp and Reggie went into his tent to lay down for a while. "Maybe I've been pushing him too hard," I thought aloud, looking for Judy's opinion. She just listened. WALKABOUT was still new to her, but she had been working with people with disabilities for a long time. "I'm not sure what the problem is. This is the nicest walking day we've had in a long time and we hardly walked."

"Steve, this is a tremendous challenge bestowed on, and expected of, a 43-year-old man with a disability," Judy suggested. "Maybe he needs to go at his own pace. Don't forget, you've done this before and it's easier for you. But that doesn't make it easy!"

"Do you think I'm pushing him too hard?" I asked.

"Do *you* think you've pushed him too hard?" Judy asked, throwing the question right back at me.

"I didn't think so until now. At first I thought he just didn't want to walk any further than the mountains. But if he really doesn't feel well, I'm wondering if maybe this steep mountain road is getting to him. I don't know. I just don't know." I was very confused and I sat for a while and thought. Judy didn't say a word. Finally, I said to her, "I haven't really given much thought to the fact that he's older or disabled. Although I might be the leader, I've thought of him as an equal partner."

"Well, that's pretty much the greatest compliment you could give him. Steve, you're not forcing him to do anything he doesn't want to do. He loves this. Can't you see that? All you're doing is helping him get in enough miles each day. You just have to find the balance. Today was an off-balance day. I'll bet that tomorrow he'll be as good as new. You can take it from there."

I was sorry I hadn't realized that Reggie wasn't enjoying the day as much as I was, but Judy was right. He needed time. I could continue to treat Reggie as an equal, push him when necessary and still be considerate of his needs.

The sun drifted west towards the ridge and it was just about dinner time when Reggie awoke from his nap. He said he felt better. He took a stroll around the campground and I did some tidying up. Judy had found more bread, and happily fattened up the ducks and geese.

I was putting an extra flashlight in Reggie's tent when I noticed something that just wasn't right. His sleeping pad was still in its sack! I could tell that his sleeping bag had been used but Reggie had not used the pad. I then realized why Reggie had so much trouble walking. He'd been hurting and sore!

"Hey, Reg, did you use your sleeping pad last night?" I asked him.

"Yes, I did. See, there it is," he pointed.

"That's your sleeping *bag*. Remember this?" I took out the sleeping pad. "This is your SLEEPING PAD. You need it so you don't sleep on the ground."

"Oh, yeah. I forgot."

"Without the pad, Reg, there is only the flimsy tent material between you and the hard, rocky ground. The sleeping pad is an important part of mountain camping gear. It keeps your body warm and comfortable. Even though the sleeping pad is only half an inch thick, it makes a big difference!"

"Oh, O.K. I make a mistake. Everyone makes mistakes."

"That's true, Reg. Of course, now I understand why you were having such a hard time today. You were stiff from sleeping on the cold, hard ground."

"No, I'm strong, Steve."

"It has nothing to do with being strong, Reggie. But that's why you have a headache today. I bet you have a bodyache, too."

"I feel better all over. We'll walk tomorrow. No breaks!"

"I wouldn't go that far, Reg," I said. I looked over at Judy. She was listening and smiling, but not saying a word. "It's not a big deal, Reg, but next time you have to make sure you unroll the sleep roll. We have all this equipment because it's important. It helps keep us strong and healthy. Now we know for next time."

"No problem, right?"

"Right. You remember to use all your gear and I'll remember not to freak out."

"Teamwork!" said Reggie.

That night Reggie slept a lot better. He slept so well that he woke up very early and from my tent I could hear him shuffling around our campsite.

"What are you doing, Reg?" I asked him.

"I'm going to make a fire."

"Oh. O.K.," I replied.

He enjoyed making our campfires and usually helped Janet with that camping ritual. I appreciated that this time he was going to try to do it all by himself.

Overnight, passing clouds had dropped some rain and our little pile of firewood was wet. I knew it wouldn't be easy to start a fire. He didn't see me watching from under my tent flap, and I was impressed when I saw that he remembered to set up the fire just the way Janet had showed him. He put little pieces of wood on the bottom and a few bigger pieces all around. He stacked it all up in the shape of a tee-pee. Then he got a box of matches and tried to set the whole thing ablaze.

He lit a match. Then another. And another. The wood was wet and Reggie was having a hard time getting the fire started. The only thing that would light was the matches! I wasn't too sure Reggie would be able to get it going by himself. Reggie lit one match after another, grumbling to himself as match after match sputtered and burnt itself out. The wood just refused to catch fire, but I didn't say a word. I laid my head back down and tried to get a little more sleep.

A few minutes later I realized that I hadn't heard Reg striking any more matches. I wondered if he had finally given up and walked away. Then I heard Reggie walk back into the campsite. "Where'd you go, Reg? Did you give up?" I called, still inside my tent.

Reggie was determined. "I'm going to make a fire!" he repeated.

I finally opened the door of my tent. I looked out and saw that Reggie's hands were full. When Reggie had left camp for those few minutes, he had gone into the campground's bathroom. In that short time he had unrolled dozens and dozens of feet of toilet paper. REGGIE WAS GOING TO MAKE A FIRE! I didn't say anything. I just watched.

"I'm going to make a fire!"

Reggie moved the wet wood and placed the pile of toilet paper under the stack. Then he put some of the twigs on top and lit another match. WHOOSH! The paper caught fire! Then, slowly, he added some small pieces of wood. Ten seconds later ...PAFOOF...a perfect fire! I was very proud of Reggie. He had tried to do something new all by himself. He'd had a problem, but he'd thought about it, and figured out a way to solve his problem. And it worked! Somehow this fire was a little warmer than usual.

We used Reggie's fire to cook a good hot breakfast of oatmeal with apples and raisins. It prepared us for some serious mountain miles. The sun came up and promised a bright, warm morning. It's amazing how a little thing like the sun can make such a big difference! At night it was 40 degrees, and without our extra warm sleeping bags, we would have been *reeeally* cold. Yet, during the day, with the sharp, glaring sun, it would get up to 80 degrees. Luckily, those nice fresh breezes blowing through the valley kept us cool.

Reggie was refreshed and ready to go. The day before I wasn't sure if Reggie had really wanted to keep walking, but it became obvious that he had just been stiff and tired from sleeping without his pad. It was hard to believe that such a simple thing had made such a big difference!

Reggie and I walked at a brisk, steady pace. The cooler weather, smoother pavement and extra rest also helped Dixie's feet and pads, and now she, too, was loving every second of our mountain trek. We all enjoyed walking in the Cascades along Kangaroo Ridge, passing by Silver Star and Liberty Bell Mountains and Early

Reggie and Dixie by Liberty Bell Mountain

Winter Spires. The weather was great and the view was fantastic! Everywhere we looked we saw trees. Some trees were saplings only two inches tall; some were hundreds of years old and 200 to 300 feet tall! In some places, we were so far above sea level in the Cascades that trees couldn't even grow. That's the timberline. It was incredible! It was beautiful! It was Washington!

Now it was my turn to say, "How about a break? Let's just sit a while and look around. It's so beautiful! Don't you think so?" I asked Reggie. He agreed. "Peace and quiet," Reggie sighed. We walked far from the road and took our packs off. Reggie sat down, put his hands behind his head and laid back to stare at the sky. Reggie knew how to relax.

"What are those sounds, Steve?" he asked me after a while.

We heard the creaking moan of the swaying trees as the wind

rushed through their branches. We listened to streams of water cascading over rocks, birds singing and woodpeckers pecking wood. We overheard squirrels and marmots talking to each other by making little squeaking or whistling sounds. Every one of our senses enjoyed the glorious mountain atmosphere. It was a great day to WALKABOUT!

"That's the sounds of the mountains, Reg," I finally answered.

"I like it here, Steve," he said.

So did I.

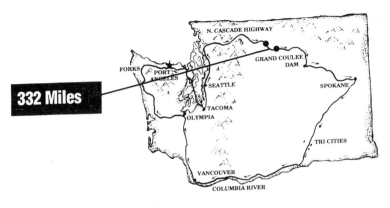

332 Miles

chapter 14

COMING OUT
of the MOUNTAINS

Down, down, downhill! Our steps brought us beyond the Cascade Mountains. Each stride pushed the mountain peaks and stout trees away from the road on which we walked. Ever so slowly, the valley opened up—before, beside and behind us. We exited the cool mountain air and entered the stifling heat of the valley. It felt as if we had walked out of an air-conditioned skyscraper and onto a muggy New York City street in mid August. Our bodies, spoiled from days in the cool mountain heaven, slowly began to wilt. We didn't push ourselves any faster than necessary.

I looked around and realized that from step one, through all the rough miles and long weeks, the only thing we had always been able to rely on was that we always had a view of green trees and snow-capped mountains. But now, as WALKABOUT continued towards Eastern Washington, the mountains, the foothills and the trees were being replaced with endless plains—hot, baking plains.

A couple hundred yards up the road, a car stopped. Two people got out and walked back towards us. It would be a while until we would be close enough to see them or talk to them. Were they reporters? Were they tourists interested in WALKABOUT? Were they just stretching their legs? Things come slowly to walkers. We had to be patient.

"That's Pat!" Reggie said, finally able to focus in and recognize the man.

"Pat?"

"Pat used to live at the group home," Reggie explained.

What a welcome surprise it was to see Pat McFarland! He wanted to be an official WALKABOUTer, so he'd driven out with Rosalie Rieck, who would now replace Judy as our substitute support driver.

After hellos and hugs, Rosalie went off to find Judy.

"Let's walk!" demanded Pat. He took off, followed by Reggie, Dixie and me. Pat was a strong supporter of WALKABOUT. "I've been listening to you every week on KONP when you call." A weekly call-in to our local radio station from different places in the state kept our friends in Port Angeles informed of WALKABOUT's whereabouts.

"How do we sound?" I asked.

"Great!" he said.

"We're famous!" exclaimed Reggie.

"Hey, Pat, Reggie told me you used to live at the group home. That must have been before Dixie and I got there." Pat fit right in to our rhythm and we walked and talked without missing a beat. Pat was walking, chin high and shoulders stout, full of determination.

"I lived there for a few years. Now I have my own apartment."

"Do you live by yourself?"

"Yes. My mother helps me sometimes and the state has a staff person who comes in once a week and helps me get my groceries."

"That's great. How do you like it?"

"It's great!" he answered. "I like living on my own."

"I'm going to have my own apartment someday, too, Steve."

"I know it, Reg," I said confidently.

I noticed that as we walked and talked, I began breathing very

Washington Pass

hard. Reggie, too, had built up quite a pouring sweat. Pat, with average-size legs, below-average shoulders, and a belly that appeared not to have too many walking miles on it, was so excited to be part of WALKABOUT that he saw what had to be done and he was doing it. Much too fast, in the opinion of Reggie and myself. Even Dixie had to quicken her over-heated four-legged trot.

"Have you noticed how fast we have to walk to keep up with Pat, Reg?" I quietly asked.

"No problem," Reggie panted.

"Yeah, sure," I thought. Another point of view is that Reggie had an ego and didn't want to walk any slower than Pat. "How silly." However, I found myself not walking any slower than Pat either. Reggie, Dixie and I were supposed to be the professionals, and we had a responsibility to keep up with the rookie. I guess I have an ego, too. Anyway, with excitement and egos leading the way, we put in 17 hard, hot miles.

Judy came by about five o'clock in the afternoon, picked Pat up and drove back over the Cascades. They headed for home. We headed for our new campsite. It was great having Judy for a few days, and having a chance to walk with Pat (even if he did make us feel like we were marching in an army), but it felt like they had come and gone in an instant. We missed them both as soon as they drove off. Of course, now we had Rosalie, and she wanted to know everything about WALKABOUT. We were never too hot or tired for that, and we talked until the last few embers of our campfire began to smoke out.

Reggie, Dixie and I were left to spend the next few days walking in the heat by ourselves. We had finally walked over the Cascades and were on the eastern side of the mountains, and that thrilled me. But, without Pat or cool mountain air to motivate us, we were back to taking breaks once or twice an hour, and that annoyed me. "Time for a break, Steve," Reggie began to *demand*. So much for my leadership. There was no rhythm to our pacing and it seemed like we weren't knocking out the miles. How many times had I felt that we were behind the schedule I had made up in my head? "It's a guideline," Janet had so often reminded me. "The schedule is not written in stone." We were doing the best we could, I reminded myself...walking, resting, walking, resting, walking, resting.

I still wondered if Reggie had much inspiration to walk now that we were out of the mountains. Open, flat land wasn't very motivating. Nor were long, hot, boring, days. There were no more mountains or cascading rivers to get to, no more woods. The emotional ups and downs of the trip were steeper than the mountains and valleys we walked through.

"Time for a break, Steve."

We didn't talk much through the heat of the day; there wasn't much to say, but we did keep moving, ever so slowly. I could feel his lack of enthusiasm like it was extra weight in my pack. "That's the way it is, Reg," I offered, as if it was my fault that walking had become boring and tiresome. "Sometimes it feels like we can walk around the State of Washington in one day. And other times, it feels like we can walk and walk and never get anywhere." Reggie just sighed.

We passed a mile marker. "Hey, Steve?" Here it came, a request for another break.

"Yes, Reg."

"We're walking the United States, Steve!" bubbled Reggie, full of cheer. He couldn't have surprised me more if he had thrown a bucket of cold water on my head.

"Yeah, you're right, Reg, we're walking the United State of Washington!"

"No problem, right, Steve?" Whining was no way to WALKABOUT, Reggie decided. "I like to walk!"

"You haven't appeared to enjoy it much lately."

"I hate the heat."

"You know something, Reg? We've made it all the way to the middle of Washington!"

"NO PROBLEM!" he said, putting some pep in his step.

Yes, WALKABOUT was moving right along and awaiting new adventures.

We were out of the mountains, but we were still camping out. Our "home" (for the next few days, at least) was going to be Pearrygin Lake State Park, just outside the town of Winthrop. The days were hot but at least the night air was comfortably cool, rejuvenating our bodies and our minds.

With our tents set along the shore of Pearrygin Lake, we ate dinner and burned wood in the fire pit. It was almost bedtime when we saw streaks of light shooting across the clear, night sky. We stared. At first I thought it was the light reflecting off the moon onto some clouds, but the clear night with millions of twinkling stars washed away that thought. People all over the campground, sitting by their campfires, gazed into the heavens.

"Maybe it's an alien spaceship over the next ridge shining lights over our heads," I imagined out loud. Rosalie looked at me strangely, but said nothing. Reggie laughed at me. He enjoyed the thought. So did I. We looked back at the sky. Then I realized what the lights were. "Hey!" I cried out. "That's the Aurora Borealis!"

What an incredible sight! Also called "The Northern Lights," these long beautiful streaks of white light danced in the sky. Bouncing and gleaming lights filled the sky like music fills a concert hall. It was a performance from Heaven! Reggie, Rosalie and I felt very inspired.

"I've slept outside hundreds of times before, but I have never seen anything as spectacular as this rare light show," I said, staring in awe. "The sky is actually singing to us!"

"I like this!" said Reggie.

"I've only been on WALKABOUT for a short time," said Rosalie, staring into the heavens, "but already I've seen two things I have never seen before. The glow of the Northern Lights and the glow on Reggie Feckley." I looked at Rosalie and then Reggie. What a trip!

We finally retired into our tents. I went to bed with a feeling that everything was going to be great! "You know what?" I said to Dixie as I zippered up my sleeping bag, "I don't think we should even doubt if we're going to make it or not. I know we will!" I settled down with Dixie by my side and we both fell into a deep, comfortable sleep.

We slept through the night and awoke ready to eat up the miles. We began the morning walking at a hearty pace. Unfortunately, because of the oven-like heat on the black pavement, we were being toasted like bread. We were slowing down. Our cool and confident attitude quickly melted away, shriveling in the heat of the late morning–early afternoon. There was no escape from the stifling heat.

"It's real hot today, Steve," Reggie said.

"Sure is, Reg," I replied, breathing deeply and blowing air out of my mouth and onto my face. "Perhaps the weatherman doesn't realize that it's late September and that summer actually ended last week. You would think that would mean something." Reggie gave a short laugh. "I don't know who hates the heat more—you, me or Dixie. I sure hope it doesn't stay this hot."

"Me, too," he said.

As we walked through the "oven" of Central Washington, I began to tell Reggie how Dixie and I had dealt with the heat when we had walked all by ourselves.

"You know, this reminds me of when Dixie and I walked through the desert of Eastern Oregon. The sun beat on us like a horsewhip. There wasn't a speck of shade, a wisp of cloud, or even the slightest hint of a breeze. We were in the middle of nowhere in the middle of summer with absolutely no escape from brutal torture. There weren't any buildings, trees, tall bushes or even big rocks in sight. With the sun so high in the sky for most of the day, not a shadow was cast! Every step was torment yet I couldn't even consider resting because without any shade to protect us, I couldn't bear the thought of sitting down and doing nothing but thinking about how the rays of the sun were cutting into our bodies like laser beams. I couldn't handle that helplessness. So we kept moving, hoping that sooner or later we'd find some shade somewhere.

"Unfortunately, Dixie had other plans. Once the morning coolness burned off, and the heat set in, she would walk right at my heels. I could hear her I.D. tags just barely jingling and I could feel her hot breath on my ankles. These sensations were as much a part of me as the hat on my head. We were walking, slowly, and I was trying to think of nothing but cool thoughts. Suddenly, I became aware that something was missing. I mean, not immediately. Once I recognized that something was out of place, I realized that the emptiness had existed for a few moments. I look down at my legs and saw nothing but asphalt. Then I looked back. For the first time in over 2,000 miles, Dixie had collapsed! Dixie was lying on the side of the road staring in my direction but not quite at me. Now, understand Reg, I've seen Dixie run over and hide under shady bushes in Louisiana, but this time she just laid down on the side of the road! Back then she would stick her head out from under the bush, smile as if she was saying, 'Look Dad, I found a great place to rest!' But she would always come running when I told her it wasn't time for a break yet. This time her legs just gave out, and it scared the living daylights out of me! This was no game she was playing, and I had to do something. But what? We couldn't lay there to bake in the sun, and yet we couldn't move, either."

"My goodness! What did you do?" asked Reggie. We were still walking, but instead of behind me, Reggie walked beside me, stride for stride. Every twenty seconds I would notice that he looked down at Dixie, who, because of the heat of this day, was walking at our heels.

"Well, my first reaction was to panic," I continued. "I didn't know what to do. I wasn't sure what happened. I felt so helpless! Dixie had proved to be such an incredible dog. She was only three years old and had already done what few other creatures could ever live through. It was hard to accept that all of a sudden she would just lay down and give up. My head begin to spin, and I felt like I had to throw up. I sat down and stroked her head. I wasn't even sure if maybe there was something else wrong with her than just exhaustion. The sun had been zapping my body and my mind of all energy, and now I was forced to think hard. I couldn't even get help. It wasn't like I had a telephone in my backpack to call a veterinarian." I looked at Reggie and I could tell by the look on his face that in his mind's eye he could picture Dixie sprawled out on the hot pavement, unable to get to her feet. "The look on your face is exactly how I felt."

"Did somebody help you?"

"That was just it. There was nobody! There weren't any cars, we hadn't passed any houses, and the closest town was five to ten miles away. I sat down next to Dixie, tears of fear and frustration welling up in my eyes, and I prayed that somebody would help me figure out what to do. But there was nobody! Nobody but Dixie, me, a hot sun and a barren desert."

"Wow! Poor Schlicky."

"That's for sure. I felt so bad for her, and for myself, because I didn't know what to do. Dixie was laying there on the hot sandy pebbles. At least her head was up, but she was panting harder than I had ever seen. Of course, I gave her some water from the canteen, but I had to ration it out. Water was scarce and I had to make it last. On the other hand, she needed some right away and it didn't do her any good if the water stayed in the canteen. She gulped down the water as quick as I poured it in her dish, but it was not nearly as much as she wanted or needed. After a while, she finally stood up. I felt a lot better about that, but I knew we couldn't keep walking in this sun or we'd have the same problem, and next time we may not have enough water! We had walked through heat before, but it had never been across land that had absolutely no streams, irrigation canals, water troughs for cows or even a farm house. We had never been so alone!" Reggie had become so enthralled he stopped walking just to listen to this tale of desperation.

I turned to him and continued the tale. "I knew it was no time to freak out, and it was reassuring to see that she felt a little better. I got my head together and scanned the landscape. Way up the road I was able to make out what looked like a small shack of some kind. Whatever it was, it was the only thing taller than a two-foot-high sagebush and I figured we could hide behind it. It took a lot of encouragement, but I convinced Dixie to walk what I figured had to be less than a mile or so. Loyal and tough, Dixie followed me as we slowly dragged ourselves up the road. It seemed to take so long to get to it I began to wonder if it was a mirage, always just beyond our grasp. A very long forty-five minutes later we caught up with it and spent the rest of the day hiding from the sun, but it still left us with a problem."

"Schlicky was O.K.?" asked Reggie. "That makes me happy," he added before I could reply. "I don't want that to happen again."

"That's exactly what I was thinking. We were still in the middle of nowhere, with little food and even less water. We couldn't stay put and yet we couldn't move. It took forever for the sun to begin its descent and for the temperature to cool down. By then we had recovered enough to believe we could make it to the town. I thought maybe I could figure something out once we got there, like talk to a veterinarian or a doctor, maybe spend a few days in a motel. But the town, if you could call it that, didn't seem to have more than just a few houses and one store—a combination gas station/post office/grocery/cafe. It wasn't very inviting, and even though we were somewhere, we still felt as if we were nowhere. We refilled the canteens, restocked our food supply, and learned that the next town was over 60 miles away. We were told that the only water we could expect would be found every twenty miles or so in the occasional house. It wasn't very encouraging. I even got the feeling Dixie understood what we were being told. She was listening to the old man who was telling us this, and her ears went back and her face dropped. I looked down at her and my heart sank like the sun setting below the horizon. We couldn't stay and yet we couldn't go.

"And then a thought struck my mind like a thunderbolt. 'Sunset!' I shouted. 'That's it! We'll walk at night!' Drastic times call for drastic measures! All of a sudden I knew exactly what had to be done. We were walking across America and nothing was going to stop us! We couldn't change nature, but we could certainly work around it."

"You walked at night?" Reggie said, cocking his head. "Wasn't that dangerous?"

"Well, maybe, but at the time my only thought was that it was too dangerous to walk during the day," I answered. "Anyway, we hung out by the store until after dark and then hit the road. Since we had spent most of the last few hours resting, and with the excitement of this new plan, we had energy to burn."

"You walked at night, huh?" Reggie repeated, thinking about the possibilities. It was the blasting heat that we were presently experiencing that had brought up this whole story. My story took our minds off of it for a while, but it didn't make it go away.

"Yup. For the next few days we would sleep in some shade during the day, hopefully near the occasional house where we could get water to wash up and refill our canteen, and then wake up at night and walk until dawn. We would walk in the light of the full moon. There was such a quietness about the night, and I could hear all the night animals, like lizards and rabbits, scurrying through the desert. A few times owls soared right in front of our faces. They must have thought we were giant mice. There was a serene beauty to it all."

Reggie liked what he was hearing and threw in a "Let's walk at night, Steve."

I smiled, but continued my story without hesitating. "Of course, I worried about the rattlesnakes. You see, during the day, the black road absorbs heat from the hot sun. Then at nighttime, the rattlers lie on the edge of the road to keep warm during the cool night," I added, remembering back. "Dixie was especially prone to them since she didn't wear thick boots like me. Of course, since it was dark, we wouldn't be able to see them until it was too late. Then we would really be in trouble! Walking at night was cooler, but it was definitely dangerous. Even with the moonlight we couldn't see very far ahead, and it was hard for the drivers of the 18-wheelers to see us as they passed by. Few truckers were expecting anybody to be walking on the road at three o'clock in the morning! We had to use our ears more than our eyes. We had to move way off the road every time a big truck approached. Once again, walking was great for both of us—fun, exciting, interesting, peaceful and spiritual—but after a few days our bodies felt way out of whack and we were incredibly tired. Our body clocks were all messed up. We finally made it to a stretch of road where there were more towns and more water, and then took a day and half off to readjust before we started back in with our daytime walking."

"Let's not walk at night," replied a sweating Reggie. I could see that he had understood the pros and cons of the situation and had changed his mind.

"Are you sure?"

"I'm sure."

"What makes you say that?" I asked.

"It's too dangerous. Washington has snakes, too," he said, thoughtfully. "I don't want Dixie to get bit."

"I agree," I said, wiping the sweat from my forehead. "But, believe me, at the time it was the best thing to do. Besides, WALKABOUT is on the road to be seen. We'd defeat the purpose if we walk when everyone else is asleep."

We kept walking. Like Eastern Oregon, this part of Washington had very few trees. Some trees were quite a distance from the road and some were fairly close. Unfortunately, *all* were too far away to provide shade or help us escape the heat, but there were a few other tricks Dixie and I taught Reggie. We took breaks in the shade of road signs, tall sagebush, the WALKABOUT-Mobile or wherever else we could find it. Sometimes all it took was a bit of creative thinking and imagination. Just when we started to get used to suffering, we were amazed to see a small stand of trees by an irrigation canal.

"Let's go rest by the water, Steve."

"Just follow Dixie. She's already found a good spot."

What luck! That stand of trees was just the beginning of what turned out to be a small forest. We were approaching Loup Loup Pass.

"Hey, another mountain!" said Reggie.

"Yeah, and it's steep, too," I added. What a relief! What a surprise! Either I hadn't studied the map very well or it had left out some minor details. The higher we climbed up the road of the mini-mountain, the crisper and cooler the air became. "It feels like during the last week we were in heaven, then went to the other place and now we're back in heaven." The 4,020 foot mountain pass, lined with trees, made walking fun again.

For two days the air was cooler, and trees growing by the side of the road provided plenty of shade. Walking was fun, and we counted off the mile-markers.

"This is the way it's supposed to be, right, Reg?"

"I like the mountains, Steve."

"We'll conquer this mountain in no time!"

"No problem!"

Well, maybe one problem—it only took us two days! Walking down the other side of the pass, we passed fewer and fewer trees. Finally they were gone. Once again, I was sure that these would be the last shade trees we'd see for five hundred miles, except for a few in private apple and peach orchards. Unfortunately, orchards were usually too far from the road to be any help to us. Although it was late September and should have been a little cooler, we had to push ourselves through the heat.

Reggie, sweat pouring down his back, wanted to stop walking when it got really, incredibly hot. Even Dixie, with the hot sun shining on her permanent fur coat, was thinking that maybe she should learn how to drive. She was panting so hard that her tongue was almost dragging on the road. There were no canals or streams on the side of the road, and I could never carry quite enough water to satisfy her. I hated the intense heat, too, but I knew we had to keep going. Someone had to keep the troops moving forward! Reggie wasn't going to do it. Dixie was no longer an inspiration. That left me. I figured that if we waited until it got cooler to walk, we would have to change our name to MOPE-ABOUT!!

"Come on gang, let's be all that we can be!"

That mentality was all well and good until we entered the town of Okanogan.

"Look at that sign, Reg. Ninety-five degrees! It's 4:30 in the afternoon and it's ninety-five gosh-darn degrees. Reggie, Dixie, let's call it a day!" Sometimes there was no one to keep us going!

"No problem," agreed Reggie. I hadn't expected an argument.

We knew Rosalie wouldn't meet up with us for a while, and we sat down to rest on a brick wall under a tree. Reggie looked around and noticed a grocery store. In a flash, as if he spontaneously combusted, he was gone! Five minutes later he returned with a carton of chocolate milk for each of us. Then he grabbed his canteen, went back into the store, came out with a quart of fresh, cold water and let Dixie take a good long drink! Then he shared some of his chocolate milk with her. She gulped that right up, too.

"Dixie *loves* her Uncle Reggie," I said as she slurped up more of the refreshing water. She was lapping the water up so fast, half of it spilled onto the street. Then I raised my chocolate milk in the air as a toast. "Here's to refreshing chocolate milk, cold water, good friends and prayers for cool weather!"

"Praise the Lord!" replied Reggie as we touched milk cartons.

"Praise the Lord, Reg!" I repeated as we ended another WALKABOUT walking day.

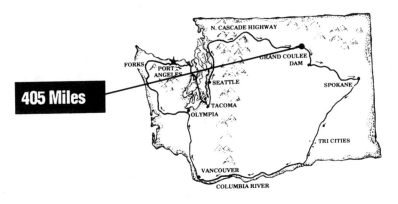

405 Miles

chapter 15

The GRAVEL PIT

"Wake up, Janet!" Reggie had walked over to Janet's tent and gently shook the walls. It was our last morning in national forest campgrounds.

"Unhh," came the strange sound from within her tent. Janet had driven back to rejoin WALKABOUT the day before, and we had said good-bye to Rosalie. Obviously, Janet needed to be reacquainted with the WALKABOUT lifestyle. Reggie chose to accept that responsibility.

"Time to get up," Reggie said again.

"Wake Steve up, Reggie. It's too early for me!" came the muffled reply.

Reggie was an early riser and his roaming around the campsite would always wake Dixie up. She, in turn, would wake me up—usually with a cold nose in the eyeball or a wet tongue up my left nostril!

I was not an early riser—usually, that is. Reggie and Dixie's prompting helped, but I had other motivation—escaping the heat of the afternoon sun. I unzipped my tent door, walked into the morning and stretched. Reggie was by his tent rolling up his sleeping pad and stuffing his sleeping bag into its stuff sack. Dixie ran out and gave him a good-morning lick.

"Good morning, Schlicky. Hi, Steve." He was almost too jolly even for me so early in the morning. But Janet was back and I was happy to see her.

"Morning, Reg. YOU UP, JANET!?" I called in a sweet voice.

"What's the matter with you people? It's six o'clock in the morning!" came a slumber-filled whine from behind the tent walls.

"Oh, didn't we tell you? We have a new strategy," I began to explain. She was in the tent so I made sure I spoke loudly enough as to not let her fall back to sleep. "Reggie and I figured that the more miles we walk in the coolness of the morning, the fewer miles we have to make in the blistering heat of the afternoon."

"I don't care. Let me sleep."

"If we can walk ten miles before lunch and five miles after, we figure we could call it a good day."

"I'll tell you what kind of day it's going to be if you don't let me sleep!" she groaned. Or, more accurately, roared!

"Is Janet mad?" Reggie asked seriously.

"C'mon, let's make her some coffee. She'll be a happy camper in a little while."

"I hope so," he muttered, walking towards neutral territory. Slowly, Janet unzipped her door, and fell out of her tent.

The morning was cool and crisp but the clear sky and the sun shining above the horizon screamed out the weather prediction of the day—HOT! Our plan was a good one!

Janet didn't say much, drank her coffee, and finally dragged herself over to the WALKABOUT-Mobile. It was about 7:15 when I drove us over to our starting spot to start our walking day.

Just chock full of energy with the cool morning air and the thrill of driving again, I asked, "By the way Janet, did you get a chance to enjoy all your stuff?"

"Huh?" groaned Janet, lifting open one eyelid. Obviously, her coffee hadn't been strong enough. She had no idea what I was talking about.

Judy and Rosalie were wonderful, and provided some fresh conversation, but there was nothing like having Janet back. I needed someone special to be obnoxious to. "You know, all your *stuff*. Your television, your bed, your living room, your books, your typewriter. I hope you gave them my best."

"Shut up, Steve," Janet replied, still quite grumpy from her early awakening. Unfortunately, she *was* awake enough to give me a sharp smack on the leg.

"Yes, Ma'am." I said, cowering. O.K., so maybe it was too early to be too obnoxious.

"Didn't your stuff miss you, Janet?" asked Reggie.

"Shut up, Reggie!"

"Yes, Ma'am," said Reggie.

Janet gave us both a sharp look, sharp enough to cut our tongues out and make us both want to keep our mouths shut. Now that she'd stifled us, she was content, and once again shut her eyes. She was still not ready to wake up completely.

I, on the other hand, was full of too much energy to stay quiet for long. I did realize, however, that it would be best to change the subject. "You know," I said, "I didn't realize how much I missed driving. I haven't driven once since we left Port Angeles."

"You know something," said Reggie "I want to learn how to drive, too."

I looked at Reggie in the rear-view mirror, sharing the backseat with Dixie. "Well, first you have to pass a lot of tests. You have to study a book, take a written test, and then pass a driving test."

"I want to drive tomorrow. Tomorrow is my turn," he said, convincingly.

That woke Janet up faster than the strongest coffee. She turned directly around and said, "Over my dead, lifeless body, Mr. Feckley!"

"O.K.," he countered. "I'll wait."

Janet wasn't sure she knew exactly what he meant by that. I just laughed and looked at Reggie in the mirror. He looked back at me, but didn't smile and just gave a shrug. Suddenly I wasn't too sure, either. Luckily, we arrived at our starting spot and the subject was dropped (at least until Janet became dead and lifeless).

Reggie, Dixie and I hitched up our packs, and Janet moved over to the driver's seat. Reggie's conversation woke Janet up completely, and she headed back to the campgrounds. Reggie, Dixie and I began our walking day.

"Now don't go back and fall asleep. You've got work to do," I cheerfully reminded her.

"Good luck finding a place to sleep," Reggie said. Without any group homes and very few campgrounds around, he was well aware that Janet's main duty was not about to get any easier.

"Thanks, Reg. I'll need it," she replied.

"Isn't she just too cute in the morning, Reg?"

"Just like a baby." Reggie and I laughed. Janet kind of smiled, I think, and drove off.

Each day when Janet left us, we had no idea what she would come up with for sleeping arrangements. In the Cascades, Judy and Rosalie looked at the map, read where the campgrounds were located and that's where we planted our tents. That luxury was a thing of the past. We were now even too far away to go back to the Loup Loup Campgrounds. But we had to sleep somewhere, and I was confident that Janet would find that "somewhere." When Janet caught up with us for lunch, she told us about the great "somewhere" she had found.

"Today, as I was driving around, I went over a little pass and saw a sign that said 'Pit Site.' It looked like it might have possibilities, but then I thought it looked like an abandoned logging road. Since it's not quite safe to sleep on a road, I kept searching for a better campsite, maybe one with some water. Unfortunately, the only place where I found water was at a gas station in a little settlement about 30 miles away. And the attendant there didn't know of any campgrounds. So, back I went, figuring that maybe I should really check out that 'Pit Site.'

"I began to wonder if maybe it meant PIT toilets and camp SITE. Wrong! It meant *gravel* pit! So I followed the road beyond the huge hole and found a nice large grassy spot behind it. It looked like it used to be the old parking lot, but I figured with a little imagination and some improvising, it could be our new home. There's no water, but I think we could still have a small campfire. I filled all our water containers at the gas station, and I've already put up the tents—so our new temporary home is just waiting for you guys, but first you have to walk a few afternoon miles!" she said. (Sometimes Janet pushed us on!)

We liked the gravel pit as much as Janet did. Apparently some cows had liked our nice grassy campsite, too, because traces of their visit could be seen, and stumbled over, everywhere. BIG traces! Janet enjoyed the pine trees. Reggie enjoyed the peace and quiet. Dixie enjoyed the smells of the former residents (the cows) and all their traces. I enjoyed our privacy. Without other campers or new friends at a group home to talk to, we enjoyed a nice evening "at home" with just the "family." The "pit" wasn't exactly a luxury hotel, but for the time being, it was private and it was ours!

We scrounged around the debris and the trees to gather wood. When we had a good-sized pile, Reggie built the fire. We roasted hot dogs over the flames, and cooked a can of beans on the coals. A thin line of light on the horizon marked where the sun had set. Far away from the lights of any town, we could see a million stars shining bright in the clear night sky. Reggie went to bed early, leaving Janet and me to watch the fire burn down to embers. Finally we buried the fire with sand and went to bed.

The next day, after we started walking, Janet spent time straightening up camp. When she finished, she headed into town to pick up some supplies. Mainly what we needed was water and ice for the cooler. With all of this heat in the afternoons, we were going through two big bags of ice each day. Janet passed us by, and boy, was Dixie confused! The WALKABOUT-Mobile drove by without stopping! "Hey, the WALKABOUT-Mobile always means rest, fresh water and a treat!" I could imagine Dixie thinking.

"Whoa, Dixie! Not this time!" I called to her. Janet watched in the rear-view mirror as poor Dixie chased after her on the side of the road. Reggie and I got a good laugh at Dixie's expense. "Just a little WALKABOUT humor, Dixie," I said as I patted her on the head after she ran back to us looking for an explanation.

When Janet came back at lunchtime, she parked about a quarter mile further up the road in a pull-out on the highway. Dixie went trotting up to her as if she hadn't been ignored earlier. Dixie can be *very* forgiving...especially when all of our canteen water was gone and Janet had the only water for miles around!

We finished the day only a few miles from the store where Janet had bought supplies that morning. Janet refilled every container we had with water, picked all of us up, and headed back to our "Pit." Once again, we made ourselves "at home." After a supper of canned beef stew and Ramen noodles, we settled in by the fire.

"This reminds me of some of the strange places Dixie and I slept when we were walking from Louisiana to Washington," I

Two wild and wacky walkers

said, speaking in a drawl as if I were an old man remembering back to the good ol' days.

"Ooh, tell us, Grandpa Steve!" Janet said playfully. She nestled up to Reggie as if they were two children ready for a bedtime story.

"Aw heck. We used to sleep anywhere we could. Way off the road and way out of town, so nobody could find us. We slept in cow pastures, inside old abandoned shacks, between haystacks. In the rain we slept under bridges with the cars shaking the bridge so hard we almost rolled into the river below. Why, even once," I said, using a stick as if I was puffing on a corn-cob pipe, "we even bedded down in a cemetery by Interstate 30 in Texas. Now, I'll tell ya, we had some strange dreams that night."

Before I could even go into details, Reggie offered his opinion of what my life was like back then. He sat straight up and looked at me and said, "Steve! You were a bum!"

So much for respect for old grandpa. "Look who's talking, Feckley," I said in my normal voice, but quite amused. "You're sleeping in a gravel pit!"

He was laughing and I'm sure he was kidding. At least, I hope he was kidding. Janet thought Reggie's comment was as funny as he did, and the two of them ended up rolling on the ground, laughing their heads off. I didn't think it was *that funny*, and caught myself just waiting for the pair of them to roll right into the fire pit!

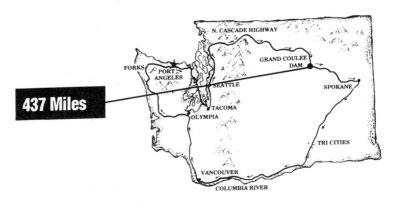

chapter 16

The GRAND COULEE DAM

"I hate having to leave our gravel pit behind," I said, sorrowfully. We had been walking well and would be too far away by the end of the day to come back. We stood around the campsite drinking cooler-cool orange juice, preparing some cold cereal.

"Yeah, it's the first place we've stayed that was private and felt like our own home away from home," said Janet, perfecting the classic pout.

"Yes, moving on *is* part of the life we've chosen," I said quietly, yet ever so profoundly. Reggie passed the milk and I poured it on my bowl of cereal.

"I want to come back and build my house right here," stated Reggie.

"Right here," Janet asked quizzically. I was ready for him this time, said nothing and watched it unfold.

"Yup!" Reggie said, quite sure of himself.

"I mean, I like this place too, a lot, and I'm

going to miss it as a campsite, but I don't think I'd want to move here, Reggie."

"I like it," said Reggie. He appeared quite serious.

Janet looked at me. I was holding back a smile. "Is he serious? Or just being silly?"

Reggie burst into laughter. "Just giving you a bad time!"

"Gee whiz, Janet, get a sense of humor," I cracked, and slapped Reggie on the back. He got her, too. I was glad we didn't have a morning fire, or I believe she would have pushed us both into it.

We finally got around to packing up our gear. We cleaned up our camp so that it looked like we'd never been there. So much for an early start. Finally, Janet dropped us off to walk while she went in search of a new home.

The land had become vast, open, spacious plains again as WALKABOUT entered Washington's Coulee Area. Thousands of years ago the Columbia River had become blocked by a gigantic glacier. The river backed up for miles in the center of the state and formed a huge lake. Then slowly, the climate of North America got warmer and the glacier slowly melted. One day, the glacier softened in just the right spot and...WHOOSH! The naturally formed dam burst—and out gushed, surged, and poured *billions* of gallons of water! The rushing waters spilled over most of Eastern Washington. Anything in the way got washed out. All that was left were deep, water-chiseled cuts in the earth. These were the "coulees," and we had an up-close and personal experience with them.

"Poor Janet," I said to Reg. "She misses so much by driving. I just love looking at the carvings in the Earth."

"It's better to walk," replied my thoughtful companion. "I like this. It's very pretty."

As Janet drove along through this desert, she, too, was struck by its beauty. I would have guessed that she was jealous of us walkers. Little did I know that she enjoyed it in her own way. Janet was not one to miss out.

"I *was* jealous for a while," she said when we met up with her. "But then I hit the brakes, slowed down the WALKABOUT-Mobile, and viewed the desert at a nice, easy 20 miles per hour. Unfortunately, the cars behind me didn't appreciate the beauty as much as I did, and they let me know it with their horns! Finally, as I got to the top of a hill, the Columbia River came into view. That was just

Photo by Janet Phipps

**The "Coulees" of
Eastern Washington**

too much. I pulled over, parked and stared at it for an hour."

If Janet had been driving slowly, we were walking even more slowly. It was still awfully hot, but every hill we walked over showed us something new. We were captivated by the shapes of the Earth and the colors of the mud and rocks and bushes and shadows. It was as if an artist had sculpted the planet. The beauty made walking so much easier. We were motivated just knowing that soon we would get to the greatest "coulee" of them all: The Grand Coulee. And of course, the Grand Coulee Dam.

Janet drove through town and found a "regulation" campground just west of the Dam. "Our new home is the lovely and shady Spring Canyon State Park on the shores of Roosevelt Lake," she told us when she found us for lunch. "Did you know that Roosevelt Lake is really a large reservoir? And did you know that it was created by the Grand Coulee Dam when the dam was built to create hydroelectricity for a large portion of Washington State? Did you know that President Roosevelt O.K.ed the money for all this?"

"Nope," we both said.

"And did you know that by supplying water to much of the dry but very fertile desert, it helped make the Palouse Wheatfields of Eastern Washington world famous?"

"Nope. I didn't know that. Did you know that, Reg?"

"Nope."

"Well, now you do," Janet said. "You may see more, but I can drive around and find more signs to read."

"Great! Did you find us a shower?" One thing the WALKABOUT team was in great need of was a shower!

"Well," she said slowly, "the campgrounds are really nice, but don't expect it to be nearly as nice or as private as our gravel pit. I'm sure Dixie is going to miss all those 'traces.'"

"Great. Did you find us a shower?"

"It has real bathrooms. Running water and flush toilets!"

"Great. Did you find us a shower?" we both demanded to know.

"Not a one," she confessed.

"We stink," said Reggie, squeezing his nostrils shut with his fingers.

"Tell me about it, Reg. I've been thinking about pouring some liquid soap on you and throwing your naked butt into the Columbia River," I told him.

"Good joke!" he cried. I didn't say a word. I just shrugged my shoulders and smiled. "Right?" he asked, beginning to wonder.

"I don't know, Reg. We might have to consider changing our name again...this time to 'STINKABOUT!'"

Reggie and Janet laughed. "We may smell pretty gross, but at least we still have a sense of humor," said Janet. "Right?"

"Hmmmm. Maybe. We'll see." I liked to keep them wondering.

Janet played it safe and went back to finish setting up camp, leaving Reggie to take his chances with me.

After she completed her chores, Janet drove into the town of Grand Coulee to see if the local newspaper was interested in the WALKABOUT story. Boy, were they! Janet was interviewed right in the newspaper office. Then the reporter requested an interview with the star himself, and Janet gladly escorted the reporter to the WALKABOUT-Mobile. She drove back up the highway, and when she passed by a small store on the side of the road, Janet noticed Dixie sitting near the doorway next to our backpacks. "There's Dixie watching the packs," Janet explained to the reporter. "They must be in the store buying some snacks."

Janet parked the WALKABOUT-Mobile, and Jim, the reporter, went inside and found Reggie and me buying chocolate milk. Jim introduced himself, and we all went outside and sat in the shade of the store building. We made ourselves comfortable as we sat on some crates, and Jim began to ask us questions. He was very interested in what Reggie's life was like—both before and during the walk. He also wanted to know what life was like at a group home.

"How many people do you live with at the group home?" Jim asked Reggie.

Reggie thought about it, but he wasn't sure of the number. Janet broke in and said, "There are 24 tenants."

"Do you have any roommates, Reggie?"

"Little Ricky, and Harvey and Shannon." Reggie wasn't nearly as nervous about answering questions as he used to be. We had been practicing answering questions since Seattle.

"It's a pretty tough day to be walking out in the desert, Reggie. What do you think about that?"

"I don't mind the heat," answered Reggie, sipping his chocolate milk through a straw. (Didn't mind the heat? Oh, yeah, sure! I could only guess that with the refreshing chocolate milk, the cool shade and the exciting newspaper interview, the last thing Reggie was concerned about was the annoying heat!)

"You like to walk, Reggie?" Jim continued.

"Real good!" Reg answered. There was certainly no doubt about that.

"What's your favorite part of the trip, Reggie?"

Reggie thought for a second and then said, "I like the peace and quiet. I like the mountains." Although I had to occasionally repeat Reggie's answers for Jim, who had a little difficulty understanding, Jim always directed his questions toward Reggie. Reggie appreciated the fact that Jim spoke directly to him. "I like to camp in the woods. It's fun!" Reggie added.

"Do you like living in a group home?"

"It's O.K."

"What's it like at the group home?" Jim asked next.

Reggie scrunched up his face, as if he were thinking deeply, but he didn't answer the question. He wasn't sure how to express that opinion. I finally broke into the conversation and said, "Basically, our job at the group home is to help people reach their potential. Of course, it's up to them to decide what goals, if any, they want to reach. We're making the walk to introduce Reggie, a person with a developmental disability, to the general public. WALKABOUT helps prove what a person with a developmental disability or developmental delays *can* do, not what he *can't* do. Reggie is a walker. I'm a walker. We're walking together because we like it. I'm teaching him what I've learned about long-distance walking. We put those skills to use and now we share the thrills together."

"Steve teaches me a lot of things," said Reggie. "That's TEAM-WORK!" Reggie added.

"The group home attempts to support our tenants to have as normal a life as possible," Janet added. "It's a place that gives them a chance to be a part of a community and to learn new things. Many of our tenants used to live in an institution and therefore they have had to unlearn some of the bad habits and other questionable things they learned due to abnormal living situations. One thing I've enjoyed on WALKABOUT is the remarkable improvement I've noticed in Reggie's speech. Even at the group home he is still surrounded by many people with speech defects. Out here, on the road, he is mostly around people who can speak very well and therefore he has had a chance to listen to people that speak fairly well on a consistent basis. This opportunity has given him a chance to improve his speech as well as other skills. Even his sense of humor has really blossomed. Anyway, the main purpose of the group home is to give people with disabilities the opportunity to lead as normal a life as possible. As men and women, they want to be treated as such."

"I'm a man," chimed in Reggie.

"Of course, it's still not perfect and that's why we're walking. Reggie is 43 years old and still has roommates and that is not what he wants. I hope that someday we can provide our tenants with their own apartments and houses, just like anybody else. They should choose where they want to live—and if they want to live with other people."

"I want my own house!" said Reggie, with a gleam in his eye.

"Do you want to live by yourself?" Jim asked.

"I learn how to cook, clean, take care of myself," explained Reggie.

"Is it hard to find a house to live in, Reggie?"

"I want to build my own house!" Reggie replied.

"Wow! That would be great," stated Jim.

"Unfortunately, that might be a bit difficult, buddy," I said to Reggie. "I won't say impossible, but difficult."

"We have a hard time finding enough landlords who will rent to people with developmental disabilities, as well as affording enough staff to allow all our tenants to get everything they want and all the services they need," explained Janet. "It takes a long time to change a system! Before, almost all people with disabilities were put into institutions, or hidden from society. We want to turn it around so that the people in need can have their own houses or apartments like everyone else—if that is indeed what they want. We have to find the balance between accepting the time it takes to change a system and being assured of forward momentum and definite progress. If it's done right, everyone will benefit!"

"When you say change the system," Jim wondered, "what exactly are you referring to, and how will everyone benefit?"

"Well, in a nutshell," answered Janet, "we want a system that understands and supports free choice, opportunity and equality when it comes to the individual lives of people with disabilities. It's a combination of trying to match up the policies of the government agencies, distributing the allotted money, and convincing the average person on the street to accept people with developmental disabilities as neighbors, employees and co-workers.

"When people with developmental disabilities were living in institutions, they didn't have much of a chance to learn about nondisabled people, and nondisabled people didn't have a chance to understand what it was like to be a person with a developmental disability.

"That ignorance has created fears and stereotypes which still get in the way today. Prejudice and discrimination keep us *all* in the dark. But as we continue to push for our goals, and people get to know and understand each other, the light gets brighter. The sooner we start, the better understanding there will be between people, generation after generation." Just then Janet paused for a moment, reflecting on what she had just said and giving Jim a chance to catch up as he wrote down her words. When he looked up from his pad, she added, "That's what life's all about, isn't it?"

"You'll get no argument from me," Jim answered, looking straight into Janet's eyes. Janet's words made her even more attractive than she already was, and even I could feel the admiration Jim was building for this insightful lady.

"We also explain the financial benefit," she went on to say. "When people live on their own with only as much services as they need, it doesn't cost the taxpayer as much in round-the-clock services such as caretakers, counselors, or medical professionals. The only people who would receive such benefits are the people who absolutely need it. Right now Reggie is surrounded by staff twenty-four hours a day. A tremendous waste!"

"The worst part of having all these adults live in a group setting, the thing I find so incredibly irritating, is the tenants' lack of privacy," I added. "I live at the group home too, and there are many things I see that, at the moment, we can't do anything about. We do the best we can to provide as normal a life as possible, yet some of our tenants can only be guaranteed complete privacy in the bathroom."

My last remark seemed to bother Jim quite a bit. He tried to imagine what it must be like to *never* have any privacy, except in the bathroom. "Wow," Jim quietly said, almost to himself. "Imagine being my age and not even having the opportunity to lie in bed without someone else watching me." Jim looked up and said, quite strongly, "No one should have to live like that."

"We know. That's why we're walking!" said Janet and I at the same time.

"That's teamwork!" Reggie said once again.

Jim smiled. Then all of a sudden he looked confused. "You give me the impression," he was saying, "that even if you walk one thousand miles in record time, there is no reason to believe Reggie will be any closer to getting his own apartment."

"This is true," said Janet.

"Then what's the point? How will his life change?"

"First of all," I answered, "you can't experience such a journey as this and not be affected in a very profound way. That's the only guarantee, though. Afterwards, who knows? We're walking for two reasons. One, it's hard work, but still it's a lot of fun. Reggie, Dixie and I love to walk, and doing things you love to do is a wonderful part of life. Second, walking is our way to show the public that people with developmental disabilities want to enjoy free choice in life as much as anyone else, even if that choice is to walk around a state. It's a simple concept, yet one that has been ignored for much too long. Sometimes people have to do something 'bigger than life' to get the public's attention. Then, when you have their attention, you can spread your message. Hopefully people will take notice. For instance, take yourself as an example. If you didn't think it was so fascinating that anyone would be walking across Washington, especially in this heat, would you be doing a story about people with disabilities?"

"Good point," admitted Jim. I felt he really understood the value and importance of WALKABOUT when he said, as if he was thinking aloud, "How a person is treated is more important than the disability itself." He was genuinely sympathetic to the ideals and motivation of why a person would walk 1,300 miles. By the look on Jim's face, I could see that learning what life could be like for a person with a disability might be quite fascinating, but also a bit disturbing. As a reporter, Jim had the means to share these new insights with the general public. Our conversation and interview would have an effect reaching far beyond our back-alley confines!

Jim took some pictures and then gathered his things. "I can't wait to type up this story," he said. "I really wish I could do more. Is there anything you need?"

"A shower!" we all chimed in. Hey—he asked! Jim laughed heartily and, as it turned out, that was "No problem!" He made arrangements for us to have showers at a privately-owned campground in town. What a guy! He'll never know how wonderful those showers felt! The three of us were magically transformed from Stinkabouters back to WALKABOUTers with just a bunch (a big bunch) of soap and a lot (and I mean a lot) of water!

Domestic responsibilities never give way, and with setting up camp, the interview and the showers, Janet hadn't had time to do all her chores during the afternoon. Reggie and I understood, but our feet and noses didn't. We were both out of clean socks, and laundry was a priority. We searched the town of Grand Coulee for a laundramat that evening, and were finally instructed to head to a specific address. We carried in our bag of dirty clothing and found washing machines, dryers and—bowling alleys. "A laundry/ bowl?!?" I thought. "I've walked over 4,000 miles and have been in hundreds of American towns and never have I seen such a combination!" With the wonder of the Grand Coulee Dam and the uniqueness of the laundry/bowl, the town of Grand Coulee, Washington, became another stand-out WALKABOUT experience. "If you walk enough, you'll see everything," I told Janet and Reggie.

Dixie wasn't very interested in either laundry or bowling, so she rested in the car. After a few curious moments spent observing people that like to mix and match "strikes" and solids, I went off by myself for a while. I had told Janet and Reggie that I wanted to go for a walk around town and I'd be back in a while. Janet understood that I wanted some private time, and she asked Reggie to help her with the laundry. Reggie seemed to understand my need for privacy...until I walked out of sight. Then his feelings were hurt. He thought that I didn't like him anymore, and he couldn't understand what he had done wrong. Janet and Reggie had a long talk about privacy.

"Sometimes a person needs to be alone, Reg. Steve is not mad at either of us. He likes you. He likes me. Steve just needs a little time to himself once in a while. He'll be back."

"Men need privacy?"

"Yes. Women, too." Janet explained. "Everyone needs it sometime. I'm by myself all day. I have lots of privacy."

Reggie sat with Janet a few minutes to think this over. Privacy wasn't something Reggie was used to. He'd talked about his need for privacy often and yet he'd never had much chance to learn how to use it. He thought about Janet stating that "men need privacy," and decided it was time to practice. "I need some privacy, too," he told her as he walked away from the laundry/bowl. He was gone about two minutes. "I'm back," he announced. Two minutes was enough privacy for Reggie. He probably figured something must be wrong with me if I needed more than that!

The next morning, with clean bodies and fresh clothing, we were feeling strong and powerful; ready to do some heavy-duty walking. "I feel good, Steve," said Reggie with a bounce in his step. "Let's walk around the world!"

Janet drove us from the campground back to where we finished walking the evening before, which was right next to the Grand Coulee Dam. "If we walk past the entrance to our campground, I'll tie my bandana on the 'Spring Canyon Campgrounds' sign as a signal," I explained to Janet before she drove off. "If you see my bandana, then you'll know to look for us east of the campground."

"Mine, too," added Reggie.

Janet laughed and said, "You guys will think of anything to avoid having a late lunch!"

The morning was clear and sunny and we walked at a brisk pace. The heat that we were used to had not set in yet. In fact, the heat was a little late. We noticed, but didn't complain. In no time flat we were walking beyond the campground.

"Here's the sign post. I'm going to tie my bandana to it for Janet to see," I reminded Reggie.

Reggie also decided to tie his bandana to the post. "I'll put mine up, too."

At first, I thought this was silly. One bandana was enough. Then I realized that Reggie copied things I did so that he could learn. It reminded me how much responsibility I had. "In a way, Reg, I am your teacher and you are my student, and in a way, you are my teacher and I your student."

"I'm a teacher, too."

"You're a good teacher, Reg. You are also a good student. You do a very good job of teaching me that no matter how much we walk together, and how much time we spend together, there is always something more for each of us to learn and understand."

"You're a good teacher, too, Steve. You too, Schlicky," he said.

Even with both of our bandanas blowing in the breeze for her to see, Janet was late! Finally, at about 2:15, Janet found us and gave us our noontime meal: sandwiches of peanut butter and jelly, store-bought coleslaw and potato chips.

"Didn't you see the signals?" I grumbled, almost as loudly as my belly.

"My bandana was there, too!" added a hungry Reggie. Maybe I shouldn't be teaching him how to be obnoxious. It could easily backfire.

"Sorry, guys. After I dropped you off, I took care of everything

Photo by Steve Breakstone

Two men of vision: Franklin Delano Roosevelt and Reggie Feckley

that needed to be taken care of and then took a short nap. I guess I overslept just a wee bit." Janet put on one of her cutest smiles and tried to look very innocent. I knew all her tricks, and faked an annoyed look in her direction. I didn't want her to think a late lunch was acceptable.

Reggie was much more forgiving. "That's O.K., Janet," he said. "Everyone makes mistakes. You work very hard. You deserve a special morning."

Reggie, playing teacher, had a game plan, and taught me a good trick. We didn't take any breaks after lunch, and we put in 15 miles before we were driven back to Spring Canyon. Reggie grabbed his suitcase from the back of the WALKABOUT-Mobile and went into his tent. Ten minutes later he came out wearing nice, clean clothes, and sat in the WALKABOUT-Mobile. Hint. Hint. "We all deserve something special!" he said. "Let's go out to a Chinese restaurant," he suggested, using a tone that didn't leave room for discussion.

Janet and I looked at each other and nodded. Reggie was right—we did deserve it!

Although he personally requested a Chinese restaurant, Reggie played it safe and ordered his favorite—a cheeseburger and fries.

Janet and I ordered chow mein, lo mein, some other Chinese stuff and a barbecue pork appetizer. When our appetizer came before Reggie's burger, his hunger encouraged him to try something new. Reggie decided to give it a taste.

He picked up a piece of pork, dipped it into the duck sauce, like Janet and me, and then scooped up some hot mustard...unlike Janet and me.

"Be careful with the hot mustard," warned Janet.

"Yeooow!" Reggie's eyes popped out, and steam rolled out of his ears. Don't think Janet and I didn't crack a smile at that one!

"Something wrong, Reg?" I said quite stoically. He tried another piece of pork, this time carefully avoiding that yellow stuff. That's another way to learn. Some lessons are harder than others. Some are just funnier.

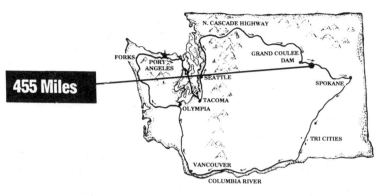

455 Miles

chapter 17

The ACTOR

The heat wave was finally over. The road took us out of the canyon of the Grand Coulee and away from the river. The highway was like an uphill roller coaster, and as we walked over the crest of yet another hill, we found ourselves looking at a seemingly endless wheat field. What a difference a few feet made!

A few paces back, at the crest, the road was wedged between two huge walls of rock. The rock fell away and the road opened up, displaying a long, straight line of rolling hills of tannish brown classic American prairie. We were in Eastern Washington, but we could see all the way to Iowa! And it was all downhill!!

Way off in the distance of forever we could see blue sky dotted with clouds shaped like anything. Halfway between here and there the sky was just blue, pure as glacial ice. Above us, keeping us cool and comfortable, and protecting us from the sun as we walked, was a light blanket of cloud.

We were in a great mood. Reggie was full of energy and spirit. Walking was so easy with the heat gone and gravity on our side. Dixie was bouncing all over the place. She welcomed the cooler weather and the wheat fields. I enjoyed walking along, watching my companions. We were all enjoying the beauty of the land. It seemed the world was at our fingertips.

We finally stopped for a break, to rest our legs as much as to just enjoy the peaceful Washington countryside. Reggie and I sat way off the side of the road, and Dixie lay down between us. We gazed out at the waving wheat, eyeballs following field swallows zipping by, darting this way and that for their insect lunches. We talked about different things—the nicer weather, where we might sleep that night, the different towns we would be walking through. We even discussed what would happen if one of us got hurt. Then we sat and stared some more.

"Well, bye, Steve. See you next year." Reggie picked himself up, grabbed his pack and walked off. I stood there with a look of amazement on my face, laughing into the breeze.

"I guess that means he's ready to walk some more," I said to Dixie.

Seeing that Reggie was happy to walk by himself, Dixie and I sat for a little while longer. Reggie was a good fifteen minutes ahead of us by the time Dixie and I were ready to hitch up our packs and get back on the road. He was always in sight, of course, and I knew I had nothing to worry about. No one could get lost out here!

With Dixie bouncing down the road beside me, I walked along lost in daydreams. There were a million things to think about…memories of things I'd done and fantasies about future fun. My mind was open to any and all thoughts that chose to enter it. Moments like these make me feel one with the universe. There was no other place I had to be or wanted to be. I was in no rush; there was nothing else I had to be doing. It was so peaceful in this time and place; I was walking, with my dog by my side, in paradise. "But just a few years ago," I remembered, "I was living in New York City. I wonder what I'd be doing if I was there now?" I looked at the watch attached to my shoulder strap. It was three hours later on the east coast—RUSH HOUR! Millions of people and tens of thousands of cars, trains and buses all yelling and honking at each other, all rushing to get from one place to another in record time.

"No one can get lost out here!"

A picture developed in my mind displaying monstrous buildings closing people in and keeping nature out. I thought it dreadful.

I stopped my legs, turned towards the open prairie and inhaled this moment of solitude in Washington State. Yes, I preferred paradise over America's busiest city. Reggie would sum it up best, I am sure. "I like peace and quiet," he would say.

I turned back towards the road. Dixie had been up the road a piece, waiting for me to continue the trek. "I'm a-comin', Doods," I called, using her nickname. Moments like these are the true glory of long-distance walking. Dixie saw that I was still rolling and not even considering a break. With an enthusiastic jump and spin, Dixie Doodles ran on. She loved it! As I've said before, Dixie was born to walk. I looked past her and saw nothing but the road to forever. It was quintessential cross-country walking!

Saw nothing?! HEY! That's not right! Something's missing. What's wrong with this picture? Reggie. Where was Reggie? WHERE *WAS* REGGIE? There was no Reggie in sight! "Reggie!" I yelled. No answer. What a change of realities! I started to talk to myself. "This is ridiculous, how can anyone get lost out here? I can see everywhere!" I turned around. "I couldn't have passed him," I thought. Nope, Reggie wasn't behind me.

Photo by Steve Breakstone

"REGGIE!" I yelled again. No answer. There wasn't even an echo. "Maybe a car stopped and Reggie decided to ride the rest of the way," I said to Dixie. "No, he wouldn't do that. Besides, I don't remember any cars."

I kept walking. "REGGIE?!" There was no way Reggie could be lost, so it seemed silly to start worrying. Dixie and I kept our eyes open and kept on walking down the road. "RE—GGIE!?" I headed to the spot where I last saw him. "We'll find him," I could hear Dixie say to me. Then, all of a sudden, out of the tall grass on the side of the road came a soft, moaning voice. "Schlicky, Schlicky." Dixie ran over to see her Uncle Reggie lying on the side of the road. She began to lick his face. She was very concerned. So was I. My heart was pounding. Did Reggie get hit by a car? Did he twist his ankle? Did he get bit by a crazed animal?

"Oh my gosh! Are you O.K.? What happened?" I asked him, bending down to his aid.

His eyes were shut. He began to speak. "O.K., Steve, now make believe I'm hurt and laying on the side of the road. What do you do?"

Thank God, he wasn't hurt. He was just testing me. "Testing me!?!" I thought. "I'll kill him! No. I'm much too nice of a guy. I'll just hurt him a little. Maybe a lot!"

I took a deep breath, as big as all outdoors. "Alright, Reg," I finally answered, plainly. "I'd see what was wrong and think what I could do to help. If you were hurt real bad, I'd either stop a car for help or find a phone and call 9-1-1. You *are* O.K., aren't you?"

"Yep," he said as he bounced back up. "I'm a good actor!"

Reggie had scared me at first, but I decided not to injure him for real. In fact, I was quite impressed. He thought up a way to test how I would handle an emergency, and with a sense of humor, too! Reggie *was* a good actor. The more we walked, the more his natural cleverness found new expression. The more we walked, the more Janet, Dixie and I learned about Reggie.

"That was a good test Reg, and good acting. You were lying still for fifteen minutes, but do me a favor—NEVER SCARE ME LIKE THAT AGAIN!!!!"

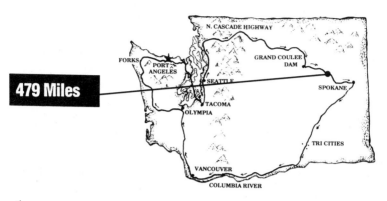

chapter 18

The WILBUR
WELCOME WAGON

"Spokane—64 miles," read the sign on the road
as we entered the town of Wilbur. Ever since
the beginning of WALKABOUT, everyone (including Janet and myself) had wondered if we would
even make it all the way across the state—let
alone all around Washington. Reggie was
quickly destroying all those doubts. Now it was
just a question of *when* Reggie would make it
across the state. A few more days of walking in
warm weather along one straight road of rolling
wheat fields would provide that answer.

Once again there were no campgrounds. In
fact, the map showed no more campgrounds
until we got all the way to the Oregon border,
and that was over three walking-weeks away!
There wasn't even a tree or a baseball field to
hide behind. We'd have to sleep somewhere.
But, where? The challenges never ended.

"Where are we going to sleep tonight?"
Reggie asked at lunch time. Janet had already
met that challenge.

"I contacted a friend of a friend of a friend. They said that they could put us up for a night."

"Good!" Reggie said. He was always more at ease when he was sure we wouldn't have to sleep on the side of the road.

"I thought you didn't mind sleeping on the side of the road," I said.

"Big joke!" he exclaimed. I wasn't sure I understood the punchline.

"Well, it might not be such a big joke," Janet said, seriously. "It's very comforting to know that we have a place set-up for tonight. Unfortunately, the sleeping arrangements for the days ahead are very uncertain. After our evening with the 'friend of a friend of a friend,' we might have to camp somewhere off the side of the road."

"Are you saying that we have run out of group homes, friends, contacts and campgrounds?" I asked.

"Yup," said Janet.

"No problem, right?" said Reggie. "We can camp out."

"I guess you're right, Reg," I said. "I'm not too worried." I looked at Janet. "Something always pops up, even if it's just a gravel pit a little off the highway."

Janet wasn't quite as certain but said, "Thanks for the vote of confidence."

Wilbur is a small town on Route 2. Jack and Jo Robertson were our Wilbur Welcome Wagon. Not only did they put us up for the night, they welcomed the WALKABOUT team with a traditional steak and potato dinner.

Jack and Jo emitted an energy that was stimulating. They were retired farmers, but far from resigned to sit around watching the sun set. "We keep busy," I remember Jack saying as we ate dinner and got to know each other. His humble tone implied that it was an understatement.

After stuffing our faces with Jo's gourmet cooking, it occurred to us that we'd forgotten about leaving room for dessert.

"No mind," said Jo, quite spry and ready to entertain, "that'll give me a chance to show off my corner of Washington."

Leaving Jack and Dixie behind to relax, Janet, Reggie and I piled into Jo's car for a riding tour of things we couldn't see while walking on the main road.

Passing fields that stretched towards the horizon and farm houses that have seen decades of harvests spurred some thoughts in all of our heads. It could have been the late 20th century, early 1920s or mid 1800s. Parts of modern-day Washington follow no calendar.

"You know," said Reggie, breaking the silence. "I used to live on a farm, too."

"That's right," I said. "I remember you telling me about that."

"When was that, Reggie?" asked Jo.

"Oh," Reggie said, thoughtfully, "when I was a little boy."

"That long ago, huh?" Janet said, kidding Reggie about his age.

"I'm becoming an ol' grandpa, now," smiled Reggie. We all laughed.

"Wait a second, weren't you in your twenties when you lived on a farm, Reg?" I said.

"Just giving you a hard time," he responded.

"I think I created a monster," I commented.

"Did your farm look like the farms around here?" Jo asked Reggie, sweeping her arm to indicate the open fields.

"Nope. We had lots of trees." Reggie had spent almost all of his life on the west side of the Cascades.

"Did you grow food or did you have animals?" I asked.

"Oh, we had lots of chickens. A cow. A cat. We had a garden. And we had a dog. He was a good woods dog. Just like Schlicky."

"I didn't know that. How interesting. What was the dog's name?"

"Hmmmm." Reggie squeezed his mouth and closed one eye trying to remember back. "Toko. I liked him. I was sad when he died."

"That happens," I said quietly.

Janet, who was sitting in the front seat, turned back to face Reggie. She gazed into his eyes, looking for the Reggie that was below the surface. For the five years that Janet had known him, she usually just thought of Reggie as a 43-year-old man living at the group home, trying to enjoy life and hoping to someday get his own apartment. Finally she said, "You know Reg, you don't talk that much about your past, but when you do I get to learn so much more about you. You have interesting things to tell us."

"No problem," said Reggie.

"That part I already know about," Janet said, playfully reaching over to smack Reggie on the knee.

Jo laughed along with us. Then she continued the tour. "See all that land?" Jo asked, pointing through all the windows in the car. "Until you can't see anymore?"

"Yes."

"That's our farm."

"Wow!" was all that Reggie, Janet or I could utter. Our eyes scanned far and wide.

"Jack's family and my family homesteaded this land over a hundred years ago."

I thought for a moment, then said in amazement, "That means that this land has been in your families since before Washington State was Washington State!"

"I guess so," Jo said. Perhaps she had not thought of it from that perspective before. "Of course, Jack and I live in town now, and the kids do most of the work." She continued the tour and showed us wheat fields and gullies and creeks and canyons where Jack had played as a little boy.

"The town was named after a man called Wilbur Condit," explained Jo. "But the local Indians called him 'Wild Goose' Bill. That's because he once mistook a gaggle of tame geese for wild ones and shot several of them. After that he was called Wild Goose Bill, but the name of the town is just plain Wilbur."

The daylight hours in the Pacific Northwest, especially in a state as far north as Washington, get shorter and shorter as October wears on. Soon it was too dark to see, so Jo took us back to her house for dessert. "In these parts, a meal ain't a meal without dessert," Jo said with a chuckle, "even if it is a little late."

We made it back to the house, and as Jo prepared to serve a delectable pound cake with fresh blackberry preserves, we had some time to chat some more with Jack. "I'll pass up a tour, but dessert is a different story," Jack said as Jo brought the pound cake to the table. A man that had seen many harvests, bumper crops and ruined fields, he was laid-back, quiet, serious, and good-humored. Jack showed a different side of himself as his eyes lit up in anticipation of the sweet tastes about to hit his lips. He showed great patience as he graciously served us all before cutting a piece for himself.

Photo by Janet Phipps

Janet: "Get going, guys."
Steve: "But it's sooo far!"

Jack took a bite, satisfying his taste buds, and then got down to business. "So, where do you start tomorrow?"

"We walked to Mount Creston today," I answered, wiping the delicious preserves off what had now become my blue chin.

"Mount Creston?" Jack was confused. He held a tasty morsel an inch from his waiting lips. "Where's that? I've lived around Wilbur all my life and I've never heard of Mount Creston," he said.

"You know," I said with a grin on my face, "the next town. The one nine miles up from here." We had actually walked past Wilbur, and Janet had to drive us back for our evening with the Robertsons.

"That's not *Mount* Creston, that's just Creston."

"Well, it seems like a mountain when you walk there, right Reg?"

"Aw heck," said Jack. "I think you guys have walked a few too many miles." Jack laughed and finally took another bite. He swallowed and added, "Wait a minute. I've driven that road millions of times. It's a flat road."

"Oh yeah? I'd bet that in all the years you've lived here you never actually *walked* to 'Mount' Creston, have you?" I asked.

"That's true. I've never even considered it."

"I'll tell you what. You walk it once and then you tell me if it's flat or uphill."

"Yes. You can walk with us," Reggie said hopefully.

"Well, maybe I'll just take your word for it," Jack said. He reached over and gave Reggie a pat on the back as he flashed a smile.

"When you walk as much as we do, you discover that there are a lot more uphills. When you ride in a car you just don't notice," I said, with a tone that appeared to be one of mocking complaint. Deep down, of course, it was moments like these, evenings with special people like Jack and Jo, that made all the uphills worthwhile.

For a few minutes, we all concentrated on dessert before I shared a thought that sparked in my mind. "Hey, I just thought of something." All heads turned toward me as if I had something very profound to say. "Reggie, you said you used to live on a farm. Who'd you say you lived with?"

Reggie swallowed his bite. "My mom and Uncle Dick," he answered.

"And what's my dog's name?"

"Schlicky!" Reggie simply answered my questions. Jo, Jack and Janet were wondering what I was getting at.

"Now, say 'DICK'," I requested.

"Dick," said Reggie, as clear as if he didn't have a speech disorder.

"Now, say 'SEE'."

"See," he said just as clearly.

"Now say Dick See."

"SCHLICKY!" he cried.

We all laughed so hard that pound cake almost came flying through our noses. "Something tells me that you're smarter than all of us put together, Reg," said Janet.

"Just giving you a bad time," Reggie said, enjoying his joke. Reggie had put the capper on the evening as it turned into night and our hosts showed us to our beds. Our first indoor beds since we had been west of the Cascades had us sleeping so deeply that we didn't even feel the passage of time.

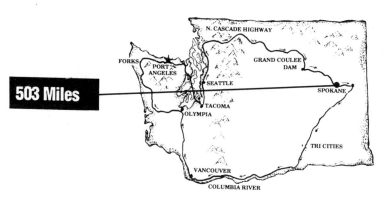

503 Miles

chapter 19

SURPRISES

When the dawn broke, there was frost on the ground. The Robertsons had saved us from sleeping outside in below-freezing temperatures. The sun rose and melted the morning ice crystals off the grass. It would be a good day to walk.

"Where are we going to sleep tonight?" Reggie asked Janet as we sat down to breakfast with Jo. Jack had been up and out before the dawn—we had seen our last of him.

Janet paused. As of yet, she didn't have a good answer. She didn't even have a bad answer. Jo broke in and asked, "Have you stayed in many churches?"

Reggie, Janet and I all looked at each other with raised eyebrows. "We forgot all about that," Janet finally said. "Until today there was always at least somewhere to pitch the tents. With all this wide open land, I figured that I'd just have to look a little harder to find a good out-of-the-way place. I've been confident that something would just pop up. It always does."

"Well, let me call a pastor in Davenport,"

said Jo. "By tonight, you should be close enough to stay there."

Jo made the call, and within moments we were all set up. "See," Janet said to Jo with a smile, "something always pops up."

We hugged Jo goodbye, and Janet dropped us off at our starting spot at "Mount" Creston. Reggie, Dixie and I headed into the rising sun as the blowing winds, pushing over the hills, tried to blow us back to Seattle. With no trees to slow it down, the wind rushed into us like the Skagit River bouncing over smooth stones.

Did it blow out our spirits? No way! Nothing, but nothing, was going to slow us down! We were averaging between 14 and 15 miles a day. Looking past the upcoming town of Davenport, we had Spokane in our sights.

We were on to new adventures—beginning with our first night in a church basement. Janet picked us up that evening and we drove to the church to meet the preacher.

We knocked on the front door of the church and out came a tall, slightly-built man with deep-set eyes. "Hello. You must be the folks that Jo Robertson called about."

"That's us!" answered Janet. She smiled her biggest smile and awaited an invitation to come right on in.

The preacher stood in the doorway, put his hands on the doorframe, blocking the entrance, and said, "Well, tell you what. I can't have you sleep in the church tonight." He paused, as if he didn't have another thing to say about it. Our faces went blank. It was getting a little late to try and find new accommodations. "But I've made arrangements for you to stay at the Circle S Motel down the street. How's that?"

Janet, Reggie and I looked at each other. We didn't know what to say. "Just tell them who you are and you'll be all set up. Well, I've got to get back to work, good luck to ya'll." He smiled, closed the door and that was the last we saw of him.

We had nothing to say or do but head to the motel. We drove to the Circle S, told the manager who we were, and the next thing we knew we were given two keys. "All bought and paid for," the woman said. "I hope you don't mind, one of them is a kitchenette."

"Did the preacher tell you that we were traveling with a dog?"

"Oh sure, that's fine. Bring her on in, I'd like to meet her. She can meet my dog."

"Do you get the feeling we are blessed?" Janet said quietly. She looked to the sky, and I was uncertain if she was joking or not.

We moved in, plopped down on the beds and turned on the T.V. It had been so long since we'd watched television that we almost forgot how to turn one on! Then we noticed the kitchen. A real kitchen made us happy, and soon Janet headed to the local grocery store. "You guys are in for a treat tonight," she promised. She went out to get some fresh food in order to attempt some real kitchen cooking! Oh, boy! (I guess.)

Reggie was also very excited to be in a motel. It wasn't too often he was a guest in one. After so many nights sleeping in a tent on the ground, sleeping on a bed had finally become a novelty.

Dixie looked around the room. I could tell she was lost in thought. I figured she was looking for the most comfortable place to snuggle into a deep sleep on the thick carpet. But Dixie's no fool. She slowly, and perhaps ever so slyly, walked over to the queen-size bed, looked at me, looked back at the bed and stepped up, one paw at a time. She made three circles with her body and plopped down. Immediately her eyes closed. She was asleep. Reggie and I watched her and laughed.

"Shhh! The baby is asleep," said Reggie, putting his index finger to his lips.

"We should tape a 'Do not Disturb' sign on her head," I whispered.

Reggie went to lay down on his bed, and I quietly crawled into bed beside my "daughter." A nap before dinner would be delightful. This was high-class living!

Back from the grocery store, Janet burst into the room. "I'M BACK!" she cried. We jumped up from our sound snoozing as if a rocket had blasted off under our backsides. By instinct, Dixie jumped off the bed, growling and showing her teeth, but stopped short of grabbing Janet's leg.

"Sorry guys," Janet said, with much too much energy. She bent down and Dixie gave her a kiss. Janet wiped her face and Dixie wagged her tail. "Hey, I forgot to tell you," Janet added, looking up. "I have two more surprises. Remember last week when I called home? Well, I asked them to send our mail to the Davenport Post Office. I picked it up today and look what they sent!"

Janet unrolled what turned out to be a HUGE banner for

Reggie, at least eight feet long. Some friends had written notes, others drew pictures, some just signed their names.

"Look, Reggie, here's Harvey's name. And here's Steve Schoos', and Greg Brack's," I said, pointing to where his friends had signed their names.

Reggie ran his hand over their names. "I miss them," Reggie said thoughtfully. "Did Rob sign it?"

"Right here," pointed Janet. "It says, 'Good job, Reggie. You are making us all very proud! Your friend, Rob Campbell'"

We looked over the banner for ten minutes. Looking at the notes and pictures made us all think about home. "I miss my friends," Reggie said. His eyes were a bit glassy.

"You ready to go home?" I asked the question as if I was truly serious, only to hear what Reggie had to say.

"No way," smiled Reggie. "Tell them to come here!"

"Way to go, Reg!" Janet said, walking over to the kitchen.

Dixie went back to sleep, and Reggie and I continued to look over the banner. Janet turned on the stove and threw some brown stuff, gray stuff, yellow stuff, green stuff and some onions into a pan and stirred it with a wooden spoon. "Eat it or starve," I quietly reminded Reggie as Janet brought it over to the small table by the window.

"Now for the second surprise."

Reggie sat down and looked at his plate. "Yup, this is a surprise alright."

Janet's eyes became laser beams. "EAT IT OR STARVE!"

"Yes, Ma'am," we said obediently. We took a mouthful and it *was* a surprise. Reggie and I didn't know what it was, but it wasn't too bad. We even complimented her.

"O.K. Now for the *third* surprise. I was fund-raising outside the grocery store today and a woman stopped to find out what WALKABOUT was all about. She became very excited about the idea and she told me that she teaches at the local grade school. She wanted to know if you guys would be walking near the school. She asked if you would be able to stop by and talk to the children."

"What did you tell her?" I asked.

"I figured that Davenport is not a very big town, and anywhere within the city limits had to be near the school. I told her I'd ask you about it, and I'd call her and let her know."

"What do you think, Reg?"

"I like that."

"This is what WALKABOUT's all about. Call her up. We'll be there!"

The next morning, after about one and a half hours of walking beside the crisp wheatfields of rural Davenport, Reggie, Dixie and I walked into the school with our packs still strapped to our backs. The teacher had met us outside the room and informed us that she had given the kids an overview of WALKABOUT. As we walked through the classroom door, we were greeted with a round of "Oohs" and "Ahhs."

"Hi, friends."

"Hi!" came the resounding greeting. Five rows of bright-eyed, energetic young students wiggled in their chairs.

"How many of you have ever walked from Davenport all the way to Reardon?" I asked energetically. Reardon is the next closest town, fourteen miles east of Davenport. The kids made comments which, roughly interpreted, made it clear they thought I was nuts. Of course, not one student raised a hand. "Well, that's how far Reggie, Dixie and I walk every day!"

"Wow," whispered one student under her breath. She turned red when she realized that I'd heard her.

"That's right! WOW! And every day, when we finish walking, we don't go back to our homes and sleep in our beds. We sleep in other people's houses or sometimes we sleep in a tent in the woods."

"We slept in a gravel pit," added Reggie.

"That's right, once we even slept in a gravel pit," I repeated for the students that couldn't understand Reggie very well. "We sleep wherever we can find a place. And each morning we wake up and walk another 14 or so miles."

Reggie and I had discussed how to best give the presentation. He preferred that I did most, but not all, of the talking. He was still shy, and he knew that with his speech disorder it would be very difficult for the children to understand him.

"Why are you doing this?" a boy in the front row asked.

"That's a great question. We are WALKABOUT! Reggie is a man who has a developmental disability. A developmental disability is a mental and/or physical disability that comes about before the age of 18 (or 22 depending on the state) and may continue for the life of that person. These disabilities can include mental retardation, cerebral palsy, autism, epilepsy, blindness, deafness, and a lot of other things."

Although I tried to make it as simple as possible so that the kids could understand, I was confident the teacher would explain the words the students didn't understand after we left. "We are walking around Washington to show people that even though it may be harder for Reggie to do the same things *non*disabled people can do, it doesn't mean that he can't *ever* do the same things. Reggie is proving that if you give a person a chance, he or she can do anything they want to. Reggie is good at walking. He is walking around the whole state to teach people that every person has the ability to accomplish anything they want. All a person needs is family and friends to give him or her a chance. Reggie wants to be accepted for who he is, just like any one of you. In fact, the most important part of WALKABOUT is that it shows that people with developmental disabilities are really no different from anybody else."

"I'm smart, too," added Reggie.

"Yes, Reggie is very smart," I said, looking over to Reggie. "Unfortunately, some people don't think he is. They see how he is a little different, or that he doesn't speak very clearly, or they don't understand why it sometimes takes him longer to understand something. For those reasons they don't show him a lot of respect. Even if he wasn't very smart or just because it takes him a long time to learn things, it is important to treat him as we all want to be treated."

"How do people become disabled?" one child asked.

"Some people are born with brain damage, and that causes a disability. Sometimes it happens after a person is born. I know some people that got very sick, and that caused brain damage. Other people have been in a car accident or have fallen down so hard that it injured their brain."

The kids were very interested and listened closely. How much they understood is a question I cannot answer.

Under a banner showing the letters of the alphabet, the teacher had posted a large Washington State map. I knew it stood out and held the students' attention. I walked over to it and traced where we had walked and where we were headed. The kids stared with eyes wide and mouths hanging open.

"Hey, wait a second. That's really far!" said one doubtful student from the back. "You're not even halfway finished yet. If Reggie doesn't make it, doesn't that mean he couldn't do it?"

There's one in every crowd, but I appreciated the question as it gave me the chance to say, "Not necessarily. All it means is that he decided not to finish. He can make that decision for any number of reasons. Hasn't anyone here ever started a project and then got bored with it?" I didn't see any volunteers so I pointed to a girl. "How about you?"

Her eyes twitched back and forth, searching for an answer. "Uh, yes," she finally answered.

"What was the project?" I asked.

She thought for a moment and then said, "I didn't finish a puzzle."

Why not?" I asked.

"I got bored," she said. "But I may go back to it someday. I still have it in my bedroom."

Another little girl held up her hand. I looked at her and nodded my head. "I started to clean my room yesterday, but then I decided to go to the living room and watch T.V."

Standing in the back, Janet and the teacher let out a giggle. So did I. We were joined by the whole classroom. I'm sure everyone was able to relate. The girl blushed deep red.

"So you see," I continued, after waiting for the class to quiet down, "it is easier to be aware of differences, but when you look deeply, everyone is basically the same. And just because you change your mind, or decide not to finish something, or don't win first prize, it doesn't mean that you are less important, or that you deserve less respect. It just means that you are an individual with the right to change your mind. So to answer the question, if Reggie decided not finish the walk around Washington, it may not mean anything except that he used his free choice to make a new decision. I looked over to Reggie and expected him to say, "I'll make it," or at least offer a "No problem," but all he did was shrug and smile.

"What's in your backpack?" popped the next question from a voice in the back.

Reggie unzipped his pack and started unpacking. After every item that Reggie took out—sunglasses, sweatshirt, rain jacket, canteen, Walkman radio, and other small things—I explained why it was important. Then Reggie took out a Snickers bar. The kids howled. I didn't even try to explain that one.

After tons of questions about our life on the road, and after every student had a chance to pet "the dog with the backpack," the whole class went outside to take a group picture with us WALKABOUTers. Then the whole class became Official Honorary WALKABOUTers as they walked us back through town.

"Hey," I yelled to our young fellow WALKABOUTers as we neared the highway, "can anyone tell me, in five words or less, why Reggie, Dixie and I are walking around Washington?"

A hand shot up. "So people can learn about people with disabilities?" a young boy said, not quite sure if he had it right.

"Good. Anything else?"

"So you can learn about people," another boy called out.

"Very good! Sometimes even I forget about that one. How about one more?"

The children were all quiet. Finally I heard a shy voice answering the question with a question. "Because you want to?"

"I like to walk," answered Reggie.

"Excellent. We like to walk. We want to walk and it's fun. And everyone's life should include doing things that are fun! Right?"

"Right!" they all answered. The kids crowded around us, shook our hands, patted Dixie, and we said our final good-byes. Our friends watched and waved as Reggie, Dixie and I headed for the horizon.

A few miles down the road I was thinking about what I had said to the students. Finally, I turned around to Reggie. He was a short distance behind me and when he caught up I asked, "Hey Reg, is it O.K. with you that I use you as an example? Do you mind that I refer to you as a man with a developmental disability?"

"That's O.K. with me, Steve," Reggie replied thoughtfully.

"Well, I'm glad. But let me know if I ever say anything that you don't like or that you feel is insulting to you. I was concerned that I may have forgotten about your feelings when I talked about you."

"No problem," he said, reassuring me with a pat on my shoulder. "I don't mind."

The Walkabouters of Davenport, Washington

The sun was shining strong and the land stretched on forever in every direction. There was a gentle breeze blowing, and we easily made it to the outskirts of Reardon by the time Janet came to pick us up.

"Hey, guys, the pastor of a church in Reardon is going to let us spend the night in a room usually set aside for weekend socials. We are on a roll!"

"Way to go, Jan!"

"No problem!"

We piled into the WALKABOUT-Mobile and headed for "home." On the way, Janet told us about two young ladies she had met. "After lunch I went back to the same store as yesterday to sell WALKABOUT buttons and T-shirts," she began. "I had just gotten the table set up when two little girls came up to me. The bigger one was dragging the smaller one behind her. They were both so cute and shy and I smiled at them.

"'Taking your friend for a drag?' I asked them," Janet said to us, describing the scene. "They both beamed smiles. Then the older girl said, 'She's not my friend. She's my sister. Giggle. Giggle.' They were about the cutest things I have ever seen," explained Janet.

"Then the bigger girl said, 'I saw you at school this morning, and Reggie, Dixie and Steve talked to my class.' She thought you were a real neat man, Reggie."

"Hey, they liked me," beamed Reggie.

"They said that you were okay, too, Steve."

"I'll take what I can get," I said. "I'll play second fiddle to you anytime, Reg."

"But she was in love with Dixie. 'Dixie even let me pet her!'" Janet said, imitating the little girl.

Janet drove up to the back door of the small brick church, and we unloaded our pillows, sleeping bags and suitcases full of clothing, soaps and toothbrushes. Staying clean was a priority, even without real showers. There were other houses nearby, but it was dinner time in the small town and we didn't see any neighbors in the street.

We also brought in our food. Janet cooked up some spaghetti in the church-sized kitchen, and Reggie asked if he could help.

"Well, here's a jar of sauce," said Janet. "Go for it."

"I like to cook," said Reggie, opening the jar. I handed him a pot and he went to work.

"You, know, I was thinking," I said, perching on a counter as the chefs were busy cooking. "Schools are great places to stress the importance that all people deserve equal chances. Most school children are very open to being friends with all kinds of people. They have a natural way of trusting that most of us older people forget about. The teacher even mentioned to me that one of the students had a developmental disability." The student was there learning new things and doing the best he could, just like everyone else.

"That makes sense," broke in Janet. "You know, Jack and Jo were really great people and very friendly. But I have no idea what they thought about people with disabilities before they met Reggie."

"They liked me. I was very nice," said Reggie. I think he wondered if the Robertsons didn't like him.

"Of course, you were as wonderful as always. But the idea of WALKABOUT is not to feel sorry for people with disabilities, but to show people that if given the chance, they can do things for themselves. I wonder if we have been getting that idea across."

Reggie listened very closely. After all the miles and weeks, I was still never quite sure exactly how much he understood. When we asked him about what he was doing, he mostly said he liked to walk and he was having a good time.

"You know," I said, "I like to believe that we are inspiring many people. Some people will never change, but I hope that we're getting some people to re-think their opinion concerning people who have disabilities. We may never know...."

"You're right," interrupted Janet. "All we can do is the best we can. We may come and go, but we are leaving behind our message. We can only hope that people understand it and take it to heart."

"I think the sauce is hot," said Reggie, watching as the sauce began to slowly bubble onto the counter.

"O.K., Reg, turn down the heat." He did, and I took a spoonful and slowly lifted it to my lips. "You can heat things up with the best of them, Reg."

"I'm a good cook!"

"You are good at a lot of things, Reg."

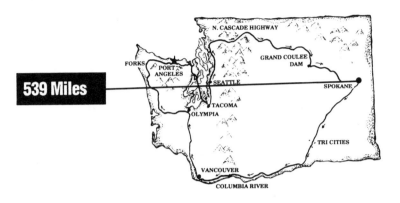

chapter 20

REGGIE'S MEETING

WALKABOUT arrived in Spokane on Friday, October 6, sometime about noon. Plowing our way alongside the thunder of traffic rushing in and out of the city, Reggie Feckley became the first man with a developmental disability to walk *across* the State of Washington!

No one noticed! The cars on the maze of streets were ungracious. No one came to greet us! No one came to offer congratulations, no photographer snapped a picture. With almost 200,000 residents, Spokane was a city big enough where you'd expect that somebody would have acknowledged this tremendous accomplishment. Nope! We were incredibly disappointed, let down, disillusioned, crushed.... Need I go on?

We couldn't even find a place to sleep! Janet called around but no one in Spokane would accept Dixie—not a church or a group home. They cringed at the thought of a dog sleeping inside their establishment. Dixie had walked every mile that Reggie and I had; she watched over us, kept us safe and kept us going. She was as much a part of WALKABOUT as anyone. It was discouraging to hear the same thing everywhere we went. "She's a dog. We can't allow dogs. Sorry."

I wanted to turn south and get out of there as fast as our legs could carry us, but Janet said we couldn't leave. "The last time I talked to the folks at home," she explained, "they told me that Mary Holden was coming out and we had to wait for her. They said she was planning a small gathering for us."

"When?" I asked. My lack of desire to hang out in Spokane was quite evident. Mary was a wonderfully, enthusiastic sprite of a woman who worked within our company, helping people with disabilities get jobs in the community. Unfortunately, I wasn't really in the mood to wait around for anyone or anything. It just didn't seem worth it. WALKABOUT deserved to be treated better than a dead fish in a big pond. Reggie's feat was unmatched, and we all deserved more respect than we were being offered here in Spokane.

"She'll be here Monday," answered Janet.

We looked at Reggie and he said nothing. He just shrugged his shoulders. He was taking his cue from us.

It didn't appear as if anyone cared if we stayed, but we couldn't leave Mary hanging. Well, if Dixie wasn't welcome at anyone's house or even a church basement, we'd find someplace where she was. "I guess there is always Plan 'B'" I said mechanically. "And if that doesn't work," I added, "we can go to Plan 'C' or Plan 'D.'"

"What are Plan 'C' and 'D'?" sighed Janet. I could tell that she thought I was just trying to cheer her up. She wasn't too far off the mark.

"I don't know. I haven't thought that far ahead yet," I replied quietly. Fortunately, Plan B worked out fine. Ten miles outside of the city was Riverside State Park, and we camped out. Dixie was welcome, even if she had to be kept on a leash. It was a little cold, but we were all together. If nothing else, we always had each other.

Janet and I moped around, wondering what we were doing out in the middle of a state park ten miles from town. No one seemed to care about us. No one even noticed that we had walked all the way across the State of Washington. WALKABOUT was supposed to be raising awareness—obviously, we weren't. As the old saying goes, "The higher the expectations, the harder the letdown." In a city as big as Spokane, we felt we should have at least found a real bed to sleep in, with a real roof to sleep under. With nothing good to say about feeling unappreciated, we quietly went about setting up camp.

"I want to have a WALKABOUT team meeting," Reggie announced. "Steve, Schlicky, Janet, I want to tell you something." Janet and I looked at each other, shrugged our shoulders, and brought Dixie over to Reggie. We all gathered around the picnic table near the fire to hear what Reggie had to say.

"I'm proud of myself. I'm happy I made it to Spokane. Steve helped me to cut down on my cigars, and he taught me how to eat smart. Schlicky's a really good dog and a good friend. Steve is a good man. He helped me out. He let us use his truck. It was fun going through the mountains. Schlicky's a good woods dog. Janet showed me how to build a fire and cut wood. She always found us a place to sleep. We wash in lakes and rivers 'cause there are no showers. I've had a great time!"

Janet and I were blown away! There were times when it seemed as if Reggie thought he was just out for a very long walk. Now it was clear that he knew that this *was* something special. And DAMMIT, it was! Walking to Spokane from Port Angeles was one heck of an accomplishment! Five minutes earlier, Janet and I were ready to pack the car and go back home. After Reggie's meeting, we were ready to walk around the planet!

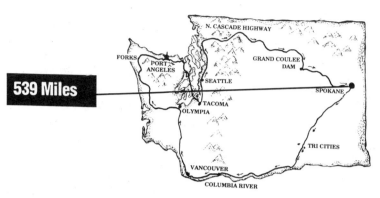

539 Miles

chapter 21

The SPOKANE 'EXTRAVAGANZA' ...and the First Lady

Sunday afternoon we packed up camp and headed for a motel. Janet had been instructed to have us cleaned up and looking our best for the people we were scheduled to meet on Monday afternoon. We dipped into our food money and invested in one room for the four of us.

After their long drive from Port Angeles, Mary Holden and a friend of Reggie's named Poncho met up with us. Mary and Poncho were both excited to come out and congratulate Reggie on his accomplishment. It was great seeing a couple of friends from home. They were people that loved us, supported us, and cared about what we were doing.

Mary told us that some people she knew wanted to congratulate Reggie, too, and that they were waiting at Spokane's famous Riverfront Park. We weren't sure what the big deal was, but whenever we had a chance to meet people, we met them. Obviously, not many people cared, but we didn't want to disappoint those that did.

The crowded city made parking difficult, but we managed to find a parking spot a few blocks from the park. With Dixie leading the way, Mary, Poncho, Janet, Dixie, Reggie and I all walked to the park together.

An island of gently rolling hills, lush lawns, and waterfalls was surrounded by the Spokane River. This island is Spokane's famous Riverfront Park. Home of the 1974 World's Fair, people come to the park on any given day to enjoy arts and crafts, theater, music, ice skating and more. Today a few people were going to be there to see something a little different, but quite special.

We crossed the last street, came around the corner of a tall office building, and noticed a tremendous crowd of people standing around an open field. We could see them milling about, chatting amongst themselves. It appeared as if they were waiting for some musicians to start playing, or a street juggler to begin performing. We walked towards them, and as we got closer, someone pointed in our direction and a cheer filled the air. They were there for WALKABOUT!?!?

Janet, Reggie and I looked at each other. Immediately, I grabbed Reggie's arm and, with clasped hands held high and smiles as big as Spokane, Reggie, Dixie and I walked ahead of the others into Riverfront Park to the cheers of the crowd.

Bright banners welcomed WALKABOUT. People from the Association for Retarded Citizens, the Washington State Centennial Commission, residents of local group homes and other people who worked at a local workshop for people with developmental disabilities cheered us with every step. Bystanders passing by or enjoying lunch in the fresh air crowded around, attracted by the electricity in the air. Standing on the side were photographers, newspaper reporters and television cameras recording it all! Microphones came at us from everywhere.

"Ladies and Gentlemen," I said, thinking quickly, "I'd like to introduce to you the first man with a developmental disability to walk across the state of Washington, MR. REGGIE FECKLEY!!!"

People cheered, clapped and crowded around to ask Reggie, Janet and me questions about WALKABOUT. Photographers and television camerapeople were taking pictures. Everyone wanted to shake hands with us. We were immersed in a spirit of humanity that established WALKABOUT as a true extravanganza of body and soul. Since Seattle, Reggie and I had practiced talking into a microphone for occasions just like this, and that practice had made him perfect! Reggie answered questions from every reporter.

We were dazed! We were overwhelmed! We were thrilled! We soaked in every last compliment. We shook every last hand. We felt like we were in dreamland. As if we were sharing a dream that sped past our eyes and seemed so real during its colorful moments, we awoke pressed to remember any of the details of the fantasy.

After a long haze-like while, the crowd dispersed. We were jolted out of our "dream come true" when we were whisked away to tour a factory whose employees included people with disabilities. We were shown that WALKABOUT was part of a much bigger family, and it was glorious.

Day turned into evening, and as we ate dinner at the house of one of the new friends we had made, we awaited the evening news.

"I don't know why they bother talking about international terrorism and how bad the economy is doing," I said. "Let's face it, all the people want to hear about is Reggie and WALKABOUT."

Everyone agreed, and just then the announcer broke in, "Coming up—meet a man who is walking over a thousand miles spreading an important message."

We anxiously waited through too many commercials, and finally the news came back on. We all quieted down to relive our moments of fame.

"'Anyone can do anything if you give them the chance'—that's the message Reggie Feckley, Steve Breakstone and Breakstone's dog, Dixie, are spreading as they walk around Washington," the news reporter announced.

"Reggie is proving that it's time to give all our friends the opportunity to show just how much they really can do," explained my voice on the television. "It's time to open our arms to everyone." The camera panned out and showed Reggie surrounded by people cheering and yelling in appreciation of his efforts.

The reporter broke in and said, "The walkers are making people aware that people with disabilities are, first and foremost, people, and are capable of doing things that some people might not think possible. Mr. Feckley is striving to raise awareness that people with developmental disabilities deserve equal respect, rights and opportunities."

"I'm famous!" cried Reggie.

"You bet you are!" exclaimed Janet, giving him a great big hug. Everyone in the apartment came over to congratulate Reggie and slap him on the back.

"I like being on T.V. It's fun!!" Reggie told me again and again. We watched ourselves getting awards and giving speeches, surrounded by so many people who looked up to Reggie for what he had done.

Knowing that we had to get our nose back to the grindstone, or rather our boots back to the pavement, we left our new friends to spend one more night at a motel. We had gotten three days of much-needed rest, and the Extravaganza had given us the boost we needed to carry us the 600 miles back home. We were ready!

But wait! Just as we were ready to pay our motel bill, a young lady working with the centennial committee drove over and told us even more good news. The Governor's wife was in town. Mrs. Booth Gardner had heard about Reggie and asked if she could meet him. "Absolutely!" we shouted. "No problem!" Reggie grinned.

So, it was back to our room for another night of luxury. This made three nights in a row that we would each have a bed to sleep in and a shower in the morning. Could life get better? We were about to find out!

In the morning we went back to Riverfront Park. As we arrived, we were once again greeted by television cameras. A black limousine drove up, and everyone focused on the back doors. A chauffeur exited from the driver's seat, came around the front of the car and opened the back door. Out stepped the beautiful and gracious Jean Gardner.

The camera caught every move as she walked over to Reggie, Janet, Dixie and me. Mrs. Gardner looked us over with a big smile and congratulated us as she shook our hands and patted Dixie on the head. "For the past year we have been celebrating Washington's past. I admire your insight and view of our future as we enter Washington's second one hundred years," she said as the camera

Photo by Janet Phipps

The First Lady meets the "First Man."
At far right: Mrs. Jean Gardner

and microphones caught every word. "As the Chairwoman of the Centennial Committee celebrating Washington State's 100th Birthday, I present to each of you this Certificate of Merit acknowledging WALKABOUT's importance to the State of Washington." She handed one to Reggie, one to me and she even handed another one to me for Dixie. Finally, Dixie had RESPECT!

"Schlicky's famous, too" laughed Reggie. He turned back to Mrs. Gardner and said, "Thank you very much. And these are for you," he said as he presented the first lady with a WALKABOUT T-shirt and button. Reggie impressed everyone as he handed her the gifts with a gentlemanly bow from the waist.

"Thank you, Reggie. I'm so sorry I can't spend any more time with you. I'd love to hear more about your walk, but I came to Spokane on business and I can't get out of those commitments," explained Mrs. Gardner.

"That's O.K. No problem," said Reggie.

"Thank you for understanding. I promise to wear the T-shirt, and I'll meet with you again when you reach Olympia."

Olympia!?! That's the state capitol way back on the other side of the state. When she said it, it seemed so far away, both in distance and in time. Olympia is close to home! Just a few days earlier Janet and I had been wondering if we could go one more mile or one more day, but the appreciation we were shown in Spokane was more than we ever dreamed. Reggie had shown us that he believed in himself and was proud of what he was accomplishing. The Extravaganza had shown us that people really did care about what we were doing. And now, Jean Gardner had shown that she believed in us, too. WALKABOUT was back on track and on its way to Olympia!

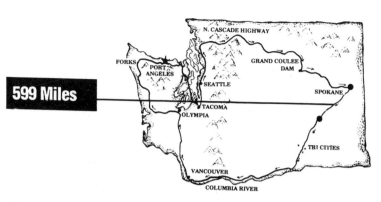

599 Miles

chapter 22

HEADING SOUTH

"You ready to head for home?"

"Nope. Let's walk the United States." Reggie would have been happy to continue east into Idaho.

Of course, Reggie knew that Spokane was the planned turn-around point for WALKABOUT, and he followed Dixie and I south as we began to circle back around the state. The multi-laned highway roared with traffic.

"Well, don't get down, Reg. 'We got a long way to go but a long time to get there. We're gonna do what they say can't be done,'" I sang, misquoting the song from the Burt Reynolds movie, *Smokey and the Bandit.* "Next stop, the Tri-cities! Let's go!"

"More cities?" asked Reggie, stopping in his tracks. The emotional drain of walking through a city was a heavy load. It could be more tiring than a 100° day.

"Don't worry. The three cities are Kennewick, Pasco, and Richland, and all together they're about half the size of Spokane."

"Oh. O.K." Reggie was relieved and continued his pace.

As big and crowded as Spokane was, it wasn't nearly as massive as Seattle. In no time flat we were out of the city limits and surrounded by countryside. We put Spokane behind us, forgetting the bad, remembering the great.

We headed southeast and soon we were walking on a highway surrounded by land that was open and bare, dotted with the occasional small town. The recently harvested wheat that had covered the land was off to the mills. Left behind were fields of short, cropped wheatstalks. Freshly-plowed fields with long straight lines scraped along the surface also stretched out before us. The lines in the brown earth sprouted short green shoots of newly planted winter wheat for next summer's harvest.

Some days the weather was warm and some days it was cool, but it was never too hot or too cold. Some days the sun shone high and bright, and other days overcast skies dropped some raindrops.

Along this peaceful road, Reggie walked at a greater and greater distance behind me as his confidence grew and he learned to appreciate his private time. Dixie ran around catching the scents of rabbits and birds. I was enjoying my private time, too, watching Dixie play, and thinking about Reggie's growth. I began to realize that every step we took now was a step closer to home.

The second half of WALKABOUT started off easy. In Cheney, Janet met Pastor Buckaloo of the Lutheran Church. Not only did he let us spend the night in his church, he gave Janet the names of pastors in the nearby towns of Sprague, Ritzville and Lind. In one fell swoop we had places to sleep for the next week!

The good Pastor also had a friend who was a professor at Eastern Washington University in Cheney. He helped arrange for me to give a speech to some of the students there. I only spoke for a few minutes, but the students understood the spirit of WALKABOUT. They came up afterward and donated money, offered us places to sleep and invited us to dinner. Friends were coming out of the woodwork!

In this area of Washington there wasn't usually much for us to do but walk. We walked through pleasant little towns separated by endless rolling fields. Towns with names like Tyler, Fishtrap and Sprague. All was pleasant and peaceful. We were all enjoying ourselves.

Reggie drifted into his own world, and I drifted into mine. Sometimes we didn't talk for miles. Occasionally, I would look back just to make sure he didn't get "misplaced" or try another shot at an "Oscar" nomination by perfecting his acting skills. It wasn't really necessary to check on him, but I did it out of habit, anyway.

Of course, there was that one time I looked back and saw only black asphalt. Reggie's body usually broke up the monotony of the background scenery, but not this time. Reggie wasn't on the road! Once again, I thought, "Where could he possibly be? Oh, Reggie, Reggie, Reggie," I remarked to myself. Through reflex and panic, and as if I had a premonition of tragedy, a hot flush rushed through my body. It covered me with a layer of sweat. Then I noticed that he was on a ridge above the slope of the road, and I chided myself for overreacting and being so silly.

"Hey, Reg," I called to him, "I think you'll find it a lot easier to walk on the hard pavement of the highway." I felt more comfortable when he was exactly where he was supposed to be. It was easier for me to relax and enjoy the walking.

"I like it up here," he replied.

"Yeah, but the ground is soft and you'll tire yourself out. All those wild bushes you have to step around make for extra walking. Come on down and walk on the road."

"I want private time, Steve."

"You can have private time here on the road. It's better down here." No reply. "Hey Reg," I called. He turned to the left and walked even further inland, where I couldn't even see him. Sometimes it was so frustrating when Reggie refused to do things the way I asked him to do them. He could be so stubborn!

"Oh, be quiet, Steve."

"Who said that?" I wondered. There was no one around. It wasn't Reggie, and I knew Dixie didn't say it. Then I realized it was me! I was telling myself to think carefully about the way I was feeling. I thought long and hard and then I said to myself, "Steve, Reg has been doing a great job of walking, and hasn't asked for an extra break in weeks. He has learned to enjoy his own space and have the confidence to walk without you right in front of him. You shouldn't be frustrated, you should be very proud!"

Later on, when Reggie met up with me on the road I said, "I'm sorry about before. As long as you walk safely, and in the right direction, you can walk anywhere you want."

"I'm a good walker, Steve," he told me. And he was right. He was a great walker! Now I could see that he was enjoying the trip more than ever. It occurred to me that the only part of this trip that Reggie might not like was that someday it would end.

Sometimes Reggie walked behind Dixie and me, and sometimes he walked ahead of us. From my perspective, Reggie was a walking stick figure way up the highway when WALKABOUT entered the town of Ritzville. He had really built up his physical stamina and mental determination. Reggie was certainly capable of walking on his own, but I wondered if he would get confused walking through strange towns with all the extra streets.

By the time Dixie and I got to Ritzville, Reggie was so far ahead of us that I couldn't even see him. I scanned the main street of town, but there was no tall stick man with a backpack in sight. I wondered if he'd walked up one of the side streets, or if he'd gone into one of the stores. If so, which one? Who knows what another man has on his mind?

When I walked into town, I went in the first store I saw, a sit-down/drive-thru restaurant, and asked a customer if another man with a backpack had walked past. "He didn't come in here," the man said, "but we saw him pass by about 15 minutes ago." I thanked him and kept on going. "He's gotta be around here somewhere!" I thought.

A few minutes later a car stopped next to Dixie and me. A large lady with curly hair and bad teeth rolled down the window. With one eye wide open and one eye squinted half shut, she asked, "Is the guy down the street with you?"

"A guy with a backpack?" I asked.

"Yeah. He's acting real peculiar, and he's hanging around the bank. Doesn't he know that banks aren't open on Sundays?" Her eyebrows lifted high as she questioned me, but her eyeballs remained fixed, staring directly into my eyeballs. It was as if she was peeking into my brain to see what was really going on in there.

I smiled and giggled, trying to calm her skepticism. "Well, I think he knows that," I said melodically. "He has an uncashed check, but I'm not sure he's aware that it's Sunday. We lose track

Photo by Janet Phipps

**Dancing in
the streets**

of the days all the time. Anyway, he's not really peculiar—he has a developmental disability."

"Oh, I'm sure!" she said in a snippy tone. "But if you don't go get him now, he'll be picked up and taken to Medical Lake Mental Hospital for observation."

The lady was very scary to me and certainly not one of the nicer people we had run into. She decided she wasn't too sure about me either. I guess she didn't like my eyes, or whatever she saw behind them. "What's your nationality?" she asked me.

"American," I answered.

"Yes, of course you are, but what else?"

"My grandparents all came from Eastern Europe. Many people think I'm Italian, though. Why do you ask?"

"I thought maybe you were a runaway Honduran," she said.

I shook my head, shrugged my shoulders and smiled. She gave me one last glare, rolled up her window, turned the car around and sped off, causing a cloud of dust and smoke. It was an interesting encounter. It reminded me that there are all types of people in the world. It would take a long time to teach everyone about all the other people sharing the Earth! People are people, whether they are American, Honduran, have a different color or a developmental disability.

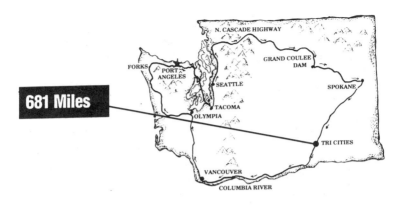

681 Miles

chapter 23

The KIWANIS CLUBS

"You must be Reggie," said a distinguished man in a business suit. He extended his hand and held it out toward Reggie. "I'm Jerry Slope." Jerry Slope was president of one of five Kiwanis clubs that we spoke to in the Tri-Cities area. Jerry had greeted us at the door of a local restaurant where the weekly meeting was taking place. WALKABOUT was the main presentation.

Reggie accepted Jerry's hand and squeezed it tightly. "Hello," he said. I noticed that he remembered how important it was to not only shake hands, but to give a good firm grip. Then he stepped aside and said, "This is Steve Breakstone."

"Nice to finally meet you, Jerry," I said, extending my hand. We had spoken on the phone, discussing details of the presentation we were to give.

"The pleasure is mine, Steve."

"And I'm Janet Phipps. I'm the support driver."

"Pleased to meet you, too, Janet," said Jerry, shaking her hand. Jerry's sincerity shined through his handshake. We were dealing with an outright friendly, intelligent man, a man who held out his heart. Jerry Slope was a man with whom I could become friends. "Hey, where's that wonderful dog I heard so much about?"

"Dixie's napping in the car," I answered. "Maybe you can come out and meet her later."

"It's too bad that she's not also a guide dog. Maybe then they would let her into the restaurant," said Janet. "Or maybe if we put her pack on, and add sunglasses and a hat, they'll think she's just a hairy hiker," she joked.

"Hey, there's an idea," Jerry said, laughing. Then he turned back to me and said seriously, "I'm a strong supporter in causes that help disabled people. I think what you're doing is great. And so exciting."

"Thank you," I said. "We believe in what we are doing." I wasn't sure, but I had a feeling Jerry was talking directly to me. He gave me the impression that he was appreciating that I was walking with Reggie more than he appreciated all of us for the whole project. Of course, Jerry didn't really know what WALKABOUT was all about. That's why he invited us to speak.

"I can't imagine what it's like to walk so many miles. I don't go anywhere without my car." He chuckled. Then he said, "It's really terrific what you are doing for him."

"What I'm doing for him? Think about what Reggie is doing for me."

Jerry flashed a hearty smile, but I wasn't sure he knew what I meant. I think he thought I was just being polite. "Yes, I'm sure you are learning a lot, too." He smiled again and then said, "Come. Let's go inside." He turned and led us to a room filled with about fifty businessmen and women. He led us to a dais table for honored guests and speakers, and said, "Order anything you want. On us!"

"Thank you, Jerry," Reggie answered.

"You're very welcome, Reggie. Excuse me, will you."

"O.K.," said Reggie.

Jerry looked into Reggie's eyes and smiled. He turned around and went over to talk to some other people. "I like him," Reggie added.

We filled our bellies with eggs and pancakes and washed it all down with a glass of chocolate milk. We joined in the singing of

the national anthem, and listened to opening speeches. Then Jerry
went up to the podium and introduced WALKABOUT to the crowd.
He told the crowd who we were and where we had walked. The
crowd applauded politely.

I walked up to the podium and described in detail some of the
adventures and experiences, physical and mental, of the past few
hundred miles. They appreciated the story about Reggie's toilet
paper fire, and laughed at how he tested my reaction to an emergency with his acting performance. Then I concluded my speech
with:

The most important aspect about people with developmental disabilities, people like Reggie, is that they are *people*—
people who should be treated with the same respect as anyone else. Yes, it's true that people like Reggie have certain
problems and disabilities. But we all have problems and disabilities or will develop them sometime in our life. The
important thing to remember is that if people have a desire to
accomplish things, then they *can* accomplish things. People
like Reggie deserve the chance and the opportunity to live a
life as fulfilling as possible. Like all of us, people with disabilities deserve to be given free choice in deciding how and
where they want to live. They deserve the opportunity to
have real jobs. Disabilities do not make *anyone* any less of a
person. All of us, regardless of our disabilities, hidden or
obvious, should have the same rights.

In the past we hid people with developmental disabilities
away from society. They were our friends and relatives, but
we were ashamed of them or we didn't know how to support
them in the community. We took away their rights. We told
them where to live, how to live, who to live with, what to
wear and what to eat—and we rationalized it by thinking that
it was for their own good. Now, at Lauridsen Group Homes,
and in programs which are set up to support people in their
own homes and apartments, we believe that everyone has a
right to be as independent as possible. We believe everyone
has the right and responsibility to become a valuable member
of his or her community. By the same token, everyone also
has the same responsibility to abide by the laws of their town.

Teamwork!

And, of course, everyone has the right to make mistakes.

We are walking to motivate people to think about accepting all people with equal respect in all phases of life and community. WALKABOUT is a 1,300 mile walk with the express purpose of proving that people with developmental disabilities can do anything they want to do if given the right support and opportunity. And if you think it's easy to just walk all day, everyday, I challenge anyone at this meeting to walk three days with us. WALKABOUT is teaching society that people with developmental disabilities, or any other disability, deserve to be treated with the same respect as anyone else.

There is an old saying that goes like this: "Give a person a fish and he eats for a day. Teach a person how to fish and he eats for life." Well, my friends, we have proved that not only can you teach people with disabilities to fish, you can teach them how to gut the fish, cook the fish, clean up afterwards, and how to get the best price on fishing gear at the store. So you can see that helping our friends become more independent is not only the moral thing to do, but it is also best for everyone!

The crowd exploded with a tremendous round of applause. I whispered over to Reggie and asked him to stand up. He did, smiled and added a wave of his hand. The whole room stood up and continued to applaud for three minutes. Reggie beamed. So did Janet and I.

The people at the Kiwanis clubs appreciated the hard work Reggie was doing. Many of them came over to shake Reggie's hand. After a while Jerry came over and said, "You know, Steve, Reggie, and you too, Janet, that was wonderful. You have really made me think."

"How's that?" I asked.

"There's a difference between feeling sorry for someone and seeing someone as an equal. It's easy to see the problems, to think that's just the way the person is and always will be. What we should be looking for is the potential. And then work together to fulfill it. I'm sure you don't want my pity," he said, looking directly to Reggie. "You just want my respect. You have made me see how important it is to not only support you with money, but with my heart. I am beginning to understand that you don't want me to just give you things to have a decent life, but you need the opportunities to make a decent life for yourself."

"I can do many things by myself," Reggie stated softly, turning his eyes toward me.

"Yes. I'm very sure that you can. Perhaps today I will start to look at other people with a little more respect—a respect I didn't realize I wasn't giving them in the first place."

"I'm a man," said Reggie.

"Yes, you are, Reggie," said Jerry, shaking his hand. "A man who should be very proud of himself."

"Thank you," said Reggie. I looked at Reggie, and my smile showed him how proud I was to be his friend. The better Reggie felt about himself, the taller he stood.

"Excuse me for a moment," said Jerry. He walked away for a few minutes and talked to some fellow members. He came back, handed Reggie a piece of paper and said, "I believe this check should help keep WALKABOUT on the road a little longer, and spread your very important message to even more people."

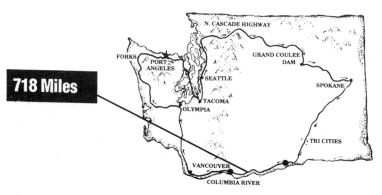

chapter 24

The COLUMBIA RIVER GORGE

Snow melts from the peaks of the Grand Teton Mountains. Drops of pristine water merge, and a trickle becomes a stream becomes a creek becomes the Snake River. After millennia of engraving grooves across the Earth, the Snake twists through Wyoming, Idaho, Oregon and Washington. For hundreds of miles it slithers through forests, around mountains and across deserts until it pours itself into the mighty Columbia River. The Snake and Columbia become one.

Twenty-three miles south of this confluence at the Tri-cities, as the WALKABOUTer walks, we found ourselves on Route 14. The road paralleled the river, and we began to share our existence with it as we walked west. It was a privilege to have the Columbia for an escort as we headed back to the western side of the Cascades.

The Columbia River runs from north to south, from east to west, and from one corner to the other in the State of Washington. Never

199

hesitating as it accepts the contribution of the Snake, and other excess fluids from North America's Pacific Northwest, the Columbia swiftly continues its potent journey to the Pacific Ocean. Growing in mass with every swirl, it is an entity unto itself.

To our left, the river ran along, functioning as border between Washington and Oregon. Looking north, to our right, it was all rock and sagebrush desert. The sun rose at our backs, but towards evening we had to wear our sunglasses as the sun set into the flowing river. All day long, the sun cast tremendously imaginative shadows as it traveled over our heads. Sometimes tattered puffs of clouds danced through the sky, and Reggie and I would walk along sharing our imaginations by describing what kinds of animals drifted above us. The earthy colors on the ground were mostly browns and grays, and once in a while some light green peeked through for a last look before winter. There was not a tree in sight.

Between the beauty of the land and the satisfaction in our hearts, we felt as if we were in heaven. Of course, we knew it was really Earth—the way it was meant to be, the way it could and should be. Such insights one learns, or is it earns, on such a pilgrimage.

We camped out nightly. There were no churches, few people, fewer stores. In fact, there were no real towns for over a hundred miles. Janet had very few chores, and there were no places to sell her wares, so she often joined us on the road. She would walk with us for a few miles, turn around and walk back to the car by herself. Then she would come pick us up and drive us to camp. One day, after a glorious walk back to the car by herself, Janet said, "This road is getting prettier and prettier with every mile. I'm beginning to believe that we are walking into the most beautiful place in the whole state. I can't take enough photographs. I think we should just stop walking and never leave." I smiled but I wasn't so sure she was kidding. I knew she loved the forests of the Olympics, but she was obviously infatuated with the sacred aura of the Columbia River and sagebrush desert under the magical sky.

"I'll build my house here," said Reggie, agreeing with Janet. He was laughing, but I was pretty sure he wasn't kidding. Nevertheless, we kept walking.

Janet sang a different tune, though, when we woke up the next morning and there was a layer of frost covering the tents. If we decided not to leave, we'd definitely have to build Reggie's house. So much for roughing it! We stayed in our sleeping bags until the sun rose high enough to warm us up. We had to work *with* desert life, not against it.

Oh yes, the breezes! How can I forget to mention the breezes? The Columbia River valley is positioned in such a way that winds blow through the river valley most of the year. These "prevailing winds" of the Columbia River valley blow out to the ocean in the winter, and inland in the summer. They are as much a part of the valley as blood is to the body. Luckily for us, it was only late fall, and the winds were light and at our backs. During the day, when the sun was sharp, they made walking pleasurable. For us, prevailing winds seemed more like prevailing breezes!

The road was long and peaceful, and with the breezes pushing us on, we did some of our best walking of the entire trip through this spectacular region. Sometimes we walked as many as 18 miles a day! Perhaps unfortunately, there was little to force us to slow down.

"You guys sure have been doing some good walking. I've noticed that you've both even lost some weight," observed Janet. "As a matter of fact, where'd you put your backsides? I'm positive that those are not the ones you had when we left Port Angeles."

Reggie and I tried to look at our backsides, but we just wound up walking around in small circles. We had to settle for looking at each other's butts. Janet was right. There wasn't much to look at.

"Well, you guys have finally done it," giggled Janet. "You walked your butts off."

"We'll call it the WALKABOUT Diet," I said, ever the opportunist. "We'll make a fortune."

"Can I buy a house?" Reggie was already calculating figures.

Every day we moved further down-river, closer and closer to the Cascades. One day I noticed a tree standing all by itself. I pointed it out to Reggie. As we kept on walking we saw more and more trees. We hadn't seen so many trees since Loup Loup Pass! The cliffs surrounding the river were getting higher, and the valley was closing in. Step by step, honest-to-God Columbia River Gorge territory encompassed us.

Eons ago, the Columbia River rushed through Washington State. The powerful headwaters, conceived in the Province of

British Columbia, Canada, carved out weird shapes as they sped towards the Pacific Ocean. The heart of the Columbia Gorge was created as the river fought its way through the many volcanic floes and uplifting thrusts of the Cascade Mountain Range. Catastrophic floods during the ice age slammed through the canyons, leaving behind hanging valleys, waterfalls, terraced cliffs and wondrous rock pinnacles.

Reggie and I could only imagine the onslaught of nature that created the world we were entering. The Columbia River, slowed by the effects of nine man-made dams, now runs quite peacefully. It seemed to drift on par with our strides, taking us closer and closer to the foothills of the Cascades, to the interior of the Gorge. There is no exact beginning or end to the Gorge, but the more we walked, the higher the mountains rose above our heads. Higher and higher they rose until they were 5,000 feet above us!

With the Columbia River on one side of us, and the majestic, water-carved cliffs towering around us, we were inspired by many thoughts and dreams. I was pondering that we had been living outdoors for over two months. We still had over a month of walking, but every step brought us closer to home! It appeared that Reggie had similar thoughts and was spending the many miles wondering about his future.

"I want to have my own apartment someday," said Reggie, breaking the silence. "Can I have my own apartment when we get home, Steve?" Reggie understood that his transition from the group home to his self-built house was one step at a time.

"I've always said that was possible Reg. But as you know, we are having a difficult time arranging that."

"Every day I have to shave, shower, and brush my teeth. I have to cook and clean up."

"Yep, that's important. But I believe that even if you lacked some of those skills, it wouldn't make a difference. It's a matter of resources. Maybe when we get back to the group home, we can talk to your caseworker at the Division of Developmental Disabilities. We'll see what they can do for you. I know you are certainly capable of living on your own. All I'd guess you would need is to have someone come in to check up on you, like Pat McFarland has, to help you manage your money and make sure you have enough food."

Mt. Hood seen from the Columbia River Gorge

"I choose you and Janet and Rob."

"We all have other jobs, Reg. We'll still be your friends, but there will be other people to help you out on a regular basis."

"O.K.," Reggie agreed.

"You've really become more confident and self-reliant on this trip, Reg. I can definitely understand that after a trip like this you are even more determined to get your own place. But remember, Reg, it depends if the department has enough money to help provide you with an apartment and a staff person. That's always been a bit of the problem. Do you know what I mean?" Reggie just shrugged. "I know how you feel," I said. "Money is such an annoying problem, but it is a fact of life."

"Of course, you could always do what Mary did," I said. On the first day of WALKABOUT, Mary, a lady who had been living at the Lauridsen Group Home for ten years, decided she wanted to go out on her own and didn't want to wait for the department to find her an apartment. It had no connection to WALKABOUT, but the timing was quite symbolic.

"Little Mary Miller?" remembered Reggie.

"That's the one. She works at McDonald's and has saved a lot of money. She found her own apartment and then moved into it.

You know, you are both doing the same thing, only differently. You are both demonstrating that if you want something badly enough, all you have to do is take it one step at a time until you have it. If you want it badly enough, you'll do it. The bottom line is that it's up to you." Reggie could, in fact, leave the group home any time he wanted. However, he felt that would be a mistake, as he wouldn't quite know how to go about making that adventure successful.

Reggie kept walking. He was smiling and talking to himself. I think I heard him say, "I'm going to build my own house." I could just imagine the pictures he was creating in his head.

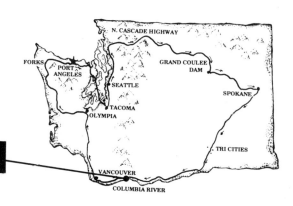

839 Miles

chapter 25

OUR SIDE of the MOUNTAIN

Trees crowded the narrowing road as we closed in on the Cascade Mountain Range. Long, dark tunnels, blasted out of the mountain-side, once again covered the road.

As we approached Vancouver, the city where we would turn north, we had to share the road with more and more cars. Walking on Route 14 over the Cascades proved much busier than the North Cascade Highway, and the shoulder of the road was getting narrower all the time. The stream of cars and trucks was only inches away! Directly to our left, beyond the guard rail, powerful locomotives pulling mile-long lines of boxcars roared along the railroad tracks.

"I don't think those honking horns mean 'Hi. How ya doin'?' Reg. I don't believe the drivers are appreciating our efforts to make society wonderful for all humankind."

"They don't like us?" Reggie asked, not believing the possibility.

"They'd like us a lot better if we weren't here making them swerve around us. I'd guess that's why they don't wave back." Reggie and I still habitually waved when we heard the beeping of a horn. Lately, no one had been waving back or smiling. "This has got to be the toughest and narrowest road we've had to walk on," I said, implying that he'd best not be too casual. "This was the kind of road mom has always warned us about." There would be no singing or howling of folk tunes here. On the road and through the dark tunnels, we concentrated on surviving.

"I'm careful, Steve. You be careful, too, Schlicky."

"Maybe we should walk on the railroad tracks, where it is safer."

"It's very dangerous to walk on train tracks, Steve."

"That's true, Reg. Now let's see. Do we get crushed to death by the occasional locomotive, or bounced off a dozen windshields like so many moths on a summer night? Decisions, decisions. How about if we take our chances on the tracks, and listen real close for any trains? I believe we can jump off before it gets dangerously close. Trains only come by every now and then, but these cars are zipping by all the time."

Staying safe was a real test of the skills and awareness Reggie, Dixie and I had learned after so much time on the road. We each had to use our wits to stay safe. Walking on train tracks is about as smart as walking through a minefield, but walking on the road was like walking across a runway at Chicago's O'Hare airport. It was one of those places where the road was *definitely* not made for walkers. The drivers whizzing by in their cars weren't too happy to share the road with two men and a dog.

Our decision made, Reggie and I stepped over the guard rail as Dixie squeezed underneath it. We climbed the short, steep embankment and crossed onto the tracks, immediately discovering that we had exchanged dangerous walking for difficult walking. Each step we took was like four steps on the asphalt. Laying perpendicular between the rails were the wooden cross-ties and large stones that supported the rails, but destroyed our walking pace. With our feet landing on the irregular stones and the edges of the ties, our ankles cramped with a pain that shot all the way up to our hips. I grumbled, Reggie stumbled and Dixie trailed behind, walking even slower as the large gravel stung her pads.

If necessity is the mother of invention, Dixie might argue that pain is a creative father. Within a couple of hundred yards Dixie figured out how to make her pads land solely on the smooth part of the railroad ties. She developed an uneven, yet steady rhythm that completely overstepped the rocks. As if she was performing a strange dance, Dixie picked up her pace and trotted ahead of us towards the tunnels. "Dixie is a teacher, too," Reggie said as we watched her run down the tracks. Reggie and I followed her lead and readjusted the length of our normal strides as we learned how to control where and how our boots landed. Under normal conditions, walking was second nature to us, but presently, we had to concentrate on every step we took.

A section of mountainside thrust out toward the Columbia River. Leaving no flat area for road or track, tunnels had to be blasted and carved out of the sheer cliff. It made this section of the Cascades look like a giant wall with holes eaten away by overgrown rats. The tunnels seemed fairly short, and we figured we could get through them in a minute or so. We entered the oval-shaped, dungeon-like passageway and felt as if we had been "Als in Wonderland," shrunk down to fit into a rathole. The haunting threat of rock, which served as the wall of the tunnel, came right up beside the track, and there was no safe alternative to walk on. With no place to hide, and forced to continue walking on the track, we quickened our pace, fearing the possibility of a train sneaking up on us. Walking was harder and strangely paced, but with ears like radar tuned in for danger, and eyes darting in all directions, we forged ahead. Our eyes had to readjust to the dark as we entered; the sounds of our footfalls bounced off the blasted caverns, causing echoes that vibrated in our heads as if the giant rat was grinding its teeth in an effort to make more tunnels. All our senses were thrown off, and we stayed close together as instinct reminded us that there is safety in numbers.

We got through the first two tunnels without a hitch, then walked towards the third, which was a bit longer than the two previous. We walked into the black hole of the mountain, intent on walking quickly towards the daylight that reflected on the rail continuing past the exit. Beyond that we could see yet another dark tunnel. As we walked, we distinctly noticed that the echoing vibrations began to grow louder. Without slowing our pace, we turned our heads to see if something was behind us, but only noticed a view that looked exactly as the one ahead. We felt as if we had lost our bearings. The grinding noise, which had been a loud hum, had begun to grow in intensity. Although we couldn't see a train, we knew that something was just not right. "Hey, Reg, I'm not sure what that sound is or where it's coming from, but I have one suggestion...RUN!!" Somewhere on the track a speeding train was coming right for us. We couldn't tell if it was from behind or ahead, but it really didn't matter. Something was causing the tracks to vibrate—we could feel it in every bone in our bodies. Running as quickly as our feet could land on every second cross-tie, we ran towards the light at the end of the tunnel. Although Dixie led the way, closely followed by Reggie and myself, we ran as a unit: men and dog as one. Our hearts pounded, our lungs gasped for breath, and adrenalin rushed through our bodies. Knowing that two men, one dog and three backpacks were just about to be cross-stitched into the railroad track, we ran with hardly a stumble, relying on the muscles and talents we had developed over the roads of Washington. The faster we ran, the greater the vibrations that encompassed us. We could just feel the hot breath of the steaming locomotive on our heels. "Hurry!" we cried as our legs pumped like pistons. "Faster, FASTER!"

Just as we made it to the daylight, we hopped over the rail. Diving down the embankment, we hoped to just barely escape the tons of metal teeth snapping at our heels. We landed on gravel, but we didn't feel a thing. We were numb! We looked around to check and make sure all three of us had made it out alive. Reggie, Dixie and I quickly cleared our heads. We stared into each other's eyes, breathing and panting deeply enough to suck in half the air on the planet. What a relief! We were all accounted for!

Nervously, Reggie and I turned to laugh at our foiled attacker. We saw nothing. Nothing but tunnel and track. We got up and walked slowly back towards the rails. We cautiously stuck our heads over the shining metal and wooden cross-ties and looked back...nothing. We looked ahead...nothing. Man, did we feel foolish! Had we run from our imaginations?! There was no train, no locomotive and no mile-long row of boxcars. There wasn't a rock-slide, a cave-in, or an avalanche. There wasn't even a rat, large or small, scurrying or nibbling on the tracks.

Reggie and I looked at each other, shrugged our shoulders and smiled ever-so-innocently. Some might call it a bonding moment, but if it was, we didn't speak of it. All we felt was embarrassment. We were thankful that there was no one nearby to see how ridiculous we had looked running for our lives from a simple echo. Without words, only confused looks, we agreed that something was causing that terrifying noise, and we stood there waiting for the inevitable culprit. We were positive that at any minute a hundred boxcars would come shooting out of the tunnel like lightening from the sky. We were right, of course. Within the next one hundred and twenty minutes that it took us to get through the last two tunnels, a speeding train came roaring down the tracks. We knew it was coming! What good senses we had developed! We had heard it while it was still dozens of miles away!

This had not been one of our more efficient days, or proudest moments, but we survived, no worse for wear, and I guess that's the bottom line. We continued on, switching from track to road and back to track, depending on which we deemed safest, and echoless, at any particular moment.

Finally, the road began to rise into the mountains. As the tracks continued to hug the riverbank along the cliffs, we chose to stay with the road. Fortunately, without the cliffs and river to determine the highway, the shoulder of the road widened and walking was safer.

Every step brought us closer to home and to heaven (the real one). The temperature dropped and the wind picked up. Dixie's fur was ruffled, and Reggie and I dug into our packs for our sweatshirts.

"Is Schlicky cold?" asked Uncle Reggie.

"I doubt it. With her fur coat, she loves this cool weather. Sometimes her fur makes her hot, but it protects her skin from the sun. And, of course, in cooler weather, it keeps her warm. This is probably her favorite temperature."

Then drops of rain slowly began to fall. Our baseball caps kept our eyes clear as we walked on. A sign up the road read "summit." We walked beside the sign and I paused. Dixie and Reggie stopped, too. I turned around to Reggie. "This is a real bittersweet moment, Reg. Do you know what that means?" Reggie shrugged. "We are now back on our side of the mountains. We're almost home. This is the beginning of the end."

*Cool, wet and
closer to home*

"I want to keep walking."

"This is a real accomplishment. Something to be very proud of," I told him.

"That makes me happy!" he responded, quite quickly and succinctly. I wasn't sure if he was sincere, or he just knew what he was expected to say. "Can we walk again next year?" he added, looking directly into my eyes.

That was a rough question being asked at a rough time. "Don't get carried away," I offered, making light of the moment. "Besides, we still have a few hundred more miles to walk." Only in our minds did it feel like we were much closer to home. In reality we were standing in an ominous cloud on a mountain top way above the Columbia River.

"Good," said Reggie. "I want to keep walking."

"Let's do it!"

"No problem, right?"

We walked on and the rain turned to soft snowflakes. We didn't feel the chill, but it must have been cold; the snow evolved into superball-sized hail. "Ouch!" laughed Reggie. The road had flattened as we walked along the table-top of the pass, and all the while we were bombarded with the hail. It was strangely fun.

"It's all downhill from here, Reg," I said as the road began to slant back towards river level. With every step closer to sea level the temperature rose, and the hail turned to a moderate rain. "The rain is almost comforting. It makes me think of home."

"We'll walk again next year," Reggie said convincingly. At least he was convinced. They say that if you think about something hard enough, it will come true. Reggie must have studied that philosophy.

Reggie and I paused to put on our rain jacket and pants.

"Does Schlicky's fur stop the rain?" Reggie asked as he pulled his orange rain-pants over his jeans.

"Nope. She's a dog, not a duck." I answered. Reggie laughed. "Dixie just gets wet," I added.

"Don't worry, Schlicky, it'll stop raining soon," Reggie told Dixie, trying to comfort her. She didn't appear to be too uncomfortable, but Reggie's hopeful, yet probably incorrect statement, made me realize that we were no longer in the eastern, and drier, half of Washington.

"I don't know, Reg. This softer, yet steady rain proves that we are definitely back in western Washington. It will probably continue to rain until next July."

"No problem, right?"

"No. I guess not. But this sure is a real welcome homecoming, isn't it?" I asked. Reggie didn't say a word. We stood there for a few minutes, looking around, taking in the moment. Finally, I turned back on the highway and walked. Reggie and Dixie followed, quietly. I'm not sure that all the water running down our faces was rain.

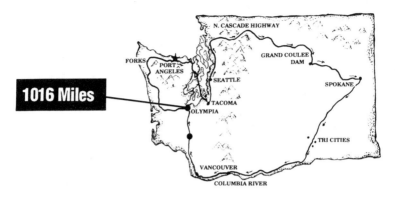

1016 Miles

chapter 26

The FIRST MAN...!

"Ha, Ha," cried a hysterical Reggie Feckley. "Schlicky looks so funny."

Reggie wore out one set of rain clothes, and we stopped at a store to buy another. That goes to show how much rain was falling! I came out with a bright orange child's poncho that I wrapped around Dixie.

"I don't know if she looks cute or stupid," Janet said, looking on in amazement.

"She'll grow to love it," I promised. I covered Dixie's body with her new rain poncho and wrapped her backpack over it to keep it in place. She flattened her ears against her head and looked up at me, quite pitifully. "Look," I explained to her, "it'll be easier for the cars to see you on these dark and gloomy days." She wasn't thrilled at first, but she took a few steps. The rain jacket didn't constrict her movements. "It's not so bad, is it?" I asked Dixie. Dixie wagged her tail once, and her ears rose back toward the sky. She stood proud and erect, showing off her proud breed. It's amazing how she learned to patronize me. Then she turned and looked at

Janet and Reggie. She flattened her ears again. "AND YOU GUYS STOP LAUGHING AT HER," I growled. "Don't make her cry! She looks up to you guys and appreciates your approval." They understood and didn't say another thing about it. Except for the occasional giggle.

It was the Pacific Northwest. It was November. We were west of the Cascades. It was raining! It wasn't raining cats and dogs, but you could say that the continual drips of small puppies and tiny kittens soaked our feet just as effectively. Janet made it a point to find a church basement to sleep in each night.

Days darkened quickly as evening crept up earlier and earlier each night. Within a few days we found that we weren't overwhelmed by the dark rainy days, we were encompassed by them. We were walking in synch with our surroundings. After living outdoors for so long, nature had become our friend. We were becoming one with nature.

At Vancouver we followed the Columbia River north for forty miles until we reached the city of Longview. We bid farewell to our tranquil, reliable river friend as it turned west to join the Pacific Ocean. We continued north, aiming for Olympia. Rain-filled clouds had taken over escort duty, chaperoning us to the capitol city.

"I talked to our friends at home," Janet told us one evening. We were spreading out our sleep rolls on the basement floor of yet another church, and unpacking our sleeping bags. "They said they talked to Mrs. Gardner's office. She's going to meet with you again like she promised."

"Hey, maybe we'll be on T.V. again," hoped Reggie as he crawled into his bag.

"Then we'll have to do some good walking. We can't keep the First Lady of Washington waiting. With the days getting shorter, we'll have to do our miles in a shorter amount of time."

"No more breaks!" demanded Drill Sergeant Reggie. He wasn't in a rush to get home, but he was on a roll. Walking was more fun than ever! He took pride in the strength and stamina he had built within his body and his mind. Reggie laid his head on his pillow and fell asleep.

Heading north on rainy Interstate 5 were three bright bubbles. Covered in our rain gear, Reggie in yellow, me in blue and Dixie in neon orange, we caught many drivers' curiosity...including that of the state patrol. A shiny white patrol car stopped us in our tracks.

"I'm sorry," said the middle-aged officer, "you can't hitchhike on the interstate." He had a barrel chest over a well-formed gut, giving him a very respectable image. Regardless of the tufts of gray hair sticking out from under his hat, there was no reason to doubt that he wasn't ready for any situation a state trooper may come up against. Secure in who he was, he gave the impression of being very fatherly, and Reggie and I appreciated it. However, we had cause to wonder why the officer felt a need to stop us as we walked peacefully along the interstate.

As we had done in the past, we explained, "we're WALKABOUT," and handed him a brochure. He read the brochure and smiled reassuringly. It was almost comforting. He was the kind of officer that made me almost hear Reggie think, "I want to be a cop."

"I think what you're doing is great," he said, "but you're not really allowed to walk on the interstate, either. It's against the law."

"Uh-oh," I said to myself. What a place to get stopped. So close, yet so far. This was no time to get hung up. We had an appointment to make. I had to think fast. "Well, we have to get to Olympia in time for our meeting with Mrs. Gardner (notice the name dropping)."

"We're going to be on television," added Reggie.

"Walking up the interstate is the only way we'll make it in time," I continued. The officer didn't flinch. "I understand that it may be illegal, but as you can see we have at least ten feet of shoulder. Besides, at twenty-five miles a day, we'll be off the interstate and in Olympia in no time." O.K., so I exaggerated, but it was for good reason.

"Well," he said softly, sympathetic to our dilemma, "there are other roads."

"Think fast, Steve," I thought to myself. I knew the roads he had in mind, but they obviously weren't my first choice. Those backroads weaved in and about the interstate, providing a quieter and prettier alternative, yet adding many more miles to our trek north. Laziness wasn't going to convince the police officer, however. I hoped my back-up argument would earn some respect. "Yes," I began to explain, "but if I know small roads that parallel the interstate, I'd bet they are narrow and dangerous. It may be legal to walk on them, but they are certainly far from safe." Reggie and I looked, ever-so-innocently, directly into the officer's eyes.

He thought for a moment as we awaited a reply. It was as if he was searching for a good logical comeback. He had none. He knew I was right about the danger of those "legal-to-walk-on" roads. He looked troubled as he tried to balance logic and the law. I wasn't confident of the outcome, as he was a cop, not Mr. Spock, and I silently prayed.

For a long ten seconds we stood uncomfortably, but finally he took a deep breath and said, "Well, you're right. There have been special occasions where it has been allowed. Of course, those people had permits," he said. He paused to wait for our excuse of why we lacked that special permission from the department of transportation or state patrol. We had no permits or excuses and said nothing. We just stood there looking pitiful with the rain falling on our faces. Finally he said, "Just be careful and stay as close to the guard rail as possible." Hey, I don't know if it was sincere prayers, a good argument or just a big heart, but Reggie and I got the permission we hoped for. I was stunned and it showed by my lack of verbal appreciation.

"Thank you, officer," said Reggie, taking up my slack.

"Yes, thank you. Very much," I finally stammered.

"See, Steve. No problem," offered Reggie. "The cop said it was O.K. Right?"

"That's what he said, Reg."

"He's a good cop."

"I think so, too," I agreed.

"Hey, Steve," asked Reggie, "can cops go to jail?"

"Well, cops are people, too," I answered. "If they do something wrong they can get arrested just like anybody else. This officer was a nice man. He seems like a real good cop."

"I think so, too." Reggie had a lot of respect for police officers, and although he asked the question, I think it was strange for him to think that even they could go to jail. He stood quietly thinking about what I had said.

"Shall we go?" I finally reminded him.

"No more breaks!"

We continued on...as did the rain...and the traffic. Interstate 5 is loud and lacks scenic beauty. The cars and trucks were the biggest and fastest we had had the displeasure of sharing the road with since day one, but it afforded us the quickest way to Olympia, and nothing was more important. WALKABOUT had been our life, exciting to us and thrilling to the people we met on the road and through the towns. Now we had hope that it would be influential to the leaders and lawmakers in Washington's capital city: men and women who could develop insightful, progressive programs. Although the rain tried to drown our enthusiasm, it only succeeded in cleansing the atmosphere of the exhaust fumes. We set our sights and thoughts on getting to the interstate exit that would bring us into Olympia and to a meeting with Mrs. Gardner. It became easy to ignore our surroundings as we walked with that one thought on our minds.

Unfortunately, our surroundings didn't ignore us. Within an hour, we were stopped by another patrol officer. Talk about deja vu. We had the exact same conversation with the exact same result...including my surprise at the flexibility of the officer. We were allowed to move along. Will wonders never cease?

"He's a good cop, too, Steve," offered Reggie.

Lunch time came and Janet met us for a roadside picnic. Janet was laughing as she said, "I believe that you guys will do anything, say anything, or try anything to avoid having to take even ten extra steps."

She was absolutely right! But I felt compelled to say, "Spoken like a true support driver." SMACK—obviously, according to Janet, I deserved it.

Soon enough Janet left us to find a church or a group home for the night, and Reggie, Dixie and I walked on, only to be stopped fifteen minutes later by yet another state patrol officer. Once again the conversation had began as the two before. Talk about deja vu. Well, you can talk about it but it didn't apply this time. This officer was a younger man and not quite as grounded. Tall and with deepset eyes, he spoke sharply and succinctly, as if he needed to prove his authority. While it appeared that the older officers saw different shades of the law, this officer saw it as only black or white.

"I'm sorry," he repeated, quite sternly, "it is *illegal* to walk on the interstate."

"Yes, but don't you agree that it's so much safer than those other roads," I said, rephrasing my earlier argument.

"I'm sorry," he said.

"But what about our appointment with Mrs. Gardner?"

"Which part of 'illegal' didn't you understand?" he snapped. And that put an end to that. He gave us a sharp look, turned, and went back to his patrol car. He waited for us to head to the exit.

"No problem?"

"No, Reg. Big problem."

"He's a bad cop. He should go to jail," was Reggie's opinion.

"Well, Reg, he's not a bad cop. He was just following the letter of the law. I'd say he wasn't the nicest guy in the world, but he doesn't deserve to go to jail. He was just doing his job, and we have to respect that."

"I like the first cop better, Steve."

"Me, too. But we have to listen to what this cop told us."

As instructed, we headed for the nearest exit. There we sat for three and a half hours, as we had no place to go until we talked with Janet. There is nothing so annoying as being forced to sit in the rain beside a busy interstate waiting for someone to pick you up, but if we trekked over to the backroads without telling Janet where we were forced to walk, we'd have been lost forever. Or if she ever did find us, she'd run us over for not waiting and telling her where we were and why we had left Interstate 5. This time I believed she'd actually do it, and with good reason.

With the loss of half a day, and with added miles of slow, narrow, more dangerous, illogical, wet, sloppy, muddy, roads, we had to walk quicker, longer and harder to get to Olympia. We griped and groaned with each and every step but we were determined not to disappoint the First Lady.

Janet was with us when we finally rolled into Olympia. The dome of the capitol building had been like a beacon, and we walked right up to the front steps. Regardless of moldy and creaking body parts made rusty from miles of rain, we bounded up the stairs of the capitol building, impatient to see Mrs. Gardner. Again we were stopped en route, but this time it was by questioning reporters and fascinated photographers. This was exciting! Through majestic doors we finally entered the capitol rotunda. Under the big gold dome was a huge and beautiful Tiffany-designed chandelier. With giant murals, portraits of past leaders, and gold-plated tiles and banisters, the hall of the rotunda impressed and inspired us.

Photo by Janet Phipps

Reggie takes Olympia by storm!

Nevertheless, nothing, but *nothing*, was greater inspiration than the welcome we received beyond those doors! Dozens of people clapped and cheered and screamed and waved banners for us! Friends from home had rented a bus and driven down to welcome us to Olympia, and they were all there to greet WALK-ABOUT as we entered the rotunda. So were other reporters, people who worked with people with disabilities, important leaders of the state, and Mrs. Gardner! Everyone was there to shake hands with the man who had walked *around* the State of Washington!

We were teary-eyed as we scanned the crowd. Amazing! Choked up (but not without something to say!), Reggie and I walked up to the podium. I said, "Ladies and Gentlemen, the first time we were honored by Mrs. Gardner, Reggie was the first man with a developmental disability to walk across the State of Washington. This time I present to our First Lady, and to all of you, a representative of people with developmental disabilities, a man who has walked around the State of Washington. I present to you a man who has helped prove that we indeed need to focus on abilities, not disabilities. A man who represents equality for all people. Ladies and gentlemen, REGGIE FECKLEY!"

The crowd roared and screamed his name. Thousands and thousands of steps, hundreds and hundreds of miles, and weeks and weeks of experiences ago, Reggie would never have attempted to speak to a large, cheering crowd. But that was then and this was now, and a more confident Reggie Feckley was well aware of his place in history:

Thank you! I have something to say. I'm very proud of myself. I like to walk. I want to live on my own some day. I thank Janet, Steve and Dixie for helping me. They teach me how to do things for myself. That's teamwork! I walked the United State of Washington!

Reggie raised his fist and flashed a smile. His glow illuminated the whole dome. He spoke more clearly than ever before. Everyone was clapping and hollering for Reggie Feckley!

Speeches and high praise were bestowed upon Reggie. Gifts and awards were presented by many people. Reggie was an inspiration for *all* people! Other people with developmental disabilities not only envied Reggie, they realized that they could have a dream and make it come true, too. Reggie showed them they could make choices in their lives, and if they work hard enough, they could have many of the things they want. Other people in the audience, people like Janet and I who worked to help others, saw that their hard work could pay off. Everyone was learning that people with differing abilities should not be treated with any less respect.

We were treated to luxurious motel rooms by the Tyee Hotel, good food and enthusiastic friends for the rest of the day. WALKABOUT wasn't over yet, though. There were still a couple of hundred miles to walk. The Olympic Peninsula was the last leg of WALKABOUT, and since it was already late November, the last leg of our journey was surely going to be wet and cold!

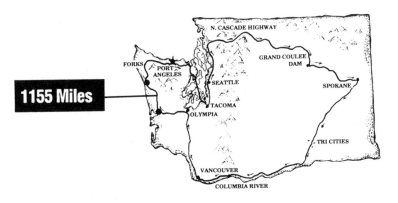

1155 Miles

chapter 27

BACK on the OLYMPIC PENINSULA

"It seems like we're on a trail deep in the woods, Reg, not on Highway 101," I said, ducking below a branch sticking out over the highway.

We had passed the first big towns west of Olympia. Highway 101 passed through Aberdeen and Hoquiam, and the trees closed in around the road. Sometimes the trees were so close to the road that Reggie and I had to bend our heads to avoid the limbs.

"Look at Dixie!" he responded, enjoying his "niece." She was running through the trees and brush.

"I don't think her nose can smell the smells fast enough," I laughed. "Who knows what elk, deer, bear, beavers, rabbits, birds, raccoons, and what all have passed through these trees?"

"Skunks, too?" asked Reggie.

"Skunks, too!"

"Uh oh. No church for her tonight." Reggie squeezed his nose and laughed.

"You mean she has to sleep in the WALKABOUT-Mobile?"

"Nope. Janet will be mad. Schlicky has to sleep in the rain. Sorry Schlicky." And that was that. "Just giving you a hard time, Schlick. Ha, Ha!"

"Speaking of rain, did you know that there are some places on the Olympic Peninsula where it rains over 150 inches a year?" I asked Reggie.

"Nope. I didn't know that," answered Reggie.

"Well, now you do. And did you know that there are over 300 plant species, 71 kinds of moss, 30 liverworts and over 70 varieties of lichen?"

"Nope. I didn't know that either."

"Well, now you do. It's a good thing I like to read all those roadside signs or our lives just wouldn't be complete. Do you think you'll remember all I just told you?"

"Yup," he assured me.

"O.K., how many different types of liverworts are there on the Olympic Peninsula," I asked.

"Uhh....."

"Yeah, me too," I said. "It's a good thing I wrote it down. Maybe I'll put it in the WALKABOUT book someday."

"I'll be famous!"

"You mean you'll be more famous, Reg."

"No problem, right?"

We walked on, absorbing some of the 150 inches of rain. One would think that the gray overcast sky would make it dark and gloomy, but in fact it brought out the vivid "greens" of the trees and bushes. We walked along tremendous fields, and mountain slopes of tall evergreens like Sitka Spruce, Hemlock, Pacific Yew, Douglas Fir and Western Red Cedar. We walked under the arch of many spectacular rainbows. For variety, sporadic red and yellow leaves of the maple and alder trees fell as if it were a strange, colorful rain. All this reminded us of the time of year. "It is definitely autumn, Reg."

"It's very pretty," he replied.

"And we are definitely back home on our peninsula." He didn't reply, but it was one of the loudest responses I've ever heard.

Photo by Steve Breakstone

Protecting the pack

He got so quiet every time I mentioned home. I felt like I had dropped a bomb. I had to remember to be more careful. We walked on.

Inevitably, and irregularly, monstrous log trucks came rolling by with their tremendous loads of freshly-cut trees. With the wind they created, we were often blown into the brush as we were sprayed with puddles from the road. "Yep, we're definitely close to home," I said, cynically.

"Stay to the side, Schlicky," Reggie called. "Those trucks can smash you flat like a pancake if you're not careful."

I laughed. "Luckily, Dixie understands, and I think we can pass up the maple syrup for a Dixie Doodle Dog pancake," I laughed. Reggie thought that was funny, too. Dixie wasn't even paying attention to us.

We walked on and then we heard something we hadn't heard in a long, long time—LOUD CRASHING WAVES! Through the trees we could hear the Pacific Ocean. Then we saw it. The crowd of trees thinned and we saw the forever of the ocean.

Janet came by just then, and the four of us sat and watched the pounding surf. A storm, raging beyond the horizon, shook the ocean, making powerful waves that beat the shore at our feet. We were home!

"I bet you can't wait to see your stuff!" I said, smiling at Janet.

"You are so obnoxious." Janet laughed and smacked me. I took pride in the statement. "But you're right. I can't wait," she humbly added. Then Janet turned to Reggie and asked, "How about you, Reg. Don't you miss your stuff?"

"Nope," he said. He shrugged and looked out to the ocean.

"Reggie and I don't have as much stuff as you," I interrupted. "Combined!" Smack!

"Don't you miss your friends?" she asked him.

"Yup. I miss them. I liked seeing them in Olympia."

"So what do you think about being home?" I asked. Reggie said nothing. "Reggie?"

Janet and I could see the wheels turning in his head. He wasn't ignoring us or blanking out, he was obviously gathering his thoughts. "Next year we'll walk the United States!" he finally replied. He smiled and his eyes brightened.

Reggie had become aware that we had walked the United State of Washington, not the United States of America, but I still wasn't exactly sure he understood all that he was asking. From experience I knew exactly what it involved. I was positive that he was capable of such a challenge, and obviously he wanted to keep walking. Reggie was trying to keep his spirits up, and we respected that. Janet and I were still concentrating on the United State of Washington, though, and for the moment the best we could say was, "Well, we'll see. We're making no promises, Reg."

Janet and I had mixed emotions about getting home, too. It had been an incredible journey, but we were tired and ready to sleep in our own beds. It was a strange feeling for us, too.

He often talked about seeing his friends, but Reggie had no desire to put an end to the greatest trip and accomplishment he had ever experienced.

Out of the blue, like a dolphin jumping out of the ocean and into the air, Reggie stood up and grabbed his pack. "Soon we'll be Home, Sweet Home," he said. I was sure Reggie was trying to convince himself of that, and I was impressed with how he'd turned his attitude around. My guess was that he was attempting to accept the end of WALKABOUT by making plans to walk every other state in the country. As always, Reggie had to inspire himself. Slowly he was accepting the inevitable end of his amazing journey.

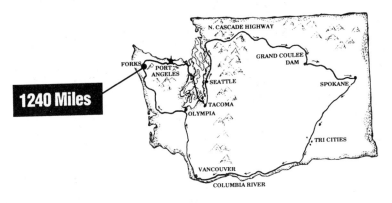

1240 Miles

chapter 28

FORKS

The timber-crowded highway curved around the Olympic Mountains. Clear-cuts (large tracts of land where all the trees are cut down for wood products) gave us the opportunity to look up the valleys to the snow-capped peaks. The road headed inland, and we walked away from the Pacific. Everywhere we looked there were trees! The road twisted and turned as we walked around the foothills of the Olympics and down through the valleys. We walked and walked until we came to the famous logging town of Forks.

Forks is Port Angeles' closest neighbor to the west. Forks and Port Angeles are separated by sixty miles of road, millions and millions of trees, and Lakes Crescent and Sutherland. Forks is a logging town of about 2,000 people, and it's only about two miles long. Because Port Angeles and Forks are such good neighbors, everyone in Forks already knew about WALKABOUT. Even nursery school children came out to the road to welcome us! They held out banners and offered the three wet, weary walkers cookies and juice.

Along the coast

Then we passed by the Forks Elementary School. Reggie and Dixie and I were celebrities! I was handed a bull-horn and was asked to talk to the students as Reggie shook their hands. Questions came shooting out of the crowd from all directions:

"What did you do if it rained?"

"We got wet."

"Where did you sleep at night?"

"With old friends, new friends, campgrounds, church basements. Wherever we could lie down."

"How many shoes did you wear out?"

"These are the boots we started with." Reggie held up his foot, and the students were amazed at how worn down the sole was. The boots were virtually on their last legs.

"What did you eat?"

"Whatever was put in front of our face."

"Did Dixie walk the whole way?"

"Every step!"

"Were you scared? Did you ever think you wouldn't make it?"

I looked at Reggie. He looked at me and smiled. "Not for a second!"

Reggie and I answered as many questions as we could. The

schoolkids were wonder-struck by the celebrities with whom they were suddenly face to face. The students swarmed around us and asked Reggie and me for autographs.

"You're famous!" I whispered to Reggie. This time I had beat him to the punch.

Finally we had to walk on. This close to home, we were drawn to the road and wanted to do nothing but walk—and keep the rain out of our eyes! Celebrations don't stop the rain on the peninsula! Four more good walking days and we would be home.

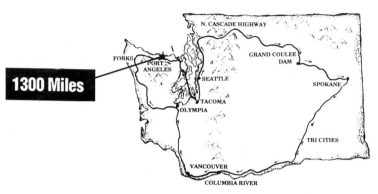

1300 Miles

chapter 29

The LAST MILE

The rain kept raining. WALKABOUT kept walking. It was the first week of December and it was
time to get home. Our friends were waiting for
us. The last 60 miles seemed like 600. The
longer we walked, the longer the road got. It
stretched on and on, never-ending before us,
but nothing could stop us now! Not this close to
home.

So close to home. What a concept. It meant
the end of WALKABOUT. Wow! WALKABOUT was
just about over. An end to everything that had
encompassed my life since that cold winter night
when WALKABOUT was conceived. Now
WALKABOUT was entering old age. It was something to think about as we came upon the last
twenty miles. Lake Crescent imposed the only
barrier between reality and memory.

The lake itself, bathed in a heavy December
fog, was quite peaceful and posed no hindrance
to our final destination. It was the road border-
ing the lake that concerned me. Ten miles of
road was carved out of the forest, right at the
point where the land poured into the lake. The

227

snake-like road was built to get people—no, passengers—from one side of the lake to the other. It was made for cars and trucks, not pedestrians. It was a million times more dangerous than the interstate we were thrown off of, yet this time we were perfectly legal. Hmmm, go figure.

Another time and place I would not only consider the dangers of the walk around Lake Crescent, I would feel anxious. I often worried too much. Or was it just enough? We had, in fact, kept safe for all these many months and miles. We had just successfully walked over 1,285 miles around Washington. Maybe I had found that ever-elusive balance.

Dixie was just ahead of me, hugging the guardrail as close as her pack would let her. Reggie was a hundred feet ahead of her, with apparently one thing on his mind..."Home, sweet home." Neither appeared preoccupied; however, through instinct and experience, both were aware of the black ice, that invisible thin layer of ice that blends into the black asphalt. As if the curves weren't bad enough, the black ice caused cars and trucks to swerve at even the most innocent of moments. Although "stay to the side, keep eyes and ears open," continued to be the standing policy, the cars couldn't slow down enough as far as I was concerned. How ironic it would be to get hit by a car so close to the end of WALKABOUT. It had been so long since Reggie tested my 9-1-1 reflexes that I wondered how I'd react if circumstances dictated I do so. Well, O.K., maybe I still worried a bit too much.

All that anxiety was real, yet I knew that little of it mattered. The concern of the highway only existed on the surface of my mind, but it didn't penetrate it. It was just a diversion. The end of WALKABOUT. It always came back to that. I was tired. Only now, with less than twenty miles to go, was I really allowing myself to ponder it. I had conveniently considered everyone's feelings but my own.

When we had gotten back on the road after our stay in Olympia, Reggie and I talked about how his life had changed. Reggie had felt that every step he had taken on WALKABOUT was a step in the right direction. He had taken steps towards a more fulfilling life full of interesting experiences, including camping out, talking to reporters and meeting people who admired him. Now when Reggie exclaimed, "I'm famous!" it really meant something to him

Dixie "Doodles" Breakstone, the German Shepherd who walked across America... and around Washington

because he knew it was absolutely true. He had seen more, done more, and made more independent choices in the last three months than in the last ten years combined. His conversation went from simple "Reggie-isms" to more complete thoughts. He had built his self-esteem, felt more accepted as an adult, acted more like an adult, and commanded more respect. While Janet and I had acknowledged Reggie's disability, his goals to achieve were similar to ours, and because of it Reggie had risen to the occasion. There was no truer statement than "I'm a man."

"You know, Reg," I had told Reggie on more than one occasion, "I believe that the actual walking of 1,300 miles wasn't the most important thing we did."

"I'm proud of myself," he would usually reply. Whereas six months before it had not even been a concept for him, I knew that it was now a sentence that Reggie said from his heart.

We had discussed these thoughts, but over the last hundred miles or so when I asked about his feelings about getting home, Reggie would only repeat "Home, sweet home," or "Next year we'll walk the United States," and then he'd walk up the road. At first I thought it was important to talk it out, and I would follow him. Repressing his deepest feelings wasn't going to help him, I believed. We would soon be home and there was no changing that.

I wanted to confront him, but I finally imagined what Janet would say to me. I had learned a lot from Janet, and I decided that I didn't have to hear her actually tell me to respect his silence. He had a right to deal with his feelings any way he wanted. It was a bitter-sweet moment for all of us, and I had no right to intrude on his way of experiencing these moments. Nothing more was said about it.

With an entirely different attitude toward dealing with the end of WALKABOUT, Janet made her feelings quite obvious. She fully accepted the inevitable and ran to greet it. She couldn't stand the suspense—it was driving her crazy. In fact, it drove her straight to town. Janet had always been the gauge measuring how rough WALKABOUT really could be. Presently, it had been easier to be 500 miles from home than twenty. We were so close she couldn't control herself, and would drive the WALKABOUT-Mobile to town to see her friends and visit her "stuff." I thought that destroyed the power of "The Moment of Return," but to each her own. I accepted Janet's actions. It was her way of dealing with the end of WALKABOUT.

The end of WALKABOUT. Finally, I couldn't ignore it any longer. At every opportunity I attempted to substitute what Reggie and Janet were going through to avoid my own feelings. Reggie and I had more in common than was obvious. Finally, I allowed myself to consider the thoughts going through my mind.

I was exhausted, physically and mentally. WALKABOUT wasn't just about walking 15-20 miles a day, in rain or traffic. WALKABOUT was speeches, interviews, raising money, finding places to sleep, and looking after each other. Although Janet and Reggie had adjusted wonderfully through each passing mile and day, it was me they looked to for leadership. It was I who had spent so many years living on the road. It was I who had taught Janet how to ask strangers if they would be good enough to lend a bed or donate a buck, and it was taken for granted that I would be the motivating force in charge of those aspects of WALKABOUT. Thankfully, Janet was a good student (and a great teacher, too!). As enjoyable as it could be, and as well as we all had adjusted to each other and to our circumstances, it was not an easy life—unfamiliar places, infrequent showers, occasional, if not strange, beds and bedrooms, picnic meals, new "friends" daily, etc.... And, of course, the four of us had to put up with each other's habits every moment of every day and every night. No matter how enjoyable certain moments can be, no matter how much you love a person, or a dog, such a lifestyle takes its toll. Rarely did a day go by when we had time to sit back, relax, do nothing and think nothing. At times our bodies rested, but never our minds.

Yet that lifestyle was a part of our lives, every second of every day, for over three and a half months. Only with time would I get a decent perspective. Presently, the emotional ups and downs of these last miles were the steepest and most draining. The last twenty miles. What a concept. Everything was about to change. The present was about to become past. And then what?

Janet was still program coordinator and would continue that role. With Dixie by my side, I would go back to being a live-in residential training counselor. Reggie would be welcomed back to New Broom Janitorial and move back into his two-man bedroom. After all this, all we walked for, strived for and talked about, there was no guarantee that Reggie's life would change in any way that was important to him. That had always been understood as we were enjoying the "here and now" of WALKABOUT; for such a long time, "when we get back home" was always the future. The future had finally arrived. What would happen to the WALKABOUT family when we all resumed our normal lives? The bond would last forever, but there would be no substitute for what we had been experiencing, day in and day out, mile after mile, since August. Would Reggie ever get his own apartment? Oh sure, maybe in a few years, but what about now? Five years is a short time in the course of social change, but it could seem like forever to a 43-year-old man. Did WALKABOUT really accomplish anything? Did we do an injustice to Reggie by giving him the opportunity to touch the stars, only to have him fall back to Earth?

"STOP!" I yelled to myself. Too much. So much for the balance I thought I had achieved. "Stop crabbing and walk. Think positive! Enjoy the moment!" It was good advice and I took it to heart.

I followed Reggie's lead. WALKABOUT was not quite over yet. There were still miles to walk, things to do, places to be and people to see. As usual we got around the lake without incident. Ten more miles and we'd be home.

The date was Saturday, December 9. Reggie, Dixie and I

arrived at the 1,298 mile marker. WALKABOUT had walked around the state and back into Port Angeles! Reggie Feckley, Dixie and I had walked completely around the State of Washington!

As we walked past Dry Creek School at the edge of town, all the students and teachers had a special afternoon and cheered us on. There were banners and questions like so many others we had seen and heard. These were special, though; these were "home town."

The last mile was just around the next curve. Reggie walked right behind me, reminding me of the first few miles. Dixie was up ahead, sniffing familiar territory. She ran up and back on the side of the road, sharing her excitement with us. She knew where we were. "Home, sweet home," I'd hear Reggie say. Inside my mind, I was cheering and crying. I didn't know how to feel. Once again I shut down my feelings. I left my mind blank, open for whatever chose to enter it. This was it. Another mile, and Reggie, Dixie and I will have successfully walked around Washington. Another mile and WALKABOUT would be all over!

You would think that by now we'd have learned to expect the unexpected. We walked the last dip and over the last rise that found Highway 101 intersecting with Lincoln Street. As we came around the curve, a crowd of people were there to greet us—no, to join us! Mile 1,300 turned out to be a Port Angeles celebration! As we waved and hugged (and licked!) the people that we had missed so very much, the crowd fell in behind us. WALKABOUT was joined by a police escort, a marching band and dozens of friends. This was going to be the hardest, longest, teariest, but best, mile of them all! This "Welcome Home Walkabout Parade"—people cheering, horns blowing, drums banging—walked the final mile with Reggie, Dixie, Janet and me through the heart of town as we waved to the hundreds of folks lining the streets. We were led to the Port Angeles City Pier, on the Strait of Juan de Fuca, where a reception awaited us. The band played "Pomp and Circumstance." Reggie, Janet, Dixie, and I were escorted up to a platform and I was handed a microphone. The crowd screamed for Reggie!

"Ladies and Gentlemen," I said,

"Do you believe that everyone is equal?

"Do you believe a dream can become a reality?

"Do you believe that anyone can do anything?

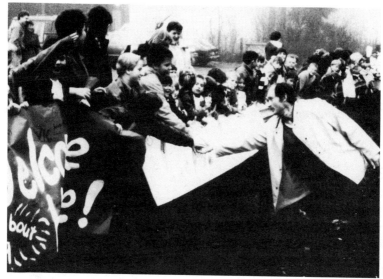

Welcome home, WALKABOUT

"Do you believe *you* can do anything?

"Are you willing to believe in yourself?

"Are you willing to work hard and think hard?

"Are you willing to believe in others?

"Are you willing to allow others the chance to fulfill their dreams?

"Are you willing to demand equality for all?

"Ladies and Gentlemen, I present to you a representative of people with Developmental Disabilities. I present to you a man who went out and allowed himself to be an example of what anyone can accomplish, given the desire and the support.

"Now, I ask you, are you willing to open up your minds and your hearts to this hero, this representative of many of our friends and relatives? Are you going to allow everyone to have a dream and work for it?

"Ladies and Gentleman, I present to you...Mr. Reggie Feckley!"

A spotlight focused on Reggie. The applause and roar were deafening. Yes, the people of Port Angeles are willing to believe that people like Reggie have all kinds of *abilities*. Reggie stood tall as they cheered for a man that made a dream come true—a man who kept going even with the pain of tired, blistering feet; a man who pushed himself when blazing sunshine tried to melt his dream, and when the rains tried to drown it. Reggie made believers of all those people who questioned his abilities, and he made the people who always believed in him so very proud!

And so closed a sensational chapter in Reggie Feckley's book of life. "Next year—the United States," dreamed Reggie Feckley as he quietly began to imagine—Volume Two.

No problem.

EPILOGUE

Less than two months after WALKABOUT returned to Port Angeles, Reggie was invited back to Olympia for a ceremony hosted by Governor Booth Gardner. Rob, Janet, and I went with him. (This time we all rode.) Governor Gardner was acknowledging those people who had done the most for people with disabilities. The woman who won the top honor had died. How could Reggie have competed with a dead woman? We wanted him to win, but it wasn't worth dying for. Second place was just as honorable.

Reggie allowed me to go up to the podium with him to receive the certificate. The Governor asked Reggie if he had anything he'd like to say. You betcha! All that practice at making speeches didn't go to waste. Mr. Gardner handed him the micro-phone, and Reggie was off and talking. In his excitement, his words were quite difficult to understand, even to Janet, Rob and myself, but I think everyone at the luncheon understood when he said, "Teamwork."

As of this printing, Reggie still lives at the Lauridsen Group Home and works for New Broom Janitorial. Dixie and I also continue to live and work at LGH, and Janet and Rob still hold their positions. Only recently has LGH been granted permission to go ahead with its plan to place (the first) six of their clients in their own apartment or house in town. It is a slow process and takes a tremendous amount of perseverance to arrange all the necessary requirements, including the financial resources. Reggie has been incredibly patient, but he has never abandoned his dream. He should be one of the first clients presently living at LGH who will move into his own apartment under this program.

We hope all his dreams come true, and we all wish him love, happiness and friendship.

ABOUT THE AUTHOR

Steve Breakstone was born, raised and formally educated in the New York City metropolitan area. Following graduation from Hofstra University, he headed out on the road.

Dixie was adopted in a shelter in New Orleans. For her efforts and accomplishments she has been named the Meaty Bones® and Jerky Treats® National Poster Dog in a contest that proves what great dogs (and cats) are always waiting to be adopted in our nation's shelters.

A three-year, 5,000-mile trip around America was the original adventure of "Steve and Dixie." That trip began with a 2,000-mile drive from New York to Louisiana, and ended with a 2 1/2-year, 3,000-mile *walk* from New Orleans, Louisiana, to Neah Bay, Washington.

Steve and Dixie have walked through a Louisiana, Texas and Oklahoma summer, over the Rockies, and across the deserts of Idaho and Oregon. They've lived on a Kansas farm where Steve drove a mighty tractor harvesting grain, wrangled horses in the mountains of Colorado (Dixie helped!), carried the luggage of movie stars at the Sun Valley ski resort, and, most recently, worked with people with developmental disabilities in Washington.

Photo by Janet Phipps

Father and daughter

FROM THE AUTHOR

My cross country walks have been a journey, not only of body but of mind and spirit. I have found, unwittingly, that I am on a never-ending path towards my goal of living in harmony, finding the balance and being one with Nature (God).

I do my best to give a hoot and not pollute; reduce, recycle and reuse; and treat *all* creatures with equal compassion and respect. Seven months after the return of WALKABOUT, I became a vegetarian. I feel great! Inside and out.

To order additional copies of *Washington Walkabout*, send a check or money order for $15.00 per copy to:

Balance Publications
P. O. Box 447
Port Angeles, WA 98362-0069

Shipping, handling and all applicable taxes are included. Discounts are given for volume orders; please inquire for details.

Reggie, Janet, Steve and Dixie enjoy and appreciate your comments. You may contact them through Balance Publications.